SURRY COUNTY, NORTH CAROLINA
DEEDS

BOOKS D, E AND F

1779-1797

By
Mrs. W. O. Absher

Please direct all correspondence and orders to:

www.southernhistoricalpress.com
or
SOUTHERN HISTORICAL PRESS, Inc.
PO BOX 1267
375 West Broad Street
Greenville, SC   29601
southernhistoricalpress@gmail.com

ISBN #0-89308-555-3

Printed in the United States of America

INTRODUCTION

Surry County was formed in 1771 from Rowan
County. It is bounded on the north by the Vir-
ginia line. In 1777 parts of Surry and the
District of Washington were taken to form Wilkes
Co. Stokes County was formed in 1789 from Surry,
and in 1849 Forsyth County was formed from
Stokes. Yadkin County was formed in 1850 from
Surry. Ashe County was formed in 1799 from
Wilkes, and in 1859 Alleghany County was formed
from Ashe. Thus, from 1771 - 1778, these Surry
County records covered the present day counties
of Ashe, Alleghany, Wilkes, Surry, Yadkin,
Stokes and Forsyth; from 1777 to 1787 the coun-
ties of Surry, Yadkin, Stokes and Forsyth. The
county seat is Dobson, North Carolina.

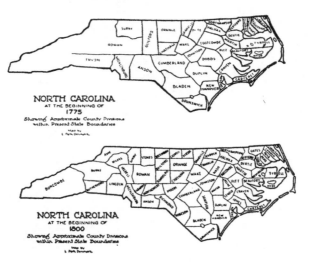

Page 1.   1 February 1789.   Christian Fredr COSSART, Gent.,
        Antrim County, Ireland and Fredr Wm. MARSHALL, his
Atty. to Peter PFAFF, planter, 5 shillings, 400 acres Muddy
Creek in Wachovia; conveyed to PFAFF by Andrew FULK and wife
Margaretha 25 July 1784. Witnesses; John LEWIS and John
KROUSE (signed in German). Signed: Christian Fredr COSSART
by Fredr Wm. MARSHALL.

Page 2.   29 September 1786.   Fredr Wm. MARSHALL, Salem, to
        Robert MARKLAND, planter of Wachovia, 52 pounds, 10
shillings, 105 acres Northeast side North branch Muddy Creek
crossing said Spangenback several times adjoining John BLAKE.
Witnesses: Jacob BLUM and Ludwig MEINUNG. Signed: Fredr
Wm. MARSHALL.

Page 3.   13 July 1781.   John LINEBACK to Philip SNIDER, 150
        pounds hard money, 400 acres adjoining SNIDER on
Elissons Creek. Witnesses: George HAUSER and Henry SPENHOWER.
Signed: John LINEBACK.

Page 4.   6 March 1788.   Martin ARMSTRONG to John SMITH, 320
        pounds, 320 acres Davidson County South side
Cumberland adjoining Capt. Samuel BUDD, part larger tract
640 acres granted M. ARMSTRONG by State of North Carolina.
Witnesses: William HUGHLETT, George CRISMAN, and Martin
ARMSTRONG, Jr. Signed: Martin ARMSTRONG.

Page 5.   27 September 1787.   Philip ROTHROCK, Yeoman, York
        County, Pennsylvania to Matthias NETTING part 4,
896 acres from Lord GRANVILLE to James HUTTON 7 August 1753;
from said HUTTON by his Attorney Fredr Wm. MARSHALL to
Philip ROTHROCK, 104 pounds Gold and Silver, 200 acres
adjoining said ROTHROCKS other tract crossing Lick Creek.
Witnesses; George HAUSER, John MORRIS, and John ROTHROCK.
Signed: Philip ROTHROCK.

Page 7.   25 June 1787.   Fredr ALBERTY to Henry KRUGER, 25
        pounds (no acres) Muddy Creek adjoining Michael
HAUSER. Witnesses: Jacob KRUGER, Francis FORDENE, and
William THORNTON. Signed: Fredrick ALBARTY.

Page 8.   12 August 1788.   Jacob KRUGER and wife Susanna to
        Henry KRUGER, 100 pounds Specie, 200 acres Muddy
Creek called the Dorothea adjoining Wachovia; part 400
acres HUTTON land sold Joseph LINEBACK by Atty Fredr Wm.
MARSHALL; by LINEBACK to Jacob KRUGER. Witnesses: Henry
SPANNHOWER, Sr. and William THORNTON. Signed: Jacob (X)
KRUGER, Susanna KRUGER.

Page 9.   9 August 1787.   North Carolina Grant John McCOLLUM,
        550 acres North fork Deep Creek adjoining REVIS.

Page 10.   11 April 1787.   Micajah CLARK, Esq. to John MARTIN,
          200 pounds, 400 acres South Double Creek adjoining
Benajah KING.   Witnesses: Jesse KNIGHTON, Bowater SUMNER, and
George MARTIN.   Signed: Mijh. CLARK.

Page 10.   9 August 1787.   North Carolina Grant Thomas TUTTLE,
          150 acres both sides Red Bank Creek adjoining
Thomas BALKAM.

Page 10.   3 October 1787.   William Justice THOMPSON and
          Edward THOMPSON to Absalom BOSTICK, 60 pounds, 100
acres both sides Huings Creek adjoining Mark HARDIN and
HUNTER.   Witnesses: Joseph LADD, Noble LADD, and John
CAMERON.   Signed: William Justice THOMPSON and Edward THOMPSON.

Page 12.   6 February 1788.   Edward THOMPSON and wife Peggy
          to Absalom BOSTICK, 100 pounds, 150 acres both
sides Heuns Creek adjoining Joseph PATTERSON, HUNTER & Mark
HARDIN.   Witnesses: John BOSTICK, Lemuel SMITH, Noble LADD,
Joseph LADD, and William LADD.   Signed: Edward THOMPSON,
Peggy (X) THOMPSON.

Page 13.   5 November 1787.   Joseph WINSTON to John HALL, 40
          pounds, 21½ acres South side Twnfork Creek adjoin-
ing Thomas GOODE Junr. and Thomas GOODE, Senr.   Witnesses;
William THORNTON and Thomas HALL.   Signed: Joseph WINSTON.

Page 14.   9 August 1787.   North Carolina Grant William
          SAMFORD, 640 acres Fall Creek adjoining HOLCOMB.

Page 14.   9 August 1787.   North Carolina Grant William COOK,
          Junr., 400 acres Roberts Branch draft of Yadkin
River adjoining McBRIDE & CARTER.

Page 15.   9 August 1787.   North Carolina Grant Philip
          PRICHARD, 200 acres waters Fishers River.

Page 15.   9 August 1789.   North Carolina Grant William RAMEY
          100 acres Forbis Creek adjoining COGBURN.

Page 16.   3 November 1786.   Benjamin WHEELESS to Lewis
          WHEELESS, 100 pounds Specie, 200 acres upper end
tract said Benjamin now lives on South side Yadkin River.
Witnesses: Abner GREENWOOD, William ATKINS, and James
DURHAM.   Signed: Benjamin (X) WHEELESS.

Page 16.   27 October 1786.   Thomas EVANS and wife Ann to
          Peter SMITH, 200 pounds, 125 acres Mill Creek
part 250 acres granted EVANS 21 October 1782 adjoining Moses
MARTIN and EVANS and crossing Creek at old horse ford.
Witnesses: Richard GOODE, Benjamin YOUNG, and Moses MARTIN,
June.   Signed: Thomas EVANS, Anne (X) EVANS.

Page 17.   27 August 1787.   Abraham LEINBACK and wife
          Annegalia to Christian SMITH, 30 pounds, 20 acres
waters Lashs Branch adjoining said LEINBACK part 232 acres
granted said LEINBACK by Fredr Wm. MARSHALL 1 August 1786.
Witnesses; William THORNTON & Edward BILLITOR.   Signed:

Abraham LEINBACK and Annegalia (X) LEINBACK.

Page 18.   3 April 1789.   Amos LONDON, Senr. to John LONDON
           5 shillings, 200 acres North side Yadkin River on
Big Seven Island.   Witnesses: Rezia JARVIS, Johnson SUMMERS,
and John PALMER.   Signed: Amos LONDON.

Page 19.   9 August 1788.   Joseph WILLIAMS, Francis POINDEXTER
           and wife Jane, Executors, estate of Robert LANIER,
deceased to Alexander DOUGLAS (Robt. LANIER by bond 21
November 1783 obligated himself to make deed to said DOUGLAS
and failed to do so in his lifetime), 20 shillings, 85 acres
adjoining SATER & LANKASTER.   Witnesses: Henry PATTILLO and
William THORNTON.   Signed: Joseph WILLIAMS, Francis
POINDEXTER, and Jane POINDEXTER.

Page 20.   25 February 1787.   Ephraim McLIMORE and wife
           Hannah to Jacob JONES, 30 pounds, 100 acres East
side Canada Creek adjoining road.   Witnesses: Sterling
McLEMORE and Nicholas MASTERS.   Signed: Ephraim (X) McLIMORE
and Hannah (X) McLIMORE.

Page 22.   8 March 1788.   James SANDERS, Senr. and wife Sarah
           to their son, James SANDERS, Junr. for love 250
acres waters Hunting Creek adjoining John ANDERSON and Geo.
WOOTEN.   Witnesses: Richard WOOTEN and John COPELAND.
Signed: James SANDERS and Sarah (X) SANDERS.

Page 23.   9 August 1787.   North Carolina Grant Moses
           WOODRUFF 200 acres waters Pipes Creek adjoining
said WOODRUFFS former tract.

Page 23.   22 March 1785.   Benjamin SAMPSON, Pittsylvania
           County, Virginia to John CROUSE, 20 pounds, 100
acres adjoining Henry HOLDER.   Witnesses; Wendal KROUSE,
Samuel SEWARD, and Francis FORDENE.   Signed: Benjamin SAMPSON.

Page 24.   15 February 1788.   Arthur TATE to John VENABLE,
           25 pounds delivered to David CUTBORSON for Arthur
TATE, 200 acres both sides South fork little Yadkin River.
Acknowledged.   Signed: Arthur TATE.

Page 25.   15 February 1788.   William VENABLE to William
           STEEL, 10 pounds, 100 acres North fork little
Yadkin, part 400 acres granted William VENABLE.   Witness:
John VENABLE.   Signed: William (X) VENABLE.

Page 25.   8 October 1785.   Valentine FREY, Senr., Rowan
           County to Henry FREY, 100 pounds, 175 acres both
sides Townfork and Buffalow Creeks waters Dan River adjoining
John FREY.   Witnesses; John COOLEY and William WALKER.
Signed: Valentine (X) FREY.

Page 26.   25 August 1783.   William CAMPBELL to Michael FREY
           100 pounds, 150 acres Townfork of Dan River adjoin-
ing said FREY.   Witnesses: Andrew ROBINSON and Gray BYNUM.
Signed: William CAMPBELL.

Page 27. 5 July 1786. Peter PERKINS, Guilford County to Peter HARISTON, Henry County, Virginia, 1.200 pounds Virginia money, 333 acres South side Dan River adjoining Lemuel SMITH and Harry TERRELL. Witnesses: Lemuel SMITH, Thomas GRAY, and Constant PERKINS. Signed: Peter PERKINS.

Page 28. 4 July 1787. James THOMPSON to Peter HARISTON, Surry County, North Carolina, 260 pounds, 13 shillings, 4 pence, 250 acres North side Dan River adjoining GAINS. Witnesses: Matt WARNOCK, Reuben LINDSAY, and Gibson SOUTHERN. Signed: James THOMPSON.

Page 29. 27 July 1787. Barnabas FARE to Michael FARE, 150 pounds, 182 acres waters Blews Creek adjoining said Barnabas FARE. Witnesses: Andrew ROBINSON and Pattr. McGIBBONY. Signed: Barnabas (X) FAIR and Elizabeth (X) FAIR.

Page 30. 9 November 1787. Edmond PETERS to Peter HAIRSTON, 100 pounds proclamation money, 200 acres North side Dan River in an Island. Witnesses: John BOSTICK, Jacob McCRAW, and Rn (Reuben) LINDSEY. Signed: Edward (X) PETERS.

Page 30. 2 February 1787. Michael HAUSER, Senr. to Jacob HOLSABECK, 100 pounds, 200 acres both sides Muddy Creek adjoining Philip SHOUSE and bank Nation Creek. Witnesses: Michael HAUSER, Jurn. (signature in German) and Maunes (X) MILLER. Signed: Michael HAUSER.

Page 31. 21 February 1788. Moses MARTIN, Junr. and wife Ann to John FLINT, 70 pounds, 200 acres both sides Mill Creek adjoining Wm. HANES, dividing line between said MARTIN and heirs Michael SPENCER, deceased, being half tract granted James MARTIN, Administrator of estate Michael SPENCER, deceased, and sold to Moses MARTIN by James MARTIN. Witnesses: Charles McANALLY, Drurias (X) WARD, and Mary McANALLY. Signed: Moses MARTIN, Anne (X) MARTIN.

Page 32. 7 August 1789. Fredr Wm. MARSHALL, Salem, to Peter MOSS and son, Henry MOSS, planters Wachovia, 59 pounds, 2 shillings, 98½ acres North side Middle fork Muddy Creek called Wach adjoining David ANDER. Witnesses: Jacob BLUM and Lewis MEINUNG. Signed: Fredr Wm. MARSHALL.

Page 33. 4 April 1788. James DUNLAP, Senr. to Peter HARISTON, 80 pounds, 150 acres North side Dan River. Witnesses: John CRITTENDEN, Reuben LINDSAY, and Daniel BOATWRIGHT. Signed: James (X) DUNLAP.

Page 34. 18 tenth month called October 1786. Micajah CLARK to Joseph JESSUP, 480 pounds, 476½ acres both sides Toms Creek. Witnesses: Moreman BALLARD, William JESSUP, and Curtis JACKSON. Signed: Mijh. CLARK.

Page 35. 18 October 1786. Micajah CLARK to Joseph JESUP, 100 pounds, 100 acres both sides Toms Creek called Baleses Mill Improvement adjoining Mill Pond. Witnesses: William JESSUP, Curtis JACKSON, and Mooreman BALLARD. Signed: Mijh. CLARK.

Page 35.   16 January 1787.   Bowater SUMNER to Thomas JESSUP
         65 pounds, 91 acres North bank Pinchen or Big Creek
of Dan River, including Thomas JESSUPS improvement.
Witnesses: Samuel PARKER and Joseph (X) JESSUP. Signed:
Bowater SUMNER.

Page 36.   8 Sept. 1788.   Henry SPEER to Fredrick SHORE, 10
         pounds, 60 acres Deep Creek adjoining Peter SHERMAN
and STANFIELD, part 200 acres surveyed for H. SPEER 1786.
Witnesses: John (X) GARNER, Thomas McCOLLUM, and Philamon
(X) WISHON. Signed: H. SPEER.

Page 37.   (No date).   Jason ISBELL and wife Elizabeth to
         Timothy JESSUP, 76 pounds, 13 shillings, 6 pence
for 100 acres Dan River. Witnesses: Isaiah MIDKIFF and
Sylvanus BAKER. Signed: Jason ISBELL and Elizabeth ISBELL.

Page 38.   13 June 1787.   Bowater SUMNER to Garret GIBSON,
         100 pounds, 134 acres Dan River. Witnesses: Curtis
JACKSON and Thomas SUMNER. Signed: Bowater SUMNER.

Page 38.   27 May 1787.   Christian MILLER to George LONG, 5
         shillings Specie, ½ acre now being inclosed within
land said MILLER for a burying place. Witnesses: William
DAVIS, Edward CLANTON, and Joseph HILL. Signed: Christian
MILLER.

Page 39.   23 August 1787.   David CRANFORD to Joseph HINSHAW,
         Randloph County, 120 pounds, 200 acres Deep Creek
adjoining HADLEY and Thomas HOLCOMB. Witnesses: William
HOUGH, Abraham (X) REESE, and Francis HINSHAW. Signed:
David (X) CRANFORD.

Page 40.   9 August 1787.   North Carolina Grant Joshua BROWN,
         150 acres North fork Deep Creek adjoining ELMORE.

Page 40.   9 August 1787.   North Carolina Grant John JOHNSON,
         190 acres waters Forbis Creek adjoining Aaron
SPEER, GALLION & FROWHAWK.

Page 41.   9 August 1787.   North Carolina Grant William PETTY
         300 acres waters Deep Creek adjoining Henry
HAMBRICK, Millington BLALOCK and Richard BLALOCK.

Page 41.   3 January 1788.   David WALKER, Yeoman, and wife
         Sarah to Nathan PIKE, planter, 20 pounds, 110
acres middle fork Muddy Creek adjoining said WALKER.
Witnesses: Joseph McPHERSON and Jon WEISNER. Signed: David
WALKER and Sarah WALKER.

Page 42.   14 May 1788.   Frederick MILLER to Gabriel JONES,
         100 pounds, 300 acres Muddy Creek adjoining Toms
Creek Road. Witnesses: Anderew ROBINSON and William
THORNTON. Signed: Frederick MILLER.

Page 43.   11 August 1787.   Benjamin PARKS, Wilkes County,
         North Carolina, to Nathaniel MORRIS, 200 pounds,
200 acres South side Yadkin River mouth Pipes Creek adjoining

PARKS, John PIPES and EATON. Witnesses: William LEWIS and Isaac SOUTHARD. Signed: Benjamin PARKS.

Page 44. 21 July 1788. Andrew RUDOLPH to Patrick BURNS, 30 pounds, 223 acres waters Turners and Deep Creeks adjoining DOWDEN. Witnesses: Rachel (X) SPEER and Henry SPEER. Signed: Andrew (X) RUDOLPH.

Page 45. 12 February 1787. William RUTLEDGE to Mary RUTLEDGE, 30 pounds, 140 acres South side South fork Deep Creek. Witnesses: John REAVIS and Henry (X) REAVIS. Signed: William RUTLEDGE.

Page 46. 8 January 1787. John PETTYJOHN to Thomas HADLEY, 21 pounds, 10 shillings, 43 acres branch Deep Creek adjoining 200 acres granted said PETYJOHN. Witnesses: John MARTIN and Simon HADLEY, Senr. Signed: John (X) PETTYJOHN.

Page 47. 1 December 1785. Richard LAURANCE to Claborn LAURANCE, 150 pounds, 200 acres Pauls Creek called the Naked Bottom on West side. Witnesses: Joseph LAURANCE, Randolph (X) LAURENCE, and James LAURANCE. Signed: Richard LAURANCE and Jesebel LAURANCE.

Page 48. 7 February 1787. James REED, Mecklenburg County, Virginia to Joseph PIKE, 100 pounds North Carolina money, 200 acres head Rutledge Creek being tract returned to Secretarys office, but grant has not yet come to hand. Witnesses: Bowater SUMNER and William FORKNER. Signed: James (X) REED.

Page 49. 15 August 1786. Margaret NELSON to Zachariah SENTER, 25 pounds, 150 acres little Fish River. Witnesses: Elijah SMALLWOOD and Thomas (X) ROSS. Signed: Margaret (X) NELSON.

Page 49. 20 November 1786. A gift from Richard GITTENS to Margaret GITTENS in behalf of her dower, 3 negroes Betty, Nelson, Roard; feather bed and furniture. Witnesses: Hugh ARMSTRONG, Moses HARRIS, and Daniel GRIFFIN. Signed: Richard (X) GITTENS.

Page 50. 15 September 1786. James SANDERS, Senr. to Daniel HOLEMAN and wife Nanny SANDERS, otherwise HOLEMAN for love said SANDERS hath for his daughter, Nanny and the heirs of her body lawfully begotten, to Nanny and her husband Daniel HOLEMAN, negro girl Hannah 7 years old. Witnesses: Thomas HOLEMAN and James SANDERS, Junr. Signed: Daniel HOLEMAN, Nanny (X) HOLEMAN and James SANDERS, Senr.

Page 51. 6 July 1786. Edmond REAVIS to Henry SPEER, 30 pounds, 640 acres waters Deep Creek adjoining William RUTLEDGE and REESE on Reeses Creek. Witnesses: Joseph REAVIS, Edward REAVIS, and Thomas CLARKE. Signed: Edmund REAVIS.

Page 52. 7 December 1786. Silas ENYART, Washington County,

Virginia to Henry SPEER, 100 pounds, 392 acres both sides Deep Creek part tract surveyed for Abraham CRESON 13 January 1759 adjoining Wyatt GARNER. Witnesses: Samuel CUMMINS, John WILLIAMS, Joshua (X) CRESON, and Abraham WINSCOT. Signed: Silas ENYART and Sarah (X) ENYART.

Page 53. 14 September 1786. Thomas SKIDMORE to Abraham SKIDMORE, 40 pounds, 113¾ acres Deep Creek adjoining Henry SPEER and John SKIDMORE. Witnesses: H(enry) SPEER, Rachel (X) SPEER, and James TODD. Signed: Thomas SKIDMORE.

Page 54. 7 September 1786. Henry SPEER to Carlton LINDSAY, 30 pounds, 540 acres Deep Creek part 640 acres granted Edmund REAVID adjoining William RUTLEDGE and RESE. Witnesses: Ann (X) MILLER, William HOUGH, and Matthew (X) BATES. Signed: H. SPEER.

Page 54. 12 February 1787. William MEREDITH, Sheriff, to Jonathan VERNON (land lost by John BEAZLEY to satisfy Jonathan VERNON), 100 acres Callahans Creek adjoining Robert HAZELETT and said VERNON including Burks old Cabbin. Witness: Robert WILLIAMS. Signed: William MEREDITH, Sheriff.

Page 55. 22 January 1787. Michael HAUSER, Senr. to John Kayser, 100 pounds, 200 acres both sides Muddy Creek adjoining Jacob HELSABECK. Witnesses: George HAUSER, Thomas HARBOUR, and Jacob SHORE. Signed: Michael HAUSER.

Page 55. 30 August 1779. Benjamin and Joseph STEWART to Matthew BROOKS, 520 pounds, 384 acres East side Yadkin River being 508 acres GRANVILLE granted to Saml STEWART, Sr. Witnesses: William THORNTON, Agness PRICE, and James BLACKWELL. Signed: Benjamin (X) STEWART, Joseph (X) STEWART, and Elizabeth (X) STEWART.

Page 56. 14 February 1786. John and Prisila GILBERT to Matthew BROOKS, 70 pounds, 640 acres waters Naked Branch adjoining Martin HAUSER and SPOONHOUR. Acknowledged. Signed: John GILBERT and Prisilla (X) GILBERT.

Page 57. 15 September 1785. James McKOIN to David JAMES, 106 pounds, 111½ acres waters Oldfield Creek adjoining said McKOIN part tract granted him 3 November 1784. Witnesses: Andrew ROBINSON and Hugh ENDSLEY. Signed: James McKOINE.

Page 57. 16 November 1786. Robert AYRES to James MATTHIS, 400 pounds, 152 acres waters Forbis Creek part 500 acres conveyed by Matthew MOORE, Esq. to Charles VANDEVER; by VANDEVER to Robert AYRES. Witnesses: John (X) BOVENDER and Royal (X) MARTIN. Signed: Robert AYRES.

Page 58. 1 February 1787. Hugh ARMSTRONG to William BURRESS, 150 acres Specie, 150 acres both sides Pauls Creek. Acknowledged. Signed: Hugh ARMSTRONG.

Page 58. 13 November 1788. Lazarus TILLY to Jesse SIMMONS, 100 pounds, 200 acres Dan River being granted said

TILLEY 13 October 1783. Witnesses: Jesse KNIGHTON and Aaron LIZBY. Signed: Lazarus TILLY.

Page 59. 13 November 1788. Lazarus TILLY to Shadrack PREWETT, 33 pounds, 6 shillings, 8 pence (no acres) waters Dan River being granted said TILLY 13 October 1783. Witnesses: Jesse KNIGHTON and Aaron LIZBY. Signed: Lazarus TILLY.

Page 60. 12 November 1789. Lazarus TILLY to Jesse SIMMONS, 20 pounds, 100 acres South side Dan River adjoining George DEATHERAGE granted TILLY by State of North Carolina 18 May 1789. Acknowledged. Signed: Lazarus TILLY.

Page 60. 16 February 1787. John Thomas LONGINO to Frederick MILLER, 40 pounds, 300 acres waters Muddy Creek, land granted James COFFEY 3 November 1784; sold at sheriffs sale to James SANDERS 10 August 1785; by SANDERS to LONGINO the same day. Witnesses: William Terrell LEWIS, Jacob BLUM, and William ARMSTRONG. Signed: John Thomas LONGINO.

Page 61. 22 December 1786. James WHITE, Spartanburg County, South Carolina to John DAVIS, 20 pounds, 50 acres East side Blackeye branch adjoining JONES. Witnesses: James DAVIS, and Samuel (X) PARFORD. Signed: James WHITE.

Page 61. 10 February 1786. Barnabas FARE and wife Elizabeth to John LOW, 100 pounds, 350 acres North fork Blews Creek adjoining Joseph CUMMINS. Witnesses; Andrew ROBINSON and Thomas LOW. Signed: (Barnabas signed in German) and Elizabeth (X) FARE.

Page 62. 16 February 1787. Matthew and Mary BROOKS to Aquilla MATTHEWS, 200 pounds, 200 acres waters Stewarts Creek adjoining MILLER, BOLEJACK, LASH & CARVER. Acknowledged. Signed: Matt BROOKS and Mary (X) BROOKS.

Page 63. 9 November 1786. Evan and Deborah THOMAS to Isaac GARRISON, 40 pounds, 100 acres waters Lick Creek adjoining John BRANSON and GARRISON being half 200 acre surveyed for David THOMAS, deceased. Witnesses: Andrew ROBINSON and John MARTIN. Signed: Evan THOMAS and Deborah (X) THOMAS.

Page 63. 9 August 1787. Isaac GARRISON and wife Martha to Stephen FOUNTAIN, 18 pounds, 18 shillings, 37½ acres adjoining said GARRISON. Witness: Joseph BITTING. Signed: Isaac GARRISON.

Page 64. 8 February 1788. Richard GOODE, Sheriff, to Thomas RAPER (land lost by Jas MOORE to satisfy Thos. RAPER), 200 acres middle fork Lick Creek adjoining Isaac GARRISON, James WARNOCK and Stephen FOUNTAIN. Witnesses: Stephen FOUNTAIN and Peter (X) FULP. Signed: Richard GOODE, Sheriff.

Page 65. 12 August 1788. Joseph LINEBACK to Jacob KRUGER, 200 pounds Specie, 400 acres waters Muddy Creek called the Dorothea adjoining Wachovia being part conveyed said LINEBACK from James HUTTON by his Atty. Fredr Wm. MARSHALL 26 December 1770 in Rowan County. Witnesses: Henry SPAENHOWER and William THORNTON. Signed: Joseph (in German).

Page 65. 13 December 1786. Daniel SWINEY and wife Sarah to William SWEATT, 250 pounds, 319 acres North side Yadkin River adjoining Philip HOWARD, Samuel DAVIS land granted Morgan BRYAN from Granville 29 October 1752; by MORGAN to James BRYAN 7 July 1753; by James to said SWINEY 23 July 1762. Witnesses: William THORNTON, Samuel MOSBY, Junr. and John (X) SWINEY. Signed: Daniel (X) SWINEY and Sarah (X) SWINEY.

Page 66. 19 March 1788. Talafero DAVIS to Agree GARNER, 100 pounds 146 acres waters Turners Creek adjoining Jacob SPEER, Roger TURNERS old tract and Purdey. Witnesses: Benjamin (X) CONNER, Thomas DAVIS, Peter PETTYJOHN, and William COLVARD. Signed: Talafero DAVIS.

Page 67. 31 August 1786. William DAVIS and wife Mary to James DAVIS, their son, 350 pounds, 120 acres South side Dan River above Upper Charow Town (land Wm DAVIS received of Thomas MULLINS and Patrick MULLINS received of Granvile) adjoining Enoch CONLEY, Punchin CAMP and County line. Witnesses: John DAVIS, John (X) DUNLAP, and Patrick (X) KINEY. Signed: William (X) DAVIS and Mary (X) DAVIS.

Page 68. 25 August 1787. John JOHNSON to Abraham VANDERPOOL 50 pounds, 150 acres Pilot Creek waters Tarrarat River. Witnesses: Ratliff BOON, Charles DUDLEY, and Micajah CLARK. Signed: John JOHNSON.

Page 69. 8 November 1788. George PHILLIPS, Senr. to George MESSICK, 30 pounds Specie, 50 acres waters North Hunting Creek. Witnesses: Josiah ROTEN and Aron LATHAM. Signed: George PHILLIPS.

Page 70. 10 February 1789. Stephen HOBSON to Isaac STUBBS, 66 pounds, 100 acres Forbis Creek part larger tract granted William JOHNSON by State of North Carolina. Witnesses: Thomas VESTAL and Samuel STUBBS. Signed: Stephen HOBSON and Rachel HOBSON.

Page 70. 8 August 1789. James JOHNSON to Robert JOHNSON, 2 pounds, 100 acres waters Abbits Creek adjoining Jesse SANDERS on Salisbury Road, Robert JOHNSON and David BROOKS. Witnesses: Lydia (X) ALLEN and Andrew ROBINSON. Signed: James JOHNSON.

Page 71. 3 June 1790. Henry SPEER and wife, Rachel to Robert JOHNSON, Stokes County, 500 pounds, 500 acres North fork Deep Creek adjoining Samuel SHINN, Peter MIERS, Simon HADLEY, George HOPPIS, Francis BAKER, Hoppis Creek being land granted Jacob FEREE. Witnesses: Henry PATTILLO, William HOUGH, and William ADAMS, Junr. Signed: H. SPEER and Rachel SPEER.

Page 72. 18 May 1789. North Carolina Grant Moses SMITH 400
acres waters Abbits Creek where Fields line inter-
sects Rowan County line.

Page 72. 18 May 1789. North Carolina Grant Reubin SHEILD
200 acres waters Abbits Creek adjoining SANDERS &
KELLY.

Page 73. 24 February 1785. Matthias RICHARDSON and wife
Fanny to Abel SHELDS, 100 pounds, 200 acres waters
Abbits Creek adjoining John TEAGUE and George VILLARDS.
Witnesses: William DOBSON, James GAMMILL, and Andrew MILLER.
Signed: Matthas (X) RICHARDSON and Fanny (X) RICHARDSON.

Page 74. 3 August 1787. Greenberry PATTERSON to John
BOHANNON, Senr., 100 pounds, 125 acres Mill Creek
mouth branch adjoining BOHANNONS fence including plantation
part tract now in possession said PATTERSON. Witnesses:
Abner GREENWOOD, Jeffrey JOHNSON, and John SUMMERS. Signed:
Greenberry PATTERSON.

Page 74. 15 May 1787. William DAVENPORT to John DOYLIN,
100 pounds, 300 acres waters Forbis Creek adjoining
Anne BAKER being tract granted DEVENPORT 8 October 1783.
Witnesses: Aaron SPEER, John WILLIAMS, and Levice (X)
HOWARD (female). Signed: William (X) DEVENPORT.

Page 75. 29 September 1786. Fredr Wm. MARSHALL, Salem, to
John BLAKE, planter, 100 pounds, 200 acres North
branch Muddy Creek adjoining Robert MARKLAND and Benj CHITTY
(part James HUTTON land vested in said MARSHALL). Witnesses:
Isaac DOUTHIT and Ludwig MEINUNG. Signed: Fredr Wm. MARSHALL.

Page 76. 18 May 1789. North Carolina Grant William DAVIS
550 acres near road crossing Shaws Creek, Simms
Creek and Little Snow Creek.

Page 77. 27 October 1785. Michael REYNOLDS, Wake County,
to Isaac COPELAND, farmer, 160 pounds, 500 acres
both sides little Beaver Creek granted said REYNOLDS 3
November 1784. Witnesses: James FREEMAN and Charles DUDLEY.
Signed: Michael REYNOLDS.

Page 79. 14 August 1786. Charles VANDEVER to Robert AYRES,
10 pounds, 152 acres waters Forbis Creek and
Beaver Dam part 580 acres sold VANDEVER by Matt MOORE, Esq.
Witnesses: Henry SPEER and Charles (X) VANDEVER. Signed:
Charles VANDEVER.

Page 80. 22 January 1787. Joseph ALLEN, Spartanburg, South
Carolina, for love to his son, Daniel ALLEN, all
his land on Beaver Dam Creek waters Yadkin River, 200 acres
part greater tract granted John BRASELL by State of North
Carolina. Witnesses: Thomas ROBINSON and John SANDERS.
Signed: Joseph ALLEN.

Page 80. 22 December 1786. James WHITE, Spartanburg County,

South Carolina to John DAVIS, 50 pounds, 100 acres Blackeye Branch adjoining JONES. Witnesses: James DAVIS and Samuel (X) PARFORD. Signed: James WHITE.

Page 81. 7 November 1784. Joseph HOBBS and wife Ann, Fredrck County, Maryland, to John SATER of Baltimore County, Maryland, 200 pounds, 500 acres in Rowan County, North Carolina, East side Yadkin River South fork Reedy Creek land granted John HOWARD by Granville 21 December 1761. Witnesses: John WEIR, Joseph WOOD, J.P., and Joshua (X) HOWARD. Signed: Joseph HOBBS and Ann (X) HOBBS.

Page 83. 6 November 1784. Joseph HOBBS, Fredrick County, Maryland appoints Robert LANIER and Phillip HOWARD both of Rowan County, North Carolina his lawful Attys to deliver above deed and future deeds, etc. Witnesses: Joseph WOOD, J.P., Joshua (X) HOWARD, and John WEIR. Signed: Joseph HOBBS.

Page 84. 1787. William ARMSTRONG to Samuel WOOD, 150 pounds, 200 acres both sides Pauls Creek on the Virginia line. Acknowledged. Signed: William ARMSTRONG.

Page 84. 1 March 1787. Elijah KIRKMAN to Aaron MOORE, 50 pounds, 250 acres waters Beaver Creek adjoining Gilbert KEEN, Thomas SPENCE and Josiah KEEN. Witnesses: David SPENCE and Thomas SPENCE. Signed: Elijah (X) KIRKMAN.

Page 85. 13 August 1787. William CLAYTON to Joel HALBERT, 120 pounds, 140 acres both sides Mill Creek of Townfork adjoining James MARTIN. Witnesses: Moses (X) MARTIN, Junr. and William (X) HEATH. Signed: William CLATON.

Page 86. 1787. Enoch CONLEY to Richard BEASLEY, 53 pounds, 10 shillings Virginia money, 184 acres Bakers Branch of Dan River adjoining James TILLEY, part 400 acres surveyed for said TILLEY. Witnesses: Joseph CLOUD, John NUNNS, and Robert (X) BEASLEY. Signed: Enoch (X) CONLEY and Sarah (X) CONLEY.

Page 87. 3 October 1785. James TILLEY to Enoch KONLE, 40 pounds, 184 acres Bakers Branch of Dan River adjoining said TILLEYS part 400 acre survey for said TILLEY. Witnesses: John BULLOCK, Matthew HARRIS, and John (X) HUNTSMAN. Signed: James (X) TILLEY and Martha (X) TILLEY.

Page 88. 1 February 1787. Fredr Wm. MARSHALL, Salem, to Gottlieb SPACH, planter Wachovia, 300 pounds, 200 acres both sides Doves Branch of Petersbach middle fork Muddy Creek adjoining late SHOEMAKER and Abraham HAUSER, part HUTTON land vested in Marshi. Witnesses: Peter YARRELL and Ludwig MEINUNG. Signed: Fredr Wm. MARHSALL.

Page 89. 2 February 1787. Mortgage Deed, Gottlieb SPACH, planter, and wife Martha Elizabeth to Gottfried PRAWZEL, Salem, County Clerk, 204 pounds, 5 shillings for 200 acres both sides Doves Branch of Petersbach middle fork Muddy Creek adjoining SHOEMAKERS corner and Abraham HAUSER

11

(if above obligation paid this deed be null and void).
Witnesses: Peter YARRELL and Ludwig MEINUNG. Signed: Gotlieb
SPACH and Martha Elizabeth (X) SPACH.

Page 91. 9 August 1787. North Carolina Grant Jacob HUTTS
          200 acres waters Harmons Creek adjoining another
100 acre tract surveyed for said HUTTS.

Page 91. 9 August 1787. North Carolina Grant Jacob HUTTS
          100 acres waters Harmons Creek adjoining HUMPHREY
and HUTTS.

Page 92. 28 March 1787. Henry SPEER to Leonard RICHARDS,
          5 shillings, 100 acres branch Turners Creek
adjoining Abraham CRESON. Witnesses: John MILLER, John (X)
BOHANNON, and Obed (X) COLLINS. Signed: H. SPEER.

Page 92. 18 May 1789. North Carolina Grant John RECTOR 300
          acres Buck Shoal Branch waters South fork Hunting
Creek adjoining Joseph MYERS and Theophilus MORGAN.

Page 93. 16 August 1787. Ashley JOHNSON to James JOHNSON,
          5 shillings, 200 acres South fork Muddy Creek
adjoining his own line tract granted Ashley by State 3
November 1784. Witnesses: William SWAIM and Auston ELMORE.
Signed: Ashley JOHNSON.

Page 94. 10 May 1785. Richard GOODE, Sheriff, to John WELLS,
          5 shillings, 600 acres waters Lick Creek adjoining
GARRISON, Sandy Branch, Samuel DAVIS, Jo HAMM (land lost by
Joseph GARRISON to satisfy John WELLS). Witnesses: Andrew
ROBINSON and Thomas GRAHAM. Signed: Richard GOODE, Sheriff.

Page 95. 10 January 1788. John HIEAT to Samuel VOGLER, 16
          pounds, 50 acres Townhawk Branch adjoining John
NULL and Andrew BLACK, part tract 200 acres granted John
NULL, but grant was lost and said land conveyed to John
HIEAT by said NULL 10 May 1787. Witnesses: William THORNTON,
Francis (X) KITNER, and Adam (X) SPOON. Signed: John HIEAT
(signed in German.).

Page 96. 9 August 1787. North Carolina Grant George HAWS
          200 acres waters Muddy Creek adjoining Jn. TEAGUE,
Moravian line, John LAUNERS and Ashley JOHNSON.

Page 96. 29 April 1786. Commissioners town of Richmond to
          John Thomas LONGINO, 4 shillings Lott #8 fronting
Broad Street on Southwest square. Witnesses: John ARMSTRONG
and William HUGHLETT. Signed: Martin ARMSTRONG, Job MARTIN,
Samuel CUMMINS, Malcum CURRY, and Robert WALKER.

Page 97. 29 April 1786. Commissioners town Richmond to
          John Thomas LONGINO, 20 shillings, ½ lott #13
Northwest square where Spring Street crosses Broad. Witnesses: John ARMSTRONG and William HUGHELTT. Signed: All the
above Commissioners signed.

Page 98. 18 November 1786. John Thomas LONGINO to Thomas

POINDEXTER, 80 pounds , lott #8 town Richmond Southwest square fronting Broad Street. Witnesses: William THORNTON, H(enry) PATTILLO, and William POINDEXTER. Signed: John Thomas LONGINO.

Page 98. 11 May 1786. John Thomas LONGINO to Hugh MORRIS, 40 pounds, 240 acres little branch Yadkin River. Witnesses: Zachariah MARTIN, John DAVIS, and Job MARTIN. Signed: John Thomas LONGINO.

Page 99. 11 November 1786. Matthias STEELMAN to James SANDERS, 20 pounds, 300 acres, waters Hunting Creek near head draft Buck Shoal Branch crossing Forbis Creek. Witnesses: Thomas McCOLLAM, Thomas GALLION, and H(enry) SPEER. Signed: Matthias STEELMAN.

Page 99. 10 May 1786. Amos LADD to Noble LADD, 45 pounds, 39¼ acres North side Dan River adjoining TATE. Witnesses: Joseph LADD, Sarah (X) SUTHERLAND, and Catron B. (X) LADD (female). Signed: Amos LADD.

Page 100. 15 November 1786. Constantine LADD to Absalom BOSTICK, 200 pounds, 87 acres waters Dan River adjoining said BOSTICK. Witnesses: William CRAWFORD, A(ndrew) ROBINSON, and Noble LADD. Signed: Constant LADD.

Page 101. 30 June 1786. Moses BAKER and wife, Mary, to Henry SPEER, 200 pounds, 50 acres waters Forbis Creek fork Joseph Branch part 550 acres deeded Robert FORBIS. Witnesses: John WILLIAMS and Robert (X) FORBIS. Signed: Moses BAKER and Mary (X) BAKER.

Page 102. 16 November 1786. Adam WOLF and Adam BINKLEY, Executors, estate of Leonard MOSER, deceased, to Anthony BITTING, 120 pounds, 200 acres Northwest corner original tract including plantation part 640 acres of Leonard MOSER, deceased. Acknowledged. Signed: Adam BINKLEY and Adam WOOLF.

Page 103. 9 November 1786. Peter MOSES to Anthony BITTING, 80 pounds, 241 acres adjoining Wachovia being tract left Peter MOSER by his father and laid off to him by Adam WOOLF and Adam BINDLEY, Executors, estate of his said father. Acknowledged. Signed: Peter (X) MOSER.

Page 103. 16 October 1785. Ambrose BLACKBURN to James COFFEY, 82 pounds, 450 acres head branch Panther and Mill Creeks. Witnesses: Martin BURRIS, Samuel HAMPTON, John EVANS, John BLACKBURN, William HEATH, and John HALBERT. Signed: Ambrose BLACKBURN.

Page 104. 9 September 1786. Christian SHOUSE, farmer, to John CONRAD, merchant, 75 pounds, 200 acres Mill Creek adjoining Fredr FISCUS, SHORE and the Richmond road. Witnesses: Henry SPEONHOWER and Jacob MILLER. Signed: Christian SHOUSE and Magdalena (X) SHOUSE.

Page 104. 9 September 1785. Benjamin GRIFFITH to John COX,

13

164 pounds, 13 shillings, 4 pence for 200 acres both sides Stewarts Creek adjoining widdow GRIFFITH, John GITTIN and Jno GRIFFITH. Witnesses: Robert HARRIS, Matthew COX, and James GITTENS. Signed: Benjamin GRIFFITH.

Page 105. 16 November 1786. Joseph AYRES to Laurence HOLCOMB, 130 pounds, 150 acres, Forbis Creek adjoining Robt AYRES, tract sold Jos AYRES by Robt AYRES 10 November 1781. Witnesses: William THORNTON and Robert AYRES. Signed: Joseph AYRES.

Page 106. 18 April 1786. John ALLEN, Senr. to John ALLEN, Junr., 5 pounds, 200 acres South side Yadkin River on Hogins Creek, tract granted Jos WOODRUFF 24 October 1782. Witness: John STREET. Signed: John (X) ALLEN, Senr.

Page 107. 18 April 1786. John ALLEN, Senr. to William ALLEN, 100 pounds, 200 acres Fishers River waters Yadkin River adjoining county road part tract 300 acres granted John ALLEN 3 November 1784. Witness: John STREET. Signed: John (X) ALLEN, Senr.

Page 108. 18 April 1786. John ALLEN, Senr. to Isaac ALLEN, 5 pounds, 200 acres Polecat Creek tract granted John ALLEN, Senr. 3 November 1784. Witness: John STREET. Signed: John (X) ALLEN, Senr.

Page 109. 12 May 1787. Edward THOMPSON to William Justice THOMPSON, 35 pounds, 100 acres both sides Huings Creek adjoining Ned HUNTER. Witnesses: Joseph LADD, Joseph DRAUGHN, and Joseph THOMPSON. Signed: Edward THOMPSON.

Page 109. 18 January 1787. George DEATHERAGE to John DEATHERAGE, 80 pounds Gold and Silver Virginia coin, 414 acres where said George now lives. (Geo indebted to John and if above obligation paid, this deed be null and void). Witnesses: Phil DEATHERAGE, John DEATHERAGE, and Sally (X) DEATHERAGE. Signed: George DEATHERAGE.

Page 110. 17 November 1790. John DURHAM, Spartanburg County, South Carolina, to Joshua May LINDSAY, Spartanburg County, South Carolina, 150 pounds Sterling, 440 acres North James LINDSAYS old line where John BITTRICKS line joins little fork Seven Island Creek on path leading to McFEES old place. Witnesses: John ALLEN, James LINDSAY, Junr., Cresy LINDSAY, Aaron MOOR, and Moses MOOR. Signed: John DURHAM and Mary DURHAM.

Page 111. 12 August 1788. James LINDSAY and wife, Mary, to John DURHAM, Spartanburg County, South Carolina, 150 pounds, 440 acres Seven Island Creek adjoining John BITTICKS and LINDSAY. Witnesses: John BITTICK and John (X) CARLTON. Signed: James LINDSAY and Mary LINDSAY.

Page 112. 18 October 1787. Joseph HAUSER to William CHILDRESS, 100 pounds, 300 acres Brusy fork branch Townfork. Witnesses: Joseph CHILDRESS, Samuel STROUT, and Henry SPANHOWER. Signed: Joseph HAUSER.

14

Page 112. 21 November 1786. James LAFOYE to Henry PATTILLO, 100 pounds, 200 acres little fork Oldfield Creek adjoining Samuel DAVIS. Witnesses: William THORNTON and Sarah THORNTON. Signed: James LAFOYE.

Page 113. 8 September 1788. Philip DEATHERAGE to Edwin HICKMAN, 80 pounds, 150 acres North Double Creek of Dan River. Witnesses: Edwin HICKMAN, Senr., Phebe HICKMAN, and William (X) HARRIS. Signed: Phil DEATHERAGE.

Page 114. 29 September 1788. John George EBERT, planter, and wife Rosina to Fredr Wm. MARSHALL, 300 pounds, 414 acres East side South fork Muddy Creek adjoining John Nicholas BOECHEL, land sold 1 March 1784 by Martin EBERT and wife Eva Barbara to John George EBERT. Witnesses: John RIGHTS and Lewis MEINUNG. Signed: George and his wife, Rosina (both signed in German).

Page 116. 10 May 1787. Richard LAURANCE to James LAURANCE, 150 pounds Virginia money, 150 acres both sides Renfro Creek East fork Tarrarat River adjoining Richard LAURANCE, land whereon said James now lives and originally granted William BURRIS. Witnesses: Thomas HUDSPETH and John BRYSON, Junr. Signed: Richard LAURANCE and Isabell (X) LAURANCE.

Page 116. 1 May 1787. Andrew MOORE to Robert CRUMP, 50 pounds, 213 acres North fork Beaver Island Creek adjoining John ROBINSON and Hugh HOLLAND. Witnesses: John BRADLEY, Anthony DEARING, and Samuel HENDERSON. Signed: Andw. MOORE.

Page 117. 1787. Commissioners town Richmond to Charles VEST, Richmond County seat, Surry County, 40 shillings, lott #16 fronting Broad Street Southeast square. Witnesses: George HAUSER and John ARMSTRONG. Signed: Martin ARMSTRONG, John RANDLEMAN, and Samuel CUMMINS.

Page 118. 18 May 1789. North Carolina Grant Allen UNTHANK, 150 acres School House Branch of Deep River adjoining LINDSAY.

Page 118. 9 August 1784. John LYNCH and wife, Mary to Mark PHILLIPS, 5 shillings, 200 acres exclusive 2 acres for use Meeting House on Salem Road adjoining CALCLEAZIER. Witnesses: Charles PARKER, John (X) DOUGLAS, and William THORNTON. Signed: John LYNCH and Mary LYNCH.

Page 119. 8 September 1788. John HARVEY, Junr. to John HARVEY, Senr., 60 pounds, 200 acres exclusive 2 acres for use Meeting House. Witnesses: William HARVEY and Clabourn (X) GENTRY. Signed: John HARVEY, Junr.

Page 120. 8 February 1788. John HARVEY, Junr. to John HARVEY, Senr., 65 pounds, 90 acres Double Creek adjoining BLACK. Acknowledged. Signed: John HARVEY, Junr.

Page 120. 10 May 1787. Edward WELBORN to John MEREDITH, Senr.

15

195 pounds, 50 acres Yadkin River. Witnesses: William COOK, Keziah (X) COOK, and Elizabeth (X) COOK. Signed: Edward WILBURN.

Page 121. 29 July 1785. Ralph SHELTON, Henry County, Virginia to Alexander BURGE, 100 pounds, 500 acres both sides Hixes fork adjoining Sanford FIELDS. Witnesses: John DEATHERAGE, Thomas ISBELL, and Phil DEATHERAGE. Signed: Ralph (X) SHELTON and Susanna (X) SHELTON.

Page 122. 23 February 1787. Elihu AYRES to William Terrell LEWIS, 150 pounds, 386 acres South side Yadkin River mouth Cobbs Creek adjoining said LEWIS. Witnesses: John JONES, Jeffrey JOHNSON, and John PARKER. Signed: Elihu AYRES.

Page 122. May 1787. John LANKFORD to Woody BURGE, Henry County, Virginia, 113 pounds, 6 shillings, 8 pence for 222 acres Peters Creek adjoining Archelous FARE. Witnesses: James GAINES and Isaac CLOUD. Signed: John LANKFORD and Elizabeth (X) LANKFORD.

Page 123. 9 August 1787. North Carolina Grant John HURT 100 acres South side Yadkin River adjoining HEADIN.

Page 124. 20 April 1787. David DOUGLAS and wife, Martha, to John HURT, 160 pounds, 300 acres North side Yadkin River adjoining McClains fork, John MASH and John COOK. Witnesses: Zach RAY, Michael GILBERT, and Joel HURT. Signed: David DOUGLASS and Martha (X) DOUGLASS.

Page 125. 18 May 1789. North Carolina Grant Reuben SHORES 400 acres waters Deep Creek in Brushy Mountain adjoining Cabbin Cadles, top Brushy Mountain and CLATON.

Page 125. 18 May 1789. North Carolina Grant Ninean RILEY 400 acres Buck Shoal Branch waters Hunting Creek adjoining MYERS and Hamblins road.

Page 126. 18 May 1789. North Carolina Grant Ninean REYLEE 200 acres waters North fork Hunting Creek adjoining James SANDERS and HINES.

Page 126. 6 November 1789. John HARVEY and wife, Mary, to Joseph HALL, 100 pounds, 116 acres Double Creek waters Yadkin River adjoining WHITAKER part 206 acres State Grant said HARVEY. Witnesses: William THORNTON and Jacob (X) BLACK. Signed: John HARVEY and Mary (X) HARVEY.

Page 127. 10 February 1787. John Christian LASH, Salem in Wachovia, to John BRINKLEY, 135 pounds, 12 shillings, 250 acres Muddy Creek, part tract Granted Jacob LASH, late of Bethlehem, Northampton County, Pennsylvania by Granville 21 January 1762, Rowan County. Witnesses: Traugott BAGGE, John MICKEY, and Jacob BLUM. Signed: John Christian LASH.

Page 128. 5 October 1786. James DOAK to Thomas BALLARD, 100 pounds, 197 acres both sides Pauls Creek.

Witnesses: Stephen K. SMITH and Chrisr. RAWLES. Signed: James DOAK.

Page 129. 13 February 1787. George HIDE to Moses RIGHT, 100 pounds, 200 acres North side Tarrarat River adjoining Samuel FREEMAN. Witnesses: John JONES, Joshua FREEMAN, and Jacob FREEMAN. Signed: George (X) HYDE.

Page 129. 19 February 1787. Robert FORBIS and wife, Mary, to John CARTER, 400 pounds, 400 acres South fork Josephs Creek. Witnesses: H(enry) SPEER, Matt BROOKS, and Joseph FORBIS. Signed: Robert FORBIS and Mary (X) FORBIS.

Page 130. 13 January 1786. Henry HOLDER to Daniel SMITH, 63 pounds, 150 acres Blanket Bottom Creek adjoining Michael MILLS. Witnesses: Nicholas DOLL (signed in German), John NULL, Jacob NULL, and Francis FORDEM. Signed: Elizabeth (X) HOLDER (signed in German).

Page 131. 18 May 1789. North Carolina Grant Henry SPEER 100 acres adjoining Aaron SPEER and FROHOCK.

Page 131. 18 May 1789. North Carolina Grant Henry SPEER 300 acres Josephs Creek adjoining SPEER, FORBIS, John COE and Giles HUDSPETH.

Page 132. 18 May 1789. North Carolina Grant Henry SPEER 35 acres Blackeye Creek adjoining James HOWELL, David HOWELL and DOWDEN.

Page 133. 10 December 1790. North Carolina Grant Henry SPEER 100 acres bank Yadkin River adjoining CRESON below Frosts old Mill above mouth Deep Creek adjoining POINDEXTER and KIMBROUGH.

Page 133. 18 May 1789. North Carolina Grant Joseph PHILLIPS 300 acres adjoining George SPRINKLE on Yadkin River adjoining HUNTER and his own line.

Page 134. 19 May 1787. Matthew MOORE, Esq., Sheriff, to Wm. Hargus GRAY, Burke County, Georgia, 200 pounds, 100 acres waters Forbis Creek adjoining said GRAY, Robert FORBIS (land lost 1781 by James SIMKINS to satisfy Henry SPEER). Acknowledged. Signed: Matt MOORE, Sheriff.

Page 134. 17 June 1791. Hugh ARMSTRONG, Esq., Sheriff, to John Thos LONGINO, Yeoman, 22 pounds, 540 acres waters Deep Creek and Swisher or Reeses Creek adjoining Benj GARRISON, Wm RUTLEDGE being part larger tract Edmund REAVIS (land lost 1787 by Calton LINDSEY indicted against him for Tresspass; he was guilty). Witnesses: Richard GOODE, James LESTER, and William THORNTON. Signed: Hugh ARMSTRONG, Sheriff.

Page 135. 10 August 1791. Hugh ARMSTRONG, Sheriff, to John Thos LONGINO, Yeoman, 21 shillings, 540 acres waters Deep Creek, Swishers or Reeses Creek adjoining Benj GARRISON, Wm RUTLEDGE being tract Edmund REAVIS (land

lost by James LINDSEY for failing to "surrender up" Calton
LINDSEY, March term Superior Court 1788). Witnesses: Joseph
WILLIAMS, and Manning (X) SUMMERS. Signed: Hugh ARMSTRONG,
Sheriff.

Page 136.   11 May 1791.   Hugh ARMSTRONG, Esq. Sheriff, to
            John Thos LONGINO, 20 pounds, 5 shillings, 440
acres Seven Island Creek adjoining road leads from Round
Hill to Critchfields fork and adjoining John BITTICK (land
lost by James LINDSAY for failing to "surrender up" Calton
LINDSAY, Superior Court March term 1789). Witnesses: Joseph
WILLIAMS and Manning (X) SUMMERS. Signed: Hugh ARMSTRONG,
Sheriff.

Page 137.   13 October 1783.   North Carolina Grant John
            BOOTHE 300 acres waters South fork Forbis Creek
adjoining FROHOCK.

Page 138.   27 December 1786.   David ALLEN, late Surry County
            to William HILL, York County, South Carolina,
1,800 pounds, 640 acres Wilkes and Surry Counties adjoining
Salathiel MARTIN, North side Big Elkin below Iron Works,
Waugh DANIELS; 640 acres Surry County, mouth Big Elkin
dividing line between Wilkes and Surry adjoining said ALLEN
and Wm. CARROLL; 5 acres Surry County Iron Mine Pit near
Thomas YATES dwelling house; 640 acres Wilkes County adjoining Wm CARROLL and Surry line; 557 acres Wilkes County
adjoining VANWINCKLE, Amos KILBOURNE, CALLEN, Samuel CARTER
on Big Elkin, being 2,482 acres granted David ALLEN by
State of North Carolina. Witnesses: Adonirum ALLEN, Job
ALLEN, and Jonathan ALLEN. Signed: David ALLEN.

Page 140.   3 April 1780.   North Carolina Grant Richard
            VARNAL 200 acres Toms Creek.

Page 140.   14 November 1787.   Matthew BROOKS and wife, Mary,
            to George LASH, 10 pounds, 20 acres Stewarts
Branch adjoining Wm YEATES, CARVER, part 220 acre Granted
BROOKS 5 November 1784. Witnesses: John MILLER, Francis
(X) KITNER, and William THORNTON. Signed: Matt BROOKS and
Mary (X) BROOKS.

Page 141.   20 February 1788.   George LASH to George HAUSER,
            100 pounds, 175 acres Gentrys Branch, Muddy Creek,
adjoining Henry HOLDER, Jacob NULL, part 350 acres Granted
James GORDON 31 November 1784; to George LASH by Seth
GORDON, heir said James 22 January 1785. Witnesses: Matt
BROOKS, Nathaniel LASH, and Allen GROCE. Signed: George LASH.

Page 142.   4 January 1787.   John STONE to Richard GOODE, 64
            pounds, 200 acres both sides little Yadkin
River adjoining LASH. Witnesses: Absalom BOSTICK, Enoch
STONE, and John STONE. Signed: John STONE.

Page 143.   18 December 1786.   John MARTIN to Richard GOODE,
            45 pounds, 100 acres both sides Lick Creek of
Townfork lower part entered by Isaac GARRISON and sold to
David THOMAS adjoining Thomas GOODE. Witnesses: John GOODE

and William BEAZLEY. Signed: John MARTIN.

Page 143. 9 June 1788. John ALLEN to John GOODE, 150 pounds,
        458 acres Panther Creek adjoining THORNTON, SPOON,
being part 640 acres State Granted Thomas JOHNSON 18 December
1778; by JOHNSON to said ALLEN 1 November 1783. Witnesses:
Sarah (X) THORNTON and William THORNTON. Signed: John ALLEN.

Page 144. 7 September 1788. John GOODE to Richard GOODE,
        100 pounds, 458 acres Panther Creek adjoining
LANIER, Adam SPOON near the pond; from JOHNSON to ALLEN;
by ALLEN to John GOODE. Witnesses: William JEAN, Betty (X)
JEAN, and Charles GOODE. Signed: John GOODE.

Page 145. 18 May 1789. North Carolina Grant Richard PARSONS
        150 acres Fox Knob head spring said Creek adjoin-
ing HARMON.

Page 145. 27 October 1786. William GUDGER, Washington
        County, to James YOUNG "full satis faction", 300
acres North fork Crooked Creek adjoining Thos JOYCE and
including James YOUNGS improvement. Witnesses: Isaac JOYCE,
Alexander JOYCE, and William MEREDITH. Signed: William
GUDGER.

Page 146. 11 February 1788. Benjamin YOUNG, Senr. to
        Benjamin YOUNG, Jr., 110 pounds, 100 acres North
side Townfork adjoining Benjamin YOUNG, Junr. and Benj.,
Senrs. old deeded line. Witnesses: Richard GOODE and
Samuel YOUNG. Signed: Benjamin YOUNG.

Page 147. 20 January 1792. Matthew MATTHIS, labourer to
        George FLYNN, labourer, 100 pounds, 150 acres
North fork Forbis Creek (land entered by Slias MORPHEW; sold
at public auction in consequence distress warrant to pay a
substitute in Militia Service of State, said SILAS refusing
to go himself and later bought by Reuben MATTHIS; later
seized and sold for some reason and said Matthew bought.).
Witnesses: James MATTHIS and James FLIN. Signed: Matthew
MATTHIS.

Page 148. 20 December 1786. Margret NELSON to John
        FLETCHER, 25 pounds, 143 acres Fish River.
Witnesses: Francis (X) RAYBON, Silvanen (X) RABON, and
Robert SAXSON. Signed: Marget (X) NELSON.

Page 149. 19 May 1787. George STEELMAN to Stephen DAVIS,
        Hanover County, Virginia, 75 pounds, 140¼ acres
Hands Creek adjoining Hands former Spring Branch. Acknowledged. Signed: George STEELMAN.

Page 149. 10 February 1787. Peter ELROD and wife, Eve, to
        Adam WAGGONER, 25 pounds "all land and tenements
left us by Will of Philip WAGGONER, deceased." Witnesses:
Barney (X) FAR and Henry STUTTS. Signed: Peter (X) ELROD
and Eve (X) ELROD.

Page 150. 1 March 1787. Fredr Wm MARSHALL, Wachovia to

Isaac DOUTHIT, planter, 120 pounds, 240 acres West part Wachovia tract North fork Muddy Creek (James HUTTON Grant). Witnesses: John BLAKE and Ludwig MEINUNG. Signed: Fredr Wm. MARSHALL.

Page 152. 2 April 1787. Henry SMITH, blacksmith, Wachovia, and Mary Barbara SMITH to George HAUSER, Junr. Esq., Bethania, 605 pounds, 502½ acres East side Bethania lot (part HUTTON Granted from Lord GRANVILLE via Atty. Fredr Wm. MARSHALL, Atty. to said SMITH in Rowan County). Witnesses: Henry SHORE, Michael HAUSER, and Adam BUTNER. Signed: Henry (X) SMITH and Mary Barbara SMITH.

Page 154. 10 December 1790. North Carolina Grant Moses BAKER 100 acres Mitchells River.

Page 155. 15 May 1789. Richard GOODE, Esq., Sheriff, to John Thos LONGINO, 16 pounds, 200 acres South side Yadkin River, Fall Creek adjoining Alex BOHANNON, James YORK, James LINDSAY, Stephen HIDE (land lost by Abner GREENWOOD and wife, Nancy by Judgment against said ABNER by County.) Witnesses: Ambrose GAINES and William THORNTON. Signed: Richard GOODE, Sheriff.

Page 155. 13 August 1789. Richard GOODE, Sheriff, to John Thos LONGINO, 40 pounds, 21 acres South side Joseph Creek adjoining BURK (land sold by Joseph BURK to Thomas ELLIOTT 2 February 1785; lost by said ELLIOTT to satisfy Thomas ADDEMAN). Acknowledged. Signed: Richard GOODE, Sheriff.

Page 156. 1 November 1789. Richard GOODE, Esq., Sheriff, to John Thos LONGINO, 40 shillings, 100 acres South side Yadkin River adjoining Wm JOHNSON and BOHANNON (land lost by Abner GREENWOOD and wife, Nancy, judgement against ABNER by County.) Acknowledged. Signed: Richard GOODE, Sheriff.

Page 157. 13 August 1787. Obediah ROBERTS, State of South Carolina, to Daniel LIVERTON, 100 pounds, 200 acres Haw Branch waters Deep Creek, part 450 acres granted John ROBERTS, deceased. Witnesses: Stasey SPRINKLE, Peter SPRINKLE, and H(enry) SPEER. Signed: Obediah ROBERTS.

Page 158. 20 January 1787. John ALLEN, Junr. to Amos CRITCHFIELD, 25 pounds, 100 acres waters Fishers River adjoining plantation where said ALLEN now lives. Witnesses: William COOK, Ben BURCH, William MEREDITH, and John CRITCHFIELD. Signed: John (X) ALLEN.

Page 159. 9 February 1786. James GAMMEL to Levin WARD, Caswell County, North Carolina, 125 pounds, 16 shillings, 207¼ acres waters Blews Creek adjoining Andrew McKILLIP and DOBSON. Witnesses: Enoch STONE, Elijah DAVIS, Daniel BARROW, and William GAMMEL. Signed: James GAMIL.

Page 160. 5 July 1787. Robert FORBIS to Henry SPEER, 100 pounds, 100 acres being tract sold by Welcom H.

HARGIS to Edmund WOOD, 1774; by WOOD to FORBIS on East side
Joseph Creek and Logans Creek, part 550 acre tract.
Witnesses: Hugh LOGAN, John BAKER, and Ann (X) MILLER.
Signed: Robert FORBIS.

Page 161.   15 August 1787.   David BROOKS to Thomas ELMORE,
            65 pounds, 150 acres West side Abbots Creek.
Witnesses: Henry JOHNSON, Thomas JOHNSON, and Robert (X)
JOHNSON.   Signed: David BROOKS.

Page 162.   17 August 1786.   Augustine BLACKBURN to Thomas
            ELMORE, 75 pounds, 600 acres Abbits Creek adjoin-
ing said ELMORE.   Witnesses: Robert (X) JOHNSON, Richard
LUNDY, and Joel SANDERS.   Signed: Augn BLACKBURN.

Page 163.   16 August 1787.   James DOAK to Jacob McCRAW, 100
            pounds, 94 acres both sides Pauls Creek adjoining
James BROWN.   Witness: Hugh ARMSTRONG.   Signed: James DOAK.

Page 164.   5 September 1787.   Thomas CAIN and wife, Lelah,
            to George BROOKS, 60 pounds, 150 acres Harmons
Creek South Yadkin River Granted Thos CAIN adjoining John
HUMPHREY.   Witnesses: H(enry) SPEER, Joseph HUDSPETH, and
John WHITLOCK.   Signed: Thomas CAIN and Lelah (X) CAIN.

Page 165.   6 August 1788.   James JONES, Senr. to James JONES,
            Junr., 5 pounds, 294 acres North fork Deep Creek.
Witnesses: Greenberry PATTERSON and Simon HADLEY.   Signed:
James JONES, Senr.

Page 165.   20 October 1788.   Barnabas and Michael FARE,
            Executors to John FARE, 50 pounds, 100 acres
waters Blews Creek adjoining Richard LINVILL, west side
middle fork said creek, Moses LINVILL and A. ROBINSON, being
tract formerly possessed by Barnabas FARE, Senr., deceased
and left by his Will to his children.   Witnesses: A(ndrew)
ROBINSON and William BEAZLEY.   Signed: Barnabas (X) FARE
and Michl. (X) FARE.

Page 167.   14 February 1788.   John LAFOYE to StephenHANDLIN,
            Guilford County, 60 pounds, 200 acres waters
Blews Creek adjoining FULP and Barney FARE.   Witnesses:
James LAFOYE, Ann WORKMAN, and Sarah (X) LAFOYE.   Signed:
John LAFOYE.

Page 167.   29 June 1791.   John LANKASTER, Davidson County,
            North Carolina, to Joseph WILLIAMS, Executor,
Robert LANIER, Esq., deceased, 400 pounds, 640 acres in
Surry and Stokes Counties on Panther Creek Northeast side
Yadkin near Shallowford road; Granted James CARTER by
GRANVILLE 15 December 1753; by CARTER to Francis CORBIN,
Edenton 18 December 1753.   Witnesses: Lemuel HARVEY, John
HARVEY, and Wiatt GARNER.   Signed: John LANKASTER.

Page 169.   18 May 1789.   North Carolina Grant Jacob FOLTZ
            100 acres waters Mudy Creek.

Page 169.   18 May 1789.   North Carolina Grant Matthew WARNOCK

21

640 acres both sides North fork Blews Creek adjoining Mary GRINDER and Henry HAMPTON.

Page 170. 18 May 1789. North Carolina Grant Moses HEAZLETT 150 acres North side Dan River adjoining John DANIEL.

Page 170. 24 December 1788. Moses KEEN, Orange County, South Carolina, to Zenas BALDWIN, 55 pounds, 150 acres Cobbs Creek and Beaver Dam Creek adjoining COBB, Gilbert KEEN and Wm T. LEWIS land. Witnesses: William T. LEWIS, Samuel DOWNEY, and Obediah Martin BENGE. Signed: Moses (X) KEEN.

Page 171. 28 February 1788. George WATKINS to John SHELTON, 25 pounds, 100 acres waters Dan River place called Duncans or Three Springs, head water Little Snow Creek. Witnesses: Jesse BUMP and Daniel CHANDLER. Signed: George (X) WATKINS.

Page 172. 3 July 1788. Joseph CUMMINS, Guilford County, to Nathan DILLARD, Guilford County, 100 pounds, 250 acres little fork Blews Creek adjoining Augustine BLACKBURN and Benjamin WATSON tract Granted Joseph CUMMINS 1783. Witnesses: William MALOGUE, Ancel (X) VELLEANT, Neley (X) VELLEANT, and Archiblad CAMPBELL. Signed: Joseph CUMMINS.

Page 173. 14 November 1788. Richard GOODE, Esq., Sheriff, to Nathan DILLARD, Guilford County, 5 shillings, 250 acres waters Blews Creek adjoining Augustine BLACKBURN, Benjamin WATSON (land lost by Joseph CUMMINS and wife to satisfy J. WINSTON and P. HAIRSTON.) Acknowledged. Signed: Richard GOODE, Sheriff.

Page 174. 14 November 1787. Aquilla MATTHEWS and wife, Elizabeth, to William ELFORD, 200 pounds Virginia money, 200 acres Stewarts Branch adjoining MILLER, BOLEJACK, LASH and CARVER; land Granted Matthew BROOKS; by said BROOKS to MATTHEWS 16 February 1787. Witnesses: William THORNTON and John GITTENS. Signed: Aquilla MATTHEWS and Elizabeth (X) MATTHEWS.

Page 175. 13 August 1789. William WEBB to Samuel EMMETT, Henry County, Virginia, 55 pounds, 200 acres Furies fork branch Snow Creek; part 450 acres tract. Witnesses: Stephen LYON, James WALKER, and Ambrouse GAINES. Signed: William WEBB.

Page 176. 24 March 1788. Jacob ROBERTSON to Samuel KERBY, 15 pounds, 23 acres, Swan Creek adjoining ROBERT-SON part 84 acre Grant Jacob ROBERTSON 24 September 1779. Witnesses: Robert WILLIAMS, John BAGLEY, Isaac SOUTHARD, and James (X) MARTIN. Signed: Jacob (X) ROBERTSON.

Page 177. 12 September 1788. Thomas SMITH, Davidson County, North Carolina to Samuel KERBY, 50 pounds, 20 acres Yadkin River adjoining his own land and David

STEWART (now John LYNCH) Granted by State to SMITH 13 October 1783. Witnesses: Joseph WILLIAMS and William THORNTON. Signed: Thomas SMITH.

Page 178. 12 September 1788. Thomas SMITH, Davidson County, North Carolina to Samuel KERBY, 300 pounds, 239 acres North side Yadkin River and both sides Swan Creek adjoining John LYNCH, Wm HOLLIMAN and Jacob ROBINSON, Granted by Jos WILLIAMS to Thos SMITH 13 August 1778. Witnesses: Joseph WILLIAMS and William THORNTON. Signed: Thomas SMITH.

Page 179. 9 August 1787. North Carolina Grant Ayres HUDSPETH 400 acres North side North fork Deep Creek, North of the Swisher draft Deep Creek adjoining John BLALOCK and John HUDSPETH.

Page 179. 10 April 1787. James DOAK to William FORKNER, 20 pounds, 34 acres each side Forkners Creek adjoining said FORKNER. Witnesses: Stephen K. SMITH and William WON. Signed: James DOAK.

Page 180. 9 February 1789. Stephen HOBSON to Thomas VESTAL, 66 pounds, 13 shillings, 4 pense, 100 acres South fork Forbis Creek. Witnesses: Isaac STUBBS and Samuel STUBBS. Signed: Stephen HOBSON and Rachel HOBSON.

Page 181. 9 August 1787. North Carolina Grant Joel LEWIS 100 acres adjoining James PERSON, HARVEL and SPARKS.

Page 181. 9 August 1787. North Carolina Grant John ALLEN 100 acres North fork Hunting Creek Southwest corner ALLENS former survey.

Page 182. 8 February 1788. Matthew CREED to Henry HERRIN, 45 pounds, 85 acres East side Stewarts Creek. Witnesses: Michael MILES, John CREED, and Colby CREED. Signed: Matthew (X) CREED.

Page 183. 9 February 1788. Matthew COX to Henry HERRIN, 100 pounds, 150 acres Buck Creek. Witnesses: Colby CREED, Michl MILES, and Bennit CREED. Signed: Matthew COX.

Page 184. 20 December 1791. North Carolina Grant Joseph MURPHY 450 acres Joseph Creek, Haugh Branch on Forbis and Bruce lines.

Page 184. 3 November 1784. North Carolina Grant William McDANIEL 200 acres middle fork Forbis Creek, Muddy Branch adjoining Jesse COUNCIL and GRAHAM.

Page 185. 9 August 1787. North Carolina Grant Rebeckah MARLATT 200 acres waters North fork Deep Creek adjoining James JONES near graveyard and Daniel HUFF.

Page 185. 18 May 1789. North Carolina Grant Joel LEWIS 300 acres waters Yadkin River adjoining Wm T. LEWIS and crossing Shores Branch.

Page 186. 3 November 1784. North Carolina Grant Wm. T.
          LEWIS 250 acres South Side Yadkin River against
Tumbling Falls.

Page 187. 3 November 1784. North Carolina Grant Christian
          WEATHERMAN 400 acres Branch South fork Deep
Creek adjoining Samuel ARNOLD, John WRIGHT and HUDSPETH.

Page 187. 13 October 1783. North Carolina Grant Terry
          BRADLEY 800 acres North side Yadkin River adjoin-
ing Matthew WARNOCK, Joshua TILLEY, Mark HARDEN and Absalom
BOSTICK.

Page 188. 22 October 1787. Philip CULCLEASURE, Westmoreland
          County, Pennsylvania to Wm. HOLAMAN, 200 pounds
proclamation money, 350 acres waters Double Creek adjoining
LYNCH. Witnesses: Peter SIGHT (signed in German), and
Francis FORDENE. Signed: CULCLEASURE (in German).

Page 189. 9 September 1788. William DOUGLASS to William
          HOLAMAN, 20 pounds, 200 acres North side Yadkin
River, branches Bishops Creek adjoining Charles PARKER.
Witnesses: William HARVEY, John B. COLVARD, and P.
DEATHERAGE. Signed: William (X) DOUGLAS.

Page 190. 31 December 1787. Thomas GLOVER to Richard
          WOOTEN "value recd", 150 acres North fork Hunting
Creek adjoining James SANDERS and line divides Surry and
Rowan Counties. Witnesses: James SANDERS, Junr. and Hardy
SANDERS. Signed: Thomas GLOVER and Ava (X) GLOVER.

Page 191. 29 July 1787. Barnabas FAIR, Senr. to Barnabas
          FAIR, Junr., 150 pounds, 150 acres waters Blews
Creek, tract Granted Barnabas Senr. 3 November 1784 plus
50 acres adjoining, being part tract sold Barnabas Sr. by
David LINVILL and wife 18 March 1774. Witnesses: A(ndrew)
ROBINSON and Parth McGIBBONY. Signed: Barnabas (X) FAIR,
Senr. and Elizabeth (X) FAIR.

Page 192. 25 February 1787. James McKINNEY to John JACKSON,
          110 pounds North Carolina currency, 200 acres
Chinquepin Creek. Witnesses: Bowater SUMNER and Rebeckah
(X) SUMNER. Signed: James McKINEY.

Page 192. 20 January 1787. Stephen JAYNE to James McKINEY,
          100 pounds, 133 acres both sides East fork Toms
Creek including Stephen JAYNES improvement. Witnesses:
Bowater SUMNER and John BURRIS. Signed: Stephen JAYN.

Page 193. 29 October 1792. North Carolina Grant Henry
          PATTILLO 270 acres Deep Creek North side below
mouth adjoining Robt ADAMS, John SKIDMORE, David HOWELL;
formerly Morgan BRYANS.

Page 194. 8 September 1786. Gideon BROWN to Abraham WOOD,
          Senr., 130 pounds, 320 acres Bean Shole Creek.

24

Witnesses: John WILLIAMS, John KERR, and Jesse SCOTT. Signed:
Gideon (X) BROWN and Drewsilla (X) BROWN.

Page 195. 18 September 1787. Spencer BALL to Joel GURLEY,
          Wayne County, North Carolina, 600 pounds, 200
acres Rutledge Creek land Granted said BALL 3 November 1784.
Witnesses: Benjamin HUMPHREY, Elijah HUMPHREY, and Sol(omon)
HUMPHREY. Signed: Spencer BALL.

Page 196. 8 October 1787. Thomas WOOTEN to James GUNSTON,
          20 pounds, 100 acres Tarrarat River including
plantation where GUNSTON lately lived and ½ WOOTENS survey.
Witnesses: Jesse BUMPS and Providence (X) WHITEHEAD (female).
Signed: Thomas (X) WOOTEN.

Page 197. 28 March 1788. Thomas HOLCOMB to Abraham REESE,
          8 pounds, 100 acres North fork Deep Creek adjoin-
ing CRAWFORD; land Granted Thomas HOLCOMB by State 9 August
1787. Witnesses: Simon HADLEY and Greenberry PATTERSON.
Signed: Thomas HOLCOMB.

Page 198. 10 March 1788. Joshua BROWN to James PILCHER,
          Junr., 40 pounds, 150 acres waters North fork
Deep Creek adjoining ELMORE; Granted said BROWN by State of
North Carolina. Witnesses: John WILLIAMS, Thomas (X)
GATTON, and Daniel PILCHER. Signed: Joshua (X) BROWN.

Page 199. 1 November 1788. William COCKSEY to Benjamin
          WIGFIELD, 60 pounds "all that remains of 200
acres after Edward RILEY has got his 100 laid off" adjoining
said RILEY. Witnesses: Stephen WOOD, Andrew YOUNG, and
Samuel WALES. Signed: William COXSEY.

Page 200. 4 October 1791. Ninian RILEY, Senr. to Nimrod
          LUNSFORD, 50 pounds Specie, 100 acres Northwest
corner Isaac JOHNSONS land. Witnesses: Stephen WOOD and
John PINNELL. Signed: Ninian RILEY.

Page 200. 29 September 1787. Fredr Wm. MARSHALL, Salem, to
          Daniel HUFF, planter, Wachovia, 117 pounds, 195
acres 30 perches both sides head branch middle fork Muddy
Creek adjoining Thomas MARSHALL and Jesse ADAMSON. Witnesses:
John RIGHTS and Lewis MEINUNG. Signed: Fredr Wm. MARSHALL.

Page 202. 11 August 1789. John DURHAM "now at this time
          residing in Surry County" to Jacob DOBBINS, 175
pounds, 300 acres waters North fork Deep Creek near Round-
Hill, small gutt in Abrm REESES line adjoining John CALTON,
Thos HADLEY and STRICKLAND. Witnesses: Simon HADLEY and
Lindsay (X) CALTON. Signed: John DURHAM.

Page 203. 12 August 1788. William HEAD to John STEPHENS,
          75 pounds Specie, 320 acres Brooks Creek adjoining
said HEAD and place Zachariah MARTIN formerly lives.
Witnesses: Thompson GLEN and Michael HAUSER. Signed:
William HEAD.

Page 204. 18 May 1789. North Carolina Grant William ZACHARY

100 acres waters Deep Creek North fork adjoining
Peter MIERS and HUDSPETH.

Page 205.   18 February 1788.   Valentine REESE to William
            ZACHARY, 140 pounds, 136 acres South fork Deep
Creek adjoining Peter SPRINKLE; GRANVILLE Granted Jacob
REESE 20 February 1761; by JACOBS Will to Valentine REESE.
Witnesses: H(enry) SPEER, William HOUGH, and Simon GROSE.
Signed: Valentine REESE.

Page 206.   7 September 1790.   Hugh MORRIS, Orange County,
            North Carolina, to Abraham VANDERPOOL, Stokes
County, 85 pounds, 240 acres waters branch empties into
South side Yadkin River through Thompson GLENS plantation
adjoining said GLEN, Andrew SPEER, George RIDENS and John
Thos LONGINO including plantation tract being tract from
John Thomas LONGINO to Hugh MORRIS. Witnesses: Matt BROOKS,
and Mary BROOKS. Signed: Hugh MORRIS.

Page 206.   18 May 1785.   Thomas FROHOCK, Rowan County, to
            Benjamin HUTCHINS, Gootchland County, Virginia,
250 pounds, 360 acres South fork Joseph Creek, now called
Forbushes Creek, Southwest side Yadkin River; GRANVILLE
Granted David JONES 28 February 1755. Witnesses: John
JOHNSON and Jonas REYNOLDS. Signed: Thomas FROHOCK.

Page 207.   13 October 1786.   David DOAK, Montgomery County,
            Virginia, to John HANNA, 100 pounds, 200 acres
Moors fork, waters Tarrarat River adjoining said HANNA.
Witnesses: James MATTHEWS and Samuel HANNA. Signed: David
DOAKE and Mary DOAKE.

Page 208.   20 February 1788.   George HAWN, planter, and wife,
            Barbara, to Philip SNIDER, planter, for love said
SNIDER and wife Elizabeth, their God-Daughter, 100 acres
near waters Muddy Creek adjoining said HAWN, John LANIER,
part 200 acre surveyed for HAWN by William THORNTON, surveyor
for Surry County. Witnesses: Frederick Miller (signed in
German). Signed: George HAWN and Barbara HAWN (Philip
signed in German), Elizabeth (X) SNIDER.

Page 211.   31 April 1789.   Abraham WINSCOTT and wife, Mary,
            to George LASH, 100 pounds, 100 acres waters
Yadkin River, part 200 acre originally Granted William
WOOLDRIDGE; by WOOLDRIDGE to Abraham WINSCOTT 10 May 1785.
Witnesses: Allen GROCE and Charles HUDSPETH. Signed:
Abraham WINSCOTT and Mary (X) WINSCOTT.

Page 212.   23 May 1789.   Abraham WINSCOTT and wife, Mary to
            George LASH, 300 pounds, 147½ acres West side
Yadkin River, part 295 acres Granted said WINSCOTT 10 August
1762. Witnesses: William THORNTON and H(enry) SPEER.
Signed: Abraham WINSCOTT and Mary (X) WINSCOTT.   Mary
WINSCOTT freely gives up her right of dower before William
THORNTON and H(enry) SPEER, J.P.'S.

Page 213.   2 July 1790.   Moses LAWS to George LASH, 12 pounds,
            30 acres waters Yadkin River, North fork Dills

26

Creek in the bent to tail of certain Mill Seat where Justice REYNOLDS lately had an overshot mill adjoining William DEVONPORT, Benjamin PETTIT and aforesaid Mill Seat. Witnesses: John Thomas LONGINO and Caleb SAPP. Signed: Moses LAWS.

Page 214. 7 December 1789. John SAYLOR, joiner, to Joseph MILLER, gunsmith, 200 pounds, 268 acres Long Run Mill Creek, waters Muddy Creek adjoining Jacob MILLER and HAUSER, Wachovia line part two tracts Granted John SAYLOR by State of North Carolina. Witnesses: George HAUSER and Henry SHORE. Signed: John SEILER.

Page 214. 10 December 1790. North Carolina Grant John LYNCH 138 acres in Surry County.

Page 215. 9 February 1790. Giles HUDSPETH to Benjamin HUDSPETH, 400 pounds, 200 acres West side Yadkin River, South side Joseph Creek and "where said Benjamin Hamine HUDSPETH do now live", part 558 acres GRANVILLE Granted to Robt FORBIS adjoining Abraham CRESON. Acknowledged. Signed: Giles (X) HUDSPETH.

Page 216. 9 February 1790. Giles HUDSPETH to Charles HUDSPETH, 400 pounds, 208 acres West side Yadkin River and North side Joseph Creek "where Giles HUDSPETH do now live", part 558 acres GRANVILLE Granted to Robert FORBIS, mouth Joseph Creek adjoining H(enry) SPEER and Edmond WOOD. Acknowledged. Signed: Giles (X) HUDSPETH.

Page 217. 31 December 1787. William BLEDSOE to Silvaner RABON, 25 pounds, 100 acres little Fish River. Witnesses: Thomas (X) RABON, William (X) RABON, and Henry NORMAN. Signed: William BLEDSOE and Lisebeth BLEDSOE.

Page 219. 12 June 1787. John MARTIN to Bowater SUMNER, 45 pounds, 640 acres North branch Pinch Gutt or Big Creek of Dan River including the widow SUMNER, Thomas SUMNER and Bowater SUMNER plantations. Witnesses: Jesse KNIGHTON and Peter BILLETER. Signed: John MARTIN.

Page 220. 20 December 1791. North Carolina Grant Ameriah FELTON 312 acres waters South fork Deep Creek adjoining Nicholas GENTRY, Allen GENTRY and WADDLE.

Page 220. 20 December 1791. North Carolina Grant Moses WOODRUFF 400 acres Fox Knob adjoining Henderson and Samuel GENTRY.

Page 221. 20 December 1791. North Carolina Grant Isaac COPELAND 200 acres head little Beaver Creek, waters Fishers River adjoining said COPELANDS former line.

Page 221. 20 December 1791. North Carolina Grant Christopher KERBY 62 acres Camp Creek.

Page 222. 20 December 1791. North Carolina Grant Amos LONDON 200 acres waters Yadkin River, North side adjoining Moses AYRES and SUMMERS.

Page 223. 9 August 1787. North Carolina Grant Andrew
        Robert TURNER and John TURNER 150 acres South
side Yadkin River adjoining CRESON.

Page 223. 9 August 1787. Philip SNIDER to William FIELDS,
        35 pounds, 110 acres Ellisons Creek, part 400
acres Granted John LINEBACK 20 September 1779; by LINEBACK
to SNIDER 1781. Witnesses: William THORNTON, Sweatman BECK,
and John (X) PURDOM. Signed: Philip (X) SNIDER and Barbara
(X) SNIDER.

Page 224. 18 May 1789. North Carolina Grant Jarmon BALLARD
        150 acres Bear Branch, waters Tarrarat River.

Page 225. 18 May 1789. North Carolina Grant John HUGHLETT
        100 acres waters Big Creek adjoining TATE.

Page 225. 29 October 1788. Henry TILLEY, Junr. to Archibald
        HUGHES and George HAIRSTON, Henry County, Virginia,
95 pounds Virginia money, 190 acres two forks Snow Creek
adjoining Henry TILLY, Junr. on South fork Snow Creek, part
larger Granted to said TILLEY 3 April 1780. Witnesses: John
HUGHES, Reuben DODSON, and Robert GAINES. Signed: Henry
(X) TILLEY.

Page 226. 8 December 1788. Major WILKINSON to Peter
        HAIRSTON, 15 pounds, 100 acres Northeast corner
John DANIELS survey. Witnesses: James GAINES, Robert
LINDSEY, and George RAY. Signed: Major WILKINSON.

Page 227. 1 July 1789. Gottlieb SHOBER, tinplate worker,
        Salem, to John HANKE, shoemaker, Salem, 20 pounds,
200 acres Oldfield and Lick Creeks adjoining QUILLIN and
EDWARDS (land lost by Edmund BALL; sold by Rich GOODE,
Sheriff to SHOBER 1786). Witnesses: Jacob BLUM and Christian
STAUBER, Junr. Signed: Gottlieb SHOBER.

Page 228. 9 August 1787. North Carolina Grant John DUNN
        and Adley OSBORN 1,000 acres adjoining Michael
HENDERSON, James JONES, William HANKINS, Moses WOODRUFF and
McMICKLES.

Page 229. 2 November 1787. John WALKER and wife, Margret,
        to Edmond BOWMAN, 140 pounds, 317 acres branch
West side Blews Creek. Witnesses: William MORROW, Samuel
CLAMPETT, and Mary (X) FARRINGTON. Signed: John WALKER and
Marget (X) WALKER.

Page 230. 12 October 1790. Zopher JAYN to James RITTER,
        15 pounds (no acres), Toms Creek adjoining John
BURCHAM and said RITTER; part 300 acres Granted said JAYN
18 May 1789. Witnesses: John BURCHAM and Samuel PARKER.
Signed: Zopher JAYNE.

Page 231. 11 January 1790. Zopher JAYN, Montgomery County,
        Virginia, to John BURCHAM, 35 pounds, 104 acres
Toms Creed, South side Bear Branch; part 300 acres Granted
Zopher JAYN 18 May 1789. Witnesses: Samuel PARKER and

James (X) RITTER. Signed: Zopher JAYNE.

Page 232. 20 December 1791. North Carolina Grant Joseph
          KEYS 400 acres North fork Deep Creek adjoining
James SANDERS.

Page 232. 20 December 1791. North Carolina Grant Shelton
          GENTRY 100 acres Fishers River.

Page 233. 10 December 1790. North Carolina Grant Samuel
          SOWARD 242 acres Hulls corner adjoining Moravian
line.

Page 234. 20 December 1791. North Carolina Grant John
          McCOLLUM, Junr. 150 acres Fall Branch adjoining
WILLIAMS and BRAMBLET.

Page 235. 20 December 1791. North Carolina Grant Moses
          WILLIAMS 50 acres East side little Reedy fork
adjoining John WILLIAMS, the Wilkes County line and including a small improvement.

Page 235. 18 May 1789. North Carolina Grant William REYNOLDS
          200 acres Archers Creek in the Virginia line.

Page 236. 9 August 1787. North Carolina Grant William
          SPARKS, Junr. 100 acres Rich Knob Brushy Mountains
adjoining his former survey.

Page 236. 10 December 1790. North Carolina Grant William
          JOHNSON 300 acres Yadkin River.

Page 237. 20 December 1791. North Carolina Grant John
          JINKINS 200 acres Mounts Branch adjoining himself.

Page 237. 12 August 1786. Peter SALLE to Elihue AYERS,
          250 pounds, 386 acres South side Yadkin River,
mouth Cobbs Creek adjoining Wm. T. LEWIS and said SALLE.
Witnesses: Richard MURPHEY, Joseph MURPHEY, and Moses AYERS.
Signed: Peter SALLE.

Page 238. 30 July 1787. John BLEDSOE to FROST & SNOW,
          182 pounds, 10 shillings Virginia Currency, 300
acres Ellets Branch adjoining Michael AHART, part 446 acres
Granted to Bledsoe STEWARTS Creek. Witnesses: William
LAFOON, William HAWKS, and Michael (X) AHART. Signed: John
(X) BLEDSOE and Susanna (X) BLEDSOE.

Page 239. 10 July 1787. John BLEDSOE to Michael AHART, 75
          pounds Virginia Currency, 100 acres South side
Stewarts Creek to first Clift, part 446 acres Granted
BLEDSOE. Witnesses: FROST & SNOW, William HAWKS, William
LAFOON. Signed: John (X) BLEDSOE and Susanna (X) BLEDSOE.

Page 241. 30 July 1787. William HARDEN to William LAFOON,
          100 pounds Virginia Currency, 160 acres Stewarts
and Naked Creeks, part 320 acres Granted said HARDEN.
Witnesses: William HAWKS and Michael (X) AHART. Signed:

William HARDIN and Sarah HARDIN.

Page 242. 30 July 1787. William HARDEN to Richard SNOW,
         100 pounds Virginia Currency, 160 acres Stewarts
and Naked Creeks adjoining John BLEDSOE, part 320 acres
Granted said HARDEN. Witnesses: FROST & SNOW, William HAWKS,
and William LAFOON. Signed: William HARDIN and Sarah HARDIN.

Page 243. 22 July 1787. David DAVIS to Stephen DAVIS,
         Hanover County, Virginia, 100 pounds, 100 acres
Hanns Creek adjoining Rowan County line and Toliver DAVIS.
Witnesses: Moses BAKER, William (X) DUGLAS, and H(enry)
SPEER. Signed: David DAVIS.

Page 244. 8 August 1787. Matthew DOSS to Adonijah HARBOUR,
         112 pounds, 100 acres where said DOSS doth now
live on Yadkin River adjoining said HARBOUR and MILLER.
Witnesses: John Thomas LONGINO and Thomas EAST. Signed:
Matthew DOSS and Mille (X) DOSS.

Page 245. 20 October 1786. Matthew COX to William BRUCE,
         90 pounds Virginia Currency, 200 acres South side
Stewarts Creek adjoining John HARRIS, John GITTINS and John
McKINNEY. Witnesses: John HARRIS, Robert HARRIS, and M.
MILES. Signed: Matthew COX.

Page 245. April 1787. James DOAK to Thomas GREEN, 400
         pounds, 166 acres each side Forkners Creek adjoin-
ing William FORKNER. Witnesses: Stephen K. SMITH and William
WON. Signed: James DOAK.

Page 246. 10 August 1787. Thomas EAST to Matthew DOSS, 225
         pounds, 125 acres both sides little Yadkin River
adjoining agreed line between Henry KERBY and Jesse HORN.
Witnesses: John Thomas LONGINO and William (X) LANE. Signed:
Thomas EAST and Mary (X) EAST.

Page 247. 11 February 1788. Mark PHILLIPS and wife,
         Elizabeth, to John HARVEY, Junr., 50 pounds, 200
acres adjoining Salem road and Clazieres, exclusive of 2
acres used as a Meeting House. Witnesses: William HARVEY
and William (X) ASHER. Signed: Mark (X) PHILLIPS, (no
signature for Elizabeth).

Page 248. 10 November 1787. John NULL, Montgomery County,
         Virginia, to John HIXT, 12 pounds, 50 acres
Tomakawk Branch adjoining John NULL and Andrew BLACK; part
200 acres Granted NULL but lost before being registered.
Witness: George HOLDER (signature in German). Signed: John
(X) NULL.

Page 249. 22 February 1787. David HUDSPETH to Joseph
         HUDSPETH, 10 pounds, 15 acres East side Yadkin
River adjoining Robert LANIERS old line; part tract where
Robert LANIER formerly lived and conveyed to David HUDSPETH.
Witnesses: Airs HUDSPETH, Junr., Thomas HUDSPETH, and
William THORNTON. Signed: David HUDSPETH.

Page 250.   10 October 1787.   William and Susanna HOLBROOK to
Moses LINVILL, 65 pounds, 150 acres waters Blews
Creek adjoining Barnabas FAIR and an old line including
William LOWS plantation which was certified 16 May 1779 by
Chas McANALLY, surveyor.   Witnesses: A(ndrew) ROBINSON and
David LINVILL.   Signed: William HOLBROOK and Susanna (X)
HOLBROOK.

Page 251.   12 October 1787.   William HOLDER to William Terrell
LEWIS, 30 pounds, 150 acres little Knob of Brushy
Mountain, left hand fork Swanpon Creek.   Witnesses: J.M.
LEWIS and Robert HAMATT.   Signed: William (X) HOLDER.

Page 252.   1 September 1787.   David BRAY to William Terrell
LEWIS, 80 pounds, 200 acres Codys Creek.   Witnesses:
Micajah L. BENGE and William (X) KILBY.   Signed: David BRAY.

Page 252.   29 September 1787.   Samuel WAGGONER to Executors
of Robert LANIER, deceased, 1,000 pounds, 497½
acres Reid Creek adjoining SATER, LANIER and JOHNSON;
Granted said WAGGONER 3rd November 1784.   Witnesses: Richard
GOODE and William THORNTON.   Signed: Samuel WAGGONER.

Page 253.   19 February 1788.   Richard GOODE, Esq., Sheriff,
to Samuel FREEMAN, 5 shillings, 250 acres Tarrarat
River adjoining Samuel FREEMAN and fence between Joshua
FREEMAN and Geo HYDE (land lost by Moses WRIGHT to satisfy
Samuel FREEMAN).   Witness: A(ndrew) ROBINSON.   Signed:
Richard GOODE, Sheriff.

Page 254.   25 February 1788.   George HOLCOMB to Grimes
HOLCOMB, 200 pounds Specie, 229 acres waters North
fork Deep Creek, part 400 acres granted George HOLCOMB and
adjoining PHILIPS.   Witnesses: H(enry) SPEER, Benjamin
GARRISH, and John WILLIAMS.   Signed: George (X) HOLCOMB,
and Elizabeth (X) HOLCOMB.

Page 255.   12 February 1788.   Adam BLACK, an Executor of
Estate of Michael CARVER, deceased, Rowan County
and George ZEGLER, an Executor of said estate in right his
wife and his wife, Mary, to Christian CARVER, 165 pounds,
300 acres Gentrys Branch, part 600 acres granted to Michael
CARVER 13 October 1783.   Witnesses: John BOSTICK, John
RANDLEMAN, and A(ndrew) ROBINSON.   Signed: George ZEGLER,
Adam (X) BLACK, and Anna M. Carver (X) ZEGLAR.

Page 256.   12 February 1788.   (Same above three) to George
CARVER, 75 pounds, 300 acres Gentrys Branch
adjoining Christian CARVER and MILLER.   Witnesses: John
BOSTICK, John RANDLEMAN, and A(ndrew) ROBINSON.   Signed:
Adam (X) BLACK, George ZEGLER and Anna M. Carver (X) ZEGLER.

Page 257.   5 February 1788.   Nathaniel WOODRUFF to William
COOK, 200 pounds, 200 acres South side Yadkin
River below Joseph WOODRUFF (now John ALLEN).   Witnesses:
W(illiam) MEREDITH, David RIGGS, and Jabez HARVIS.   Signed:
Nathaniel WOODRUFF.

Page 258. 15 August 1788. Richard GOODE, Esq., Sheriff, to
Aires HUDSPETH, 6 pounds, 10 shillings for 125
acres North side Deep Creek adjoining Matthew McHAND, mouth
Schoolhouse Branch, James LINDSAY and 640 acres surveyed for
Wm. RUTLEDGE (land lost by Philamon HOLCOMB and Ellander,
his wife to satisfy John RANDLEMAN). Witnesses: William
THORNTON and John RANDLEMAN. Signed: Richard GOODE, Sheriff.

Page 259. 15 December 1790. North Carolina Grant Christian
WEATHERMAN 200 acres waters North fork Deep Creek
adjoining John BRUER.

Page 260. 10 December 1790. North Carolina Grant William
YEATES 200 acres Brooks Ferry road adjoining
GILBERT.

Page 260. 17 May 1788. Samuel KERBY, Senr. to Henry ARNOLD,
200 pounds, 200 acres both sides little Yadkin
River. Witnesses: William THORNTON and Jesse KEARBY.
Signed: Samuel (X) KERBY.

Page 261. 9 August 1787. North Carolina Grant Daniel
LIBERTINE 300 acres Forbis Creek adjoining
FROHOCK.

Page 261. 9 August 1787. North Carolina Grant James OLIVER
100 acres Double Creek of Yadkin River.

Page 262. 20 December 1791. North Carolina Grant Rezia
JARVIS 50 acres Fishers River adjoining Samuel
WEST and said JARVIS' former survey.

Page 262. 3 November 1784. North Carolina Grant Henry
SPEER 100 acres waters Turners Creek adjoining
Abraham CRESON.

Page 263. 3 November 1784. North Carolina Grant James
WHITE 50 acres East side Blackeye Branch.

Page 263. 3 November 1784. North Carolina Grant Hardy
REDDICK 450 acres waters Neatman and Flat Shole
Creeks adjoining Thomas COOK and line said REDDICKS first
tract.

Page 264. 3 November 1784. North Carolina Grant John WELLS
200 acres North fork Blews Creek adjoining Gabriel
JONES, BLACKBURN and Benjamin JONES.

Page 265. 3 November 1784. North Carolina Grant John SMITH
200 acres Flat Sholes Creek.

Page 265. 3 November 1784. North Carolina Grant James
MATTHEWS 200 acres waters Toms Creek adjoining
Abraham COOLEY.

Page 266. 3 November 1784. North Carolina Grant James
MATTHEWS 100 acres middle fork Tarrarat River
adjoining James ROBERTS and place where Jonathan OSBORN lives.

Page 266. 6 February 1787. Christian Fredr COSSART, Antrim County, Kingdom Ireland, Gent, by Fredr Wm. MARSHALL, Salem to John KRAUSE, planter and blacksmith, 5 shillings, 35 acres adjoining Abraham LINEBACK, Christian CONRAD, and Wachovia line. (John Earl GRANVILLE to late Henry COSSART de Saint Aubin d'Espuz, father of said Christian FREDR, 12 November 1754; said Christian FREDR fell heir to on November 1778; 1,280 acres West line Wachovia tract on Muddy Creek). Witnesses: Peter PFAFF (signature in German) and Ludwig MEINUNG. Signed: Christian Fredr COSSART by Fredr Wm. MARSHALL.

Page 267. 4 October 1787. Cornelius KEETH, Junr. to James STEWART, 13 pounds, 6 shillings, and 8 pense for 50 acres West side little Fisher River, part 100 acre to said KEETH by Eli NORMAN 27 September 1787. Witnesses: William (X) STEWART and Duncan KEETH. Signed: Cornelius (X) KEETH.

Page 368. (The numbering jumps from 200 to 300 here and continues.) 29 September 1786. Fredr Wm. MARSHALL, Esq. to George TANNER, planter, Rowan County, 60 pounds, 16 shillings for 189 3/4 acres both sides middle fork Muddy Creek adjoining John Jacob SCHOTT, Adam FISHEL (James HUTTON land vested in said MARSHALL). Witness: John RIGHTS (signature in German). Signed: Fredr Wm. MARSHALL.

Page 370. 7 November 1787. Thomas CHILDRESS to William MARTIN, 80 pounds, 100 acres little fork Forbis Creek. Witness: John (X) BARWONGAR. Signed: Thomas CHILDRESS and Richard CHILDRESS.

Page 370. 13 May 1788. Salathiel MARTIN to Nathan HAINES, 110 pounds, 360 acres waters Deep Creek adjoining Isaac AUSTILL; part 500 acre granted David MARTIN now deceased and to Salathiel MARTIN as heir at Law said David. Witnesses: Jonathan HAINES and Clisby COBB. Signed: Salathiel MARTIN.

Page 371. 3 May 1780. Francis HOLT and wife, Martha, to James BOHANNON, 100 pounds Virginia money, 200 acres little Peters Creek including his improvement. Witnesses: James GAINES, Elizabeth (X) GAINES, and Thomas LANKFORD. Signed: Francis (X) HOLT and Martha (X) HOLT.

Page 373. 13 May 1788. John CONNEL to Wm. LONDON, 60 pounds, 200 acres little Yadkin whereon said LONDON now lives adjoining Saml SMITH and including Long Shole. Acknowledged. Signed: John (X) CONNEL.

Page 373. 6 August 1786. Salathiel MARTIN to Isaac AUSTILL, 100 pounds, 132 acres head water Deep Creek at Fox Knobbs; part 500 acre surveyed for David MARTIN. Witnesses: Jonathan HAINES, Nathan HAINES, and Richard JACKS. Signed: Salathiel MARTIN.

Page 374. 2 February 1788. Philip PRITCHET to Benjamin BLEDSOE, 50 pounds, 200 acres Fishers River.

Witnesses: William BLEDSOE, Miner MARSH, and Henry HARDEN.
Signed: Philip (X) PRICHET and Nancy (X) PRITCHET.

Page 374.   17 September 1787.   John COX to Richard ADAMS,
            150 pounds Virginia money, 200 acres North side
Stuarts Creek adjoining widow GRIFFITHS fence, a Maprile
tree and John GITTINGS. Witnesses: Hugh ARMSTRONG, James
DICKERSON, and Collins HAMPTON. Signed: John COX.
Mary COX, wife of said John relinquishes her right of dower
before Hugh ARMSTRONG and James BRYSON, J.P.'s 10 May 1788.
(Both J.P.'S signed.)

Page 375.   20 February 1788.   Joseph JENEWAY to Archb HUGHES
            and George HAIRSTON, Henry County, Virginia, 30
pounds Virginia money, 150 acres branches Snow Creek.
Witnesses: John HUGHES, John OVERTON, John CHILDRES, and Lea
HUGHES. Signed: Joseph (X) JENEWAY.

Page 376.   1 September 1787.   Henry BAKER, Senr. to Henry
            BAKER, Junr. for love for son, 140 acres Snow
Creek, part land Henry Sr. lives on adjoining William
HICKMAN and crossing through said BAKERS Mill House.
Witnesses: John HUGHES, Absalom BAKER, and Magdalen (X)
SOUTHERN. Signed: Henry BAKER, Senr.

Page 377.   10 May 1788.   Matthew CREED to Bennett CREED, 76
            pounds, 76 acres West side Stewart Creek where
said CREED now lives adjoining John DAVIS. Witnesses: John
CREED, John DAVIS, and Bartlet CREED. Signed: Matthew (X)
CREED, and Marget (X) CREED.

Page 378.   10 May 1788.   Matthew CREED to John DAVIS, 40
            pounds, 47 acres West side Stewart Creek where
DAVIS now lives. Witnesses: John CREED, Bartlett CREED, and
Bennit CREED. Signed: Matthew (X) CREED and Marget (X) CREED.

Page 378.   24 March 1788.   James MEREDITH, Senr. to William
            MARTIN, 8 pounds, 13 shillings, 4 pense North
Carolina Currency, 6 acres North side Crooked Creek adjoining County line. Witnesses: John CHILDRES, John OVERTON,
and Thomas WHITLOCK. Signed: James MEREDITH (Senr.).

Page 379.   3 October 1787.   Carlton LINDSEY to James LINDSEY,
            Senr., 150 pounds, 540 acres Deep Creek adjoining
William RUTLEDGE, REESE and SWISHER. Witnesses: John ALLEN
and Joshua LINDSEY. Signed: Carlton LINDSEY.

Page 380.   25 March 1788.   James LINDSEY to Thomas WILES,
            150 pounds, 540 acres Deep Creek adjoining
William RUTLEDGE, REESE and SWISHER. Witnesses: John (X)
BLALOCK, Nathaniel MARLOW, Jacob (X) MILLER, Reuben GEORGE,
and Jonathan HARROLD. Signed: James LINDSEY.

Page 381.   11 August 1788.   James LINDSEY and Mary LINDSEY
            to John BITTICK, 60 pounds, 200 acres Seven
Island Creek adjoining James LINDSEY. Witnesses: John
DURHAM and John (X) CARLTON. Signed: James LINDSEY and
Mary (X) LINDSEY.

Page 381. 2 August 1788. Mary EASON to William LEWIS, 56
pounds, 13 shillings, 4 pense for 100 acres Dan
River adjoining Robert WARNOCK. Witnesses: Peter HAIRSTON,
Reuben LINDSEY, and Jo TERRELL. Signed: Mary (X) EASON.

Page 382. 14 August 1788. William Terrell LEWIS to William
MEREDITH "a certain sum", 100 acres Yadkin River
adjoining John CRITCHFIELD. Acknowledged. Signed: Wm. T.
LEWIS.

Page 383. 1 October 1787. Barnaby FAIR to William KNOTT,
Guilford County, 150 pounds (no acres), both
sides South fork Beloos Creek; adjoining Hugh McKILIP,
Guilford County line and William BOSTICK. Witnesses: William
JEAN, William HOLBROOK, and Justain KNOTT. Signed: Barnaby
(X) FAIR.

Page 384. 31 October 1787. John Thomas LONGINO to Christop-
her MONDAY, 75 pounds Specie, 100 acres North fork
Hunting Creek above Sholes; part 400 acre surveyed for
Isaac MIZE and since laid off to said LONGINO. Witnesses:
Elisha CAST and S(tephen) WOOD. Signed: John Thomas LONGINO.

Page 385. 14 August 1788. John Thomas LONGINO to John
RIGHTS, 20 pounds, 200 acres waters Bean Shole
Creek; part 300 acres granted LONGINO by State of North
Carolina. Acknowledged. Signed: John Thomas LONGINO.

Page 386. 14 September 1787. Josiah FREEMAN to James
FORESTER, 500 pounds, 320 acres North side Yadkin
River said FREEMANS and MIERS lines. Witnesses: Frederick
DESERN, Moses MIERS, and Edward (X) SMITH. Signed: Josiah
(X) FREEMAN.

Page 387. 9 November 1787. William Terrell LEWIS to John
MARSH, 25 pounds, 150 acres little Knob Brushy
Mountain left hand Swan Pon Creek. Witnesses: Moses
WOODRUFF and John Allen WOODRUFF. Signed: Wm. T. LEWIS.

Page 387. 3 March 1788. Philamon HOLCOMB to Elijah CARLTON,
100 pounds, 200 acres waters Deep Creek, head
spring Fall Branch. Witnesses: William DAVIS, Edward
CLANTON, and John (X) CARLTON. Signed: Philimon (X) HOLCOMB.

Page 388. 11 August 1788. William and Dorcas HOWARD to
John PADGET, 35 pounds Specie, 200 acres Fishers
River. Witnesses: J. MACKAY, John JARVIS, and Sarah (X)
MACKAY. Signed: William HOWARD and Dorcas (X) HOWARD.

Page 389. 29 August 1789. William FLINN to Thomas
CHILDRESS, 80 pounds, 200 acres Sunny Branch
adjoining Andrew SPEER, Peter ELDER and Michael SPRINKLE.
Witnesses: James MATTHIS and George FLINN. Signed: William
FLINN.

Page 390. 16 February 1788. David MORROW and wife, Martha,
to William DOBSON, Esq., 600 pounds, 400 acres
whereon said David MORROW now dwelleth, waters Muddy Creek,

Deep River, Haw River and Yabbits Creek including land, swamp, branch and cripple. Witnesses: Henry CAMPBELL and Henry Baker DOBSON. Signed: David MORROW and Martha (X) MORROW.

Page 391. 6 August 1788. Benjamin SPEER to Matthias STEELMAN, 50 pounds, 30 acres North side Turners Creek and Green Branch adjoining STEELMANS old line; part 150 acres from Jacob SPEER to said Benjamin SPEER. Witnesses: Joseph RUTLEDGE, John (X) SPEER, and H(enry) SPEER. Signed: Benjamin SPEER.

Page 392. 12 September 1788. William VENABLE to John VENABLE, 45 pounds, 300 acres little Yadkin River; part 400 acre tract. Witnesses: William STEEL and William (X) VENABLE (Jr.?) Signed: William (X) VENABLE.

Page 393. September 1788. Richard WEBSTER and wife, Rebecah to William WALKER, Rockingham County, North Carolina, 140 pounds, 100 acres Kings Creek adjoining said WALKERS former line and Charles McANALLY. Witnesses: John MORGAN and George RAY. Signed: Richard (X) WEBSTER and Rebecah (X) WEBSTER.

Page 394. 12 August 1788. Jacob FREEMAN to William WHITAKER, 50 pounds, 50 acres Hogans Creek. Witnesses: Job (X) BRAUGHTON, Ephraim (X) PHILLIPS, and Benjamin (X) RAY. Signed: Jacob FREEMAN.

Page 395. 15 November 1788. Isaac WRIGHT, Guilford County, to Moses LAWS, 200 pounds, 200 acres small creek, waters Yadkin River near Yellow bank ford adjoining PETTIT. Witnesses: Jo WINSTON and David POINDEXTER. Signed: Isaac WRIGHT.

Page 396. 1 April 1788. Benjamin CORNELIUS, Greenville County, South Carolina to Thomas BALL, 100 pounds, 200 acres Beaver Dam Creek of Fishers River being place Mark CADLE formerly dwelt adjoining Joel MACKEY and Elijah GILLASPY. Witnesses: Joseph LOGIN, Elijah GLASPY, and John (X) RABON. Signed: Benjamin (X) CORNELIUS.

Page 397. 3 November 1788. Mary EASON to Joseph EASON, 50 pounds, 300 acres head Widows Creek of Dan River, granted Mary EASON by State 1787. Witnesses: Charles McANALLY, James COFEY, and Harry TERRELL. Signed: Mary (X) EASON.

Page 397. 18 March 1788. Joshua MIZE to James SANDERS, Senr., 30 pounds Specie, 100 acres waters North fork Hunting Creek adjoining John COPELAND and James SANDERS. Witnesses: Richard WOOTEN and John COPELAND. Signed: Joshua (X) MIZE and Martha (X) MIZE.

Page 398. 13 February 1789. Richard GOODE, Sheriff, to John LYNCH, 1 pound, 6 shillings, for 230 acres both sides Joseph Creek adjoining Patrick LOGAN, Ro. FORBIS, Moses BAKER (land lost by Timothy COX and wife, Lucy, to

satisfy Patrick LOGAN and sold by John GOODE, D. Sheriff).
Acknowledged. Signed: Richard GOODE, Sheriff.

Page 399.   13 March 1788.   William JOHNSON to Stephen
              HOBSON, 200 pounds, 300 acres Forbis Creek.
Witnesses: George (X) WOOTEN and Isaac STUBBS. Signed:
William JOHNSON and Elizabeth (X) JOHNSON.

Page 400.   10 November 1786.   Isham THOMPSON to William
              SELBY, 80 pounds, 150 acres; part 300 acres
Fishers River granted Elijah THOMPSON; by Elijah to said
Isham 10 May 1786. Witness: Wm. T. LEWIS. Signed: Isham
THOMPSON.

Page 401.   10 February 1789.   Roger GIDEONS and wife, Sarah,
              to Thomas MARTIN, 500 pounds, 300 acres Crooked
Run adjoining Malcum CURRY: granted Roger 17 September 1778.
Acknowledged. Signed: Roger GIDDENS and Sarah (X) GIDDENS.
Sarah relinquishes her right of dower before Absalom BOSTICK,
J.P.

Page 402.   24 January 1789.   Dan HILL to Edward MERIT, 40
              pounds, 200 acres Northeast corner Wachovia, head
Branch East fork Townfork Creek; part 2,000 acre Granted
Traugott BAGGE by Jas. HUTTON. Witnesses: Abraham MARTIN,
John MERIT, and Benjamin BYNUM. Signed: Dan HILL.

Page 403.   20 December 1788.   John WILLIAMS to Grimes
              HOLCOMB, 100 pounds, 300 acres Hough Branch,
waters North fork Deep Creek being Granted John WILLIAMS.
Witnesses: H(enry) SPEER, Thomas HADLEY, and Aires HUDSPETH.
Signed: John WILLIAMS.

Page 403.   20 August 1788.   William SELBY to John MARSH,
              100 pounds, 150 acres; part 300 acres on Fishers
River granted Elijah THOMPSON; by Elijah to Isham THOMPSON
1786. Witnesses: Benjamin BLEDSOE, Miner MARSH, and John
MARSH. Signed: William (X) SELBY.

Page 404.   20 January 1789.   James and Catharine BRYSON to
              William HILL, 100 pounds Specie, 380 acres
Fishers River South side main river. Witnesses: John BRYSON,
Junr. and Thomas HILL. Signed: James BRYSON, (no signature
for Catharine.)

Page 405.   24 October 1788.   Peter COLEMAN to Stephen JAYN,
              150 pounds (no acres), Toms Creek above ford
containing all land belongint to Peter COLEMAN in survey of
Nathaniel JAYN with Mill on said Creek. Witnesses: John
BURCHAM and John (X) BURCHAM. Signed: Peter COLEMAN.

Page 406.   12 September 1779.   Thomas SMITH to Benjamin
              BENSON, 100 pounds, 150 acres Lovings Creek
middle fork Tarrarat River; part 400 acres GRANVILLE granted
to Patrick COIL, deceased, 1762; by James COIL, son, said
Patrick to Jonathan OSBURN 1774 and adjoining Stephen
OSBURN. Witnesses: David HUMPHREYS and James GITTINS.
Signed: Thomas SMITH and Rebeckah (X) SMITH.

Page 407.   23 January 1789.   James DOAK to Obed BAKER, 300
           pounds, 350 acres both sides Renfrows Creek North
fork Arrarat River. Witnesses: Charles SMITH, Stephen K.
SMITH, and William SMITH. Signed: James DOAK and Mary DOAK.

Page 408.   21 October 1788.   Toliver DAVIS to Benjamin SPEER,
           150 pounds, 156 acres Turners Creek adjoining
Jacob SPEER and Argie GARNER, old corner 337 acres GRANVILLE
Granted to Roger TURNER; by Roger TURNER to Toliver DAVIS
22 September 1784. Witnesses: H(enry) SPEER, George PRIDDY,
and John STEELMAN. Signed: Tolaver DAVIS.

Page 409.   13 February 1788.   Gray BYNUM to William COOK,
           50 pounds, 122 acres both sides Neatman Creek
adjoining Robert COOK including improvement where said
William COOK now lives; part 200 acre surveyed for said
BYNUM; the other 77 acres deeded to Hardy REDDICK by said
BYNUM. Witnesses: John MARTIN, John MERIT, and William
CAMPBELL. Signed: Gray BYNUM.

Page 409.   6 December 1787.   Thomas MOSBY to Philip HOWARD,
           10 shillings, 60 acres near said HOWARDS old
deeded line; part 150 acres Granted Samuel MOSBY, Senr.
Witnesses: Jo WILLIAMS, John McBRIDE, and Robert WILLIAMS.
Signed: Thomas MOSBY.

Page 410.   29 January 1789.   Richard LINVILL to David LINVILL,
           100 pounds, 100 acres waters Blews Creek adjoining
DOTSON including old plantation where Rich formerly dwelt.
Witnesses: A(ndrew) ROBINSON and Lydia (X) ALLEN. Signed:
Richard (X) LINVILL.

Page 411.   17 February 1789.   Henry SPEER to Standwick
           HOWARD, 30 pounds, 200 acres little Fishers River
adjoining Garner TUCKER. Witnesses: Gideon EDWARDS, S. WORD,
Stephen WOOD?, and Andrew ROBINSON. Signed: H. SPEER.

Page 412.   14 November 1788.   Lewis ELLITT to Jacob
           ELSBERRY, 60 pounds, 140 acres Branch South side
South fork Deep Creek. Witnesses: Aires HUDSPETH and
Catharene (X) HUDSPETH. Signed: Lewis ELLITT.

Page 412.   11 February 1788.   Abraham CRESON to James
           CAMPBELL, 150 pounds, 13 shillings, 4 pence for
250 acres Branch Lick Run empties into Yadkin below Deep
Creek and above Shallowford adjoining Wiatt GARNER and
STEELMAN; tract Granted CRESON 3 November 1782. Witnesses:
H(enry) SPEER and William THORNTON. Signed: Abraham (X)
CRESON.

Page 413.   20 October 1788.   James REAVIS and wife, Mary, to
           John HUTCHENS, 700 pounds, 378 acres North fork
Deep Creek adjoining Simon GROSS, Fredr SHORES Spring
Branch; part 640 acres Granted James REAVIS. Witnesses:
John JOHNSON, John REAVIS, and Edward CLANTON. Signed:
James REAVIS and Mary (X) REAVIS.

Page 414.   17 November 1788.   William LAFOON to Thomas BURRIS,

100 pounds Virginia Currency, 150 acres Stewarts and Naked Creeks. Witnesses: FROST & SNOW, William GOLDING, and Stephen K. SMITH. Signed: William LAFOON and Sarah (X) LAFOON.

Page 415. 13 July 1788. John BLEDSOE to John DAVIS, 55 pounds Virginia Currency, 46 acres on Stewarts Creek adjoining SNOW & DAVIS; part 446 acres State Granted to BLEDSOE. Witnesses: William LAFOON, William HAWKS, and Michael (X) AHART. Signed: John (X) BLEDSOE and Susannah (X) BLEDSOE.

Page 416. 25 July 1788. Mary EASON to James THOMPSON, 50 pounds, 200 acres adjoining Dan River and Mill Creek, mouth Mill Creek and South bank Dan River adjoining Robert WARNOCK; being tract Granted Mary EASON by State of North Carolina. Witnesses: Adam MITCHELL and Abner BARNES. Signed: Mary (X) EASON.

Page 417. 13 November 1788. Henry AYRES, Spartanburg County, South Carolina, to Joseph HAGERMAN, 100 pounds, 197 acres Forbis Creek adjoining Nicholas HUTCHENS. Witnesses: John AYRES and Joseph HAGERMAN. Signed: Henry AYRES.

Page 417. 7 August 1788. John ALLEN and wife, Elizabeth, to Zachariah SUGART, 100 pounds, 400 acres waters North fork Deep Creek adjoining James LINDSAY. Witnesses: Abraham (X) REESE and Nathan FARMER. Signed: John ALLEN and Elizabeth ALLEN.

Page 418. 14 May 1789. William SHEPPERD, Orange County, North Carolina, to Edmond KERBY, 100 pounds, 700 acres Yadkin River, excepting that sold to SNEED & WALKER. Witnesses: Constant LADD and Matt BROOKS. Signed: William SHEPPERD.

Page 419. 17 March 1788. William T. LEWIS to Abner PHILIPS, 75 pounds, 100 acres North side Yadkin River draft Turkey Creek. Witnesses: Zachariah RAY, Richard G. DENNIS, Zenos BALDWIN, and William COOK. Signed: Wm. T. LEWIS.

Page 420. 7 March 1788. William T. LEWIS to Abner PHILLIPS, 75 pounds, 300 acres North side Yadkin River, East side Turkey Creek. Witnesses: Zachariah RAY, Richard G. DENNIS, James DOWNEY, Zenos BALDWIN, William COOK, and Reuben SHORE, Junr. Signed: Wm. T. LEWIS.

Page 421. 20 February 1789. Thomas RABON to Nathaniel STUART, 75 pounds, 150 acres little Fishers River, mouth of a branch. Witnesses: Thomas NORMAND, Hampton STUART, and Silvaner RABON. Signed: Thomas (X) RABON and Sarah (X) RABON.

Page 422. 1 April 1789. John REDD to Robert HAMMOCK, 105 pounds Virginia Currency, 140 acres Stuarts Creek. Witnesses: Thomas PRATHER, Jacob BURRIS, and Ann

CUNNINGHAM. Signed: John REDD and Mary REDD.

Page 423. 11 December 1787. Joel GURLEY to Ratliff BOON,
          100 pounds, 200 acres formerly property Spencer
BALL by deed 3 November 1784, West side Rutledge Creek.
Witnesses: David HUMPHREYS, Elijah HUMPHREYS, and Sol(omon)
HUMPHREYS. Signed: Joel GURLEY.

Page 424. 6 November 1788. John BLALOCK to Joseph HILL, 10
          pounds Virginia Currency, 100 acres purchased by
BLALOCK from Henry SPEER, Esq. on Millers Creek. Witnesses:
Carter HUDSPETH, Junr., Edward CLANTON, and Thomas (X)
CLANTON. Signed: John (X) BLALOCK.

Page 425. 9 April 1789. Joseph GENTRY and Samuel GENTRY to
          John RIDENS, 300 pounds, 110 acres South side
Yadkin River adjoining William WOOLDRIGE and said RIDINS.
Witnesses: Matt BROOKS, Andrew SPEER, and Sarah (X) GENTRY.
Signed: Joseph (X) GENTRY and Samuel GENTRY.

Page 426. 3 June 1789. Francis CALLOWAY, Wilkes County,
          Georgia, to Isaac WINFREE, Wilkes County, North
Carolina, 200 pounds, 275 acres South Fork Mitchells River.
Witnesses: John KING, Richard HARTSFIELD, and Caleb WINFREE.
Signed: Francis CALLOWAY and Jane (X) CALLOWAY.

Page 427. 19 November 1788. John BLALOCK to Carter HUDSPETH,
          40 pounds Specie, 40 acres mouth branch on Cotobo
Creek adjoining MILLER. Witnesses: Joseph HILL, Edward
CLANTON, and Thomas (X) CLANTON. Signed: John (X) BLALOCK.

Page 428. 19 November 1788. John BLALOCK to Carter HUDSPETH,
          26 pounds, 100 acres waters Millers Creek adjoining
BLALOCKS old line, MILLER and ARNOLD. Witnesses: Joseph
HILL, Edward CLANTON, and Thomas (X) CLANTON. Signed: John
(X) BLALOCK.

Page 429. 15 May 1789. Peter MURPHEY to John FRANKLIN, 70
          pounds, 125 acres South fork Mitchells River
adjoining lower end CALEB'S field and FIELDERS old line.
Witnesses: Richard MURPHEY, Daniel WOOLF, and Mary (X) WOOLF.
Signed: Peter MURPHEY.

Page 430. 16 February 1789. Christopher MONDAY to Matthew
          BROOKS, 31 pounds, 100 acres both sides North
fork Hunting Creek above Sholes; part 400 acres Granted
Jacob MIZE. Witnesses: George LASH and George (X) LASH,
Junr. Signed: Christopher (X) MONDAY.

Page 431. 6 November 1788. John BLALOCK to Thomas CLANTON,
          150 pounds, 309 acres North side South fork
Deep Creek adjoining CLANTONS old line. Witnesses: Edward
CLANTON, Joseph HILL, and Carter (X) HUDSPETH, Junr.
Signed: John BLALOCK.

Page 432. 11 December 1787. John DAVIS to ZaZa BRESHER,
          60 pounds, 150 acres waters Blews Creek adjoining
Gabriel JONES, Augustine BLACKBURN, Benjamin JONES, and

John DOLING. Witnesses: William (X) GIBSON and Richard (X) BRO (?). Signed: John DAVIS.

Page 432. 8 February 1788. Richard GOODE, Sheriff, to Peter FULP, 5 shillings, 200 acres middle fork Lick Creek adjoining Thos RAPIER (land lost by James MOORE to satisfy said RAPER). Witnesses: Stephen FOUNTAIN and Thomas (X) RAPIER. Signed: Richard GOODE, Sheriff.

Page 433. 23 April 1789. William ALLEN to John ALLEN, Junr., 200 pounds, 200 acres North side Yadkin River, East side Fisher River near mouth on Richmond road. Witnesses: Aaron SPEER, William IDOLS, and Jeffery JOHNSON. Signed: William ALLEN.

Page 434. 10 October 1787. Moses PAGGET to Henry SCALES, Henry County, Virginia, 30 pounds North Carolina Currency, 100 acres South fork Buffalow Creek called little Buffalo adjoining Wm. WEBB. Witnesses: John CHILDRES, Elisha CHILDRES, and Henry CHILDRES. Signed: Moses (X) PADGETT.

Page 435. 26 July 1789. John SCHAUB, planter, Bethabara, to John SCHAUB, dyer, Bethabara, 110 pounds, 150 acres both sides North fork Muddy Creek adjoining West line Wachovia and Shallowford road; part 300 acre by James HUTTON, by his Atty. Fredr Wm. MARSHALL 4 August 1769; payment to be made 29 September which is feast Saint Michael the Arch Angel. Witnesses: Jacob BLUM and Charles CLAYTON. Signed: John SCHAUB, Senr.

Page 437. 28 September 1789. John McBRIDE to John TRUITT, 100 pounds, 180 acres adjoining Allens Creek, Robert ELROD, Philip WAGGONER and Daniel HOOFHINES. Witnesses: Francis POINDEXTER and Philip HOWARD. Signed: John McBRIDE.

Page 437. 18 March 1788. Joshua MIZE to John COPELAND, 600 pounds Continental Money, 300 acres Hunting Creek adjoining said MIZES original tract and 100 acres North end sold James SANDERS. Witnesses: James SANDERS, Richard WOOTEN, and James CARTER, Senr. Signed: Joshua (X) MIZE and Martha (X) MIZE.

Page 439. 8 August 1788. Isaac WILLIAMS, Yeoman, and wife Rachel, to Micajah WEISNER, planter, 18 shillings, 36 acres middle fork Muddy Creek below the Falls. Witnesses: John WEISNER, Thomas MORGIN, and William WEISNER. Signed: Isaac WILLIAMS and Rachel (X) WILLIAMS.

Page 440. 27 July 1789. Isaac WILLIAMS to Owen WILLIAMS, Chatham County, North Carolina, 200 pounds, 264 acres middle fork Muddy Creek below the Falls. Witnesses: Micajah WEISSNER and Nathan PIKE. Signed: Isaac WILLIAMS.

Page 441. 18 October 1789. Joseph PORTER and wife, Rose, to FROST & SNOW, 30 pounds North Carolina Currency, 100 acres Moores fork, Stewarts Creek. Witnesses:

John TALIAFERRO, William (X) TUCKER, and James (X) TUCKER.
Signed: Joseph PORTER and Rose PORTER.

Page 441.   9 February 1790.   Joseph WILLIAMS to Peter MOCK,
            Rowan County, 25 pounds, 10 acres Island in
Yadkin River adjoining SLONE and COLVARD. Witnesses: William
THORNTON and John Thomas LONGINO. Signed: Joseph WILLIAMS.

Page 442.   20 December 1788.   Nathaniel CHAMBLESS to Isham
            ROYALTY, 25 pounds, 100 acres Fishers River.
Witnesses: Darby RYAN, William HOWARD, and J. MACKEY.
Signed: Nathaniel (X) CHAMBLESS.

Page 443.   10 November 1789.   William RENY to John STANLEY,
            46 pounds, 100 acres Forbis Creek adjoining
COGBURN and surveyed by Henry SPEER. Witnesses: John JOHNSON,
Aires HUDSPETH, and Samuel AYERS. Signed: William RENY.

Page 443.   26 April 1790.   Amos KILBURN, Green County, North
            Carolina, to Abraham VANWINKLE, 100 pounds, 150
acres Grassy Creek, adjoining MARTIN. Witnesses: Benjamin
GOODIN, Peter SALLE, and Job SIMS. Signed: Amos (X) KILBURN.

Page 444.   27 November 1789.   Adam TATE, Rockingham County,
            North Carolina, to Joseph JESSUP, 281 pounds,
13 shillings, 4 pense, 300 acres Pinch Gut Creek, alias
Big Creek of Dan River adjoining Joseph TATES corner of
400 acres including part Joseph JESSUPS improvement.
Witnesses: Thomas LACEY, Henry HARDIN, and Jacob JESSUP.
Signed: Adam TATE.

Page 445.   27 November 1789.   Adam TATE, Rockingham County,
            North Carolina, to Joseph JESSUP, 281 pounds,
13 shillings, 4 pense, 400 acres Pinch Gut Creek, alias
Big Creek of Dan River crossing stock ford and crossing
TATES fork including part JESSUPS improvement. Witnesses:
Thomas LACEY, Henry HARDIN, and Jacob JESSUP. Signed:
Adam TATE.

Page 446.   26 October 1789.   William T. LEWIS to Humphrey
            COCKERHAM, 10 pounds, 50 acres South side Fox
Knob adjoining where COCKERHAM now lives and taken out of
tract including John CATES old plantation on head waters
Deep Creek. Witnesses: James DOWNEY and John McCONNAL.
Signed: Wm. T. LEWIS.

Page 446.   7 January 1790.   Henry SOUTHARD to Isaac SOUTHARD
            56 pounds, 100 acres waters Camp Creek crossing
Grassy fork said Creek. Witnesses: John PIPES and Abel (X)
CARTER. Signed: Henry SOUTHARD.

Page 447.   9 March 1789.   Aires HUDSPETH to Benjamin
            HUDSPETH, 40 pounds, 400 acres adjoining William
SPURGINNER. Witnesses: Richard GOODE, George HUDSPETH,
and John ALLEN. Signed: Aires HUDSPETH.

Page 448.   14 February 1789.   Benjamin HUMPHREY to George
            READ, 100 pounds, 200 acres Forkners Creek

including William FORKNERS old improvement whereon Geo READ now lives. Witnesses: David HUMPHREYS and William HAMMOND. Signed: Benjamin HUMPHREYS.

Page 449.   24 July 1788.   Joshua K. SPEER to William COOK,
                60 pounds, 150 acres McFees Creek. Witnesses:
William LOVE, John STEPHENS, and Aaron SPEER. Signed:
Joshua K. SPEER.

Page 450.   1 December 1787.   Samuel WOOD and wife, Mary, to
                William BURRIS, 150 pounds Specie, 200 acres both
sides Pauls Creek known as Lem JONES place adjoining Virginia
line. Witnesses: Jacob McCRAW, Joseph HARVEY, Wilm. ARMSTRONG,
and Hugh ARMSTRONG. Signed: Samuel WOOD and Mary (X) WOOD.

Page 450.   24 February 1790.   Simon HADLEY to Thomas HINSHAW,
                26 pounds, 100 acres waters, North fork Deep
Creek. Witnesses: John HINSHAW and Simon HADLEY. Signed:
Simon HADLEY.

Page 451.   11 August 1789.   John DURHAM, Spartanburg County,
                South Carolina, to Lindsey CARLTON, 10 pounds,
100 acres Round Hill, waters North fork Deep Creek Granted
said DURHAM 18 May 1789. Witnesses: Simon HADLEY and Jacob
DOBBINS. Signed: John DURHAM.

Page 452.   11 May 1790.   Jesse SAMFORD by Joseph MURPHEY,
                Atty. for said SAMFORD to Stephen HIDE, 100
pounds, 200 acres waters Fall Creek. Witnesses: Aires
HUDSPETH and James HIDE. Signed: Joseph (X) MURPHEY, Atty.

Page 453.   24 February 1790.   Simon HADLEY to John HINSHAW,
                25 pounds, 100 acres waters North fork Deep
Creek adjoining JOHNSON and HADLEY. Witnesses: Thomas
HINSHAW and Simon HADLEY, Junr. Signed: Simon HADLEY.

Page 454.   12 May 1790.   Richard GOODE, Esq., late Sheriff,
                to Charles BEAZLEY, 5 shillings, 100 acres
adjoining Grizel SMITH (land lost by Daniel BENNETT and wife
(n n) to satisfy Charles BEAZLEY; tried before James MARTIN,
Esq., J.P.) Acknowledged. Signed: Richard GOODE, Sheriff.

Page 455.   12 May 1790.   Richard GOODE, late Sheriff, to
                George HAUSER, Esq., 5 shillings, 400 acres South
side Yadkin River at a bush called Father Grey Beard above
Charles DUDLEYS (land lost by Job FELTON and wife, Elizabeth,
to satisfy Joseph PHILIPS for use FORBES and JONES. Witness:
William THORNTON. Signed: Richard GOODE, Sheriff.

Page 456.   2 January 1790.   William SWEATT to Orman
                KIMBROUGH, 5 pounds, 33 acres Yadkin River adjoin-
ing Sweatts Spring Branch. Witnesses: William THORNTON and
George KIMBROUGH. Signed: William SWEATT.

Page 457.   2 January 1790.   Orman KIMBROUGH to George
                KIMBROUGH, 200 pounds, 100 acres North side
Yadkin River adjoining Sweatts Spring Branch; part KIMBROUGH
tract known by the Shallowford tract together with 33 acres

this day conveyed by Wm. SWEATT to Orman KIMBROUGH. Witnesses: William THORNTON and John WILLIAMS. Signed: Orman KIMBROUGH.

Page 458. 22 June 1789. William MORE and wife, Margaret, to John SUGART, 60 pounds, 100 acres South fork McFees Creek. Witnesses: Simon HADLEY, William ADAMS, and William (X) SUGART. Signed: William MOORE and Margaret (X) MOORE.

Page 458. 22 June 1789. Wm. MOORE and wife, Margaret, to John SUGART, 15 pounds, 100 acres McFees Creek. Witnesses: Simon HADLEY, William ADAMS, and William (X) SUGART. Signed: William MOORE and Margaret (X) MOORE.

Page 459. 15 October 1780. Aires HUDSPETH to Daniel BILLS, 200 pounds, 100 acres South side Yadkin River, mouth Fall Creek adjoining George HOLCOMB. Witnesses: Moses AYERS and Garsham BILLS. Signed: Airs HUDSPETH.

Page 460. 20 October 1789. John TALIAFERRO and wife, Mary, to James TUCKER, 45 pounds, 127 acres little Fisher River adjoining Richard TALIAFERRO and James TUCKER. Witnesses: Benjamin TALIAFERRO, William (X) TUCKER, and Jo(seph) PORTER. Signed: John TALIAFERRO and Mary TALIAFERRO.

Page 461. 11 August 1790. Hugh ARMSTRONG, Esq., Sheriff, to John Thomas LONGINO, 5 pounds, 5 shillings, 200 acres Dills Creek branch Yadkin River adjoining William ROBINSON (land lost by Henry PATTILLO; on 7 June 1788 before Henry SPEER, Esq.; Abraham CRESON brought judgement against John ALLEN for which PATTILLO was secretary.) Witnesses: John HENNERY and Carter HUDSPETH. Signed: Hugh ARMSTRONG, Sheriff.

Page 462. 10 August 1790. Thomas BALLARD to Joseph HARVEY, 80 pounds, 110 acres East side Pauls Creek. Witnesses: Jacob McCRAW, Ewyl McCRAW, and William McCRAW. Signed: Thomas BALLARD.

Page 463. 11 May 1787. Thomas NORMAN to John McKINNEY, 60 pounds Virginia money, 100 acres South side Stuarts Creek adjoining John GITTEN. Witnesses: W. BRUCE, John McKINNEY, Junr., and Jesse McKINNEY. Signed: Thomas (X) NORMAN.

Page 464. 21 December 1789. Benjmain WATSON, Wilkes County, North Carolina to Augustine BLACKBURN of County Aforesaid, 500 pounds Specie, 600 acres Lick Creek of Townfork, West side. Witnesses: William JOHNSON, George JOHNSON, and John CUNNINGHAM. Signed: Ben(jamin) WATSON.

Page 465. 4 May 1790. James MATTHEWS to John FLEMMING, 200 pounds Virginia money, 192 acres Stuarts Creek in the Hollow fork Creek adjoining John HANNA and Andrew BAILEY: part survey for Andrew BAILEY and known as STUARTS old improvement. Witnesses: Stephen K. SMITH, Obed BAKER, and John MATTHEWS. Signed: James MATTHEWS and Mary MATTHEWS.

Page 466.   12 November 1790.   Thomas AYERS and wife, Ellender,
          to Jesse LESTER, Stokes County, North Carolina,
400 pounds, 150 acres North side Yadkin River mouth Branch;
being Granted to Thomas AYERS by State 3 November 1784.
Witnesses: H(enry) SPEER and Richard MURPHEY.   Signed: Thomas
(X) AYERS and Ellender (X) AYERS.

Page 466.   12 November 1790.   Thomas AYERS and wife, Ellender,
          to Jesse LESTER, Stokes County, North Carolina,
500 pounds, 50 acres Yadkin River adjoining his former
corner; being Granted to Thomas AYERS by State 18 May 1789.
Witnesses: H(enry) SPEER and Richard MURPHEY.   Signed: Thomas
(X) AYERS and Ellender (X) AYERS.

Page 467.   12 November 1790.   Thomas AYERS, Senr. and wife,
          Ellender, to Jesse LESTER, Stokes County, North
Carolina, 400 pounds, 47 acres Yadkin River adjoining
HAWKINS near White Rock ford, Nathaniel AYERS Cabbin, 53
acres conveyed by said Thomas AYERS to Commissioners of
Surry County.   Witnesses: H(enry) SPEER and Richard MURPHEY.
Signed: Thomas (X) AYERS and Ellender (X) AYERS.

Page 468.   19 May 1789.   William MARTIN and wife, Lydda, to
          James DEFREES, Rockbridge County, Virginia, 200
pounds, 250 acres surveyed for James BRUCE 28 December 1778
South side Forbis Creek.   Witnesses: James GRAHAM, Ryal (X)
MARTIN, and Henry PATTILLO.   Signed: William (X) MARTIN and
Lydda (X) MARTIN.

Page 469.   18 May 1789.   James GIBBINS and wife, Catharine,
          to William DEFREES, Rockbridge County, Virginia,
85 pounds, 281 acres South side North fork Deep Creek,
Meeting House Branch and Iron Work road.   Witnesses: H(enry)
SPEER and James DEFREES.   Signed: James GIBBINS and
Catharine GIBBINS.

Page 470.   13 March 1790.   Benjamin WHELESS to Reuben
          WHELESS, 50 pounds and for love for son, Reuben
(after decease of Benjamin and wife, Elizabeth), 200 acres
Yadkin River along fence adjoining land now in possession
of Lewis WHELESS.   Witnesses: Edmund PACE and Ann (X)
MAIES.   Signed: Benjamin WHELESS.

Page 471.   23 August 1790.   Thomas AYERS to William Terrell
          LEWIS, Edward LOVELL, Micajah OGLESBY, Charles
SMITH, and Henry SPEER, Commissioners appointed to settle
on a site for a court house and other public buildings, 5
shillings, 53 acres waters Yadkin River near White Rock Ford
below Elihue AYRES Cabbin, adjoining said AYRES back line,
Moses AYERS corner, Nathaniel AYERS Cabbin; tract originally
granted Thomas AYERS by State of North Carolina 18 May 1789.
Witnesses: John Thomas LONGINO, Daniel BILLS, and William
BILLS.   Signed: Thomas (X) AYERS.

Page 472.   23 August 1790.   Moses AYRES to William Terrell
          LEWIS, Edward LOVELL, Micajah OGLESBY, Charles
SMITH, and Henry SPEER, Commissioners appointed to settle
on a site for a court house and other public buildings,

5 shillings, 5½ acres waters Yadkin River adjoining Nathaniel AYRES Cabbin, Moses AYRES, Thomas AYRES; part 320 acres sold by Alexander HAWKINS to said Moses AYRES 10 May 1785. Witnesses: John Thomas LONGINO, Daniel BILLS, and William BILLS. Signed: Moses AYERS.

END DEED BOOK D

1. When there were no witnesses listed in a land transaction, said transaction was acknowledged in open Court by the Grantor.

2. When an X is uese it denotes his or her mark; otherwise it is assumed one could write or sign his or her name.

Page 1.   18 May 1789.   North Carolina Grant Jesse COUNCIL
            400 acres middle fork Forbush Creek adjoining John
ENGLAND agreed line William MOORE.

Page 2.   18 May 1789.   North Carolina Grant Simon HADLEY,
            200 acres waters Deep Creek adjoining JOHNSON, said
HADLEY, crossing Sanders Branch.

Page 3.   18 May 1789.   North Carolina Grant Clabourn GENTRY
            150 acres adjoining intersection Moravian and Rowan
County lines.

Page 3.   18 May 1789.   North Carolina Grant Adam PETREE 200
            acres adjoining his own land and Rowan County line.

Page 4.   18 May 1789.   North Carolina Grant Jacob PETREE 100
            acres adjoining his old line near John PETREE.

Page 4.   18 May 1789.   North Carolina Grant Robert MATTHEWS
            300 acres waters Forbis Creek.

Page 5.   18 May 1789.   North Carolina Grant Mary GRINDER 200
            acres both sides North fork Blews Creek.

Page 5.   18 May 1789.   North Carolina Grant Ludwig MEINUNG
            80½ acres adjoining Godfrey FIDLER and George
HOLDER.

Page 6.   18 May 1789.   North Carolina Grant John HALEY 300
            acres waters Muddy Creek adjoining HARROLD and
WILLIAMS.

Page 6.   18 May 1789.   North Carolina Grant John PIPES 200
            acres Camp Creek above the Falls.

Page 7.   18 May 1789.   North Carolina Grant William SPARKS
            200 acres South side Brushy Mountain crossing Deep
Creek.

Page 8.   18 May 1789.   North Carolina Grant John WILLIAMS
            640 acres waters South fork Deep Creek adjoining
Frederick LONG and WAGGONER.

Page 8.   18 May 1789.   North Carolina Grant John WILLIAMS
            400 acres South side Shoale Branch.

Page 9.   18 May 1789.   North Carolina Grant John WILLIAMS
            300 acres North side North fork Deep Creek adjoin-
ing Henry SPEER and PETTYJOHN.

Page 10.   18 May 1789.   North Carolina Grant Lazarus TILLEY
            100 acres South side Dan River adjoining George
DEATHERAGE.

Page 10.   18 May 1789.   North Carolina Grant Michael HAUSER

400 acres Mill Creek adjoining FISHER, HUGHS, BRIGGS, SHORE and MILLER.

Page 11.   18 May 1789.   North Carolina Grant Daniel HUFF 200 acres adjoining HUFF and Pattersons Creek.

Page 11.   18 May 1789.   North Carolina Grant John CHILDRESS 400 acres South side Crooked Creek adjoining Frederick COX.

Page 12.   18 May 1789.   North Carolina Grant Daniel BARNETT 100 acres South fork Snow Creek including his improvement adjoining Charles WHITLOCK and G. SMITH.

Page 12.   18 May 1789.   North Carolina Grant Joseph WALDRAM(N) 100 acres Bull Run waters of Tarrarat River.

Page 13.   18 May 1789.   North Carolina Grant John BARRON (BORREN) 300 acres adjoining said BORENS land and WEATHERMAN.

Page 14.   18 May 1789.   North Carolina Grant James BOWLES 300 acres East side Briery Branch, waters Neatman Creek.

Page 14.   18 May 1789.   North Carolina Grant Joseph WILLIAMS 10 acres Yadkin River adjoining SLOAN and COLVARD.

Page 15.   18 May 1789.   North Carolina Grant John GIBSON 640 acres Buffalow Creek adjoining William WEBB, John WILKINS, Joseph FRANCIS and William MERRIDETH.

Page 15.   18 May 1789.   North Carolina Grant William WEBB 450 acres Furies Fork adjoining County line and Ambrose WHEELER.

Page 15.   18 May 1789.   North Carolina Grant John RANDLEMAN 200 acres both sides Hugh Branch, North fork Deep Creek adjoining George HOLCOMB.

Page 16.   18 May 1789.   North Carolina Grant Stephen JARVIS 140 acres Hogan Creek adjoining SUTTON.

Page 16.   18 May 1789.   North Carolina Grant West MOSLEY 100 acres South side Codys Creek.

Page 17.   18 May 1789.   North Carolina Grant Charles DUDLEY 100 acres North fork Bull Run.

Page 17.   18 May 1789.   North Carolina Grant Stephen WOOD 200 acres Rocky Branch of Hunting Creek.

Page 18.   18 May 1789.   North Carolina Grant William HOWARD 100 acres South fork Double Creek, waters Yadkin River adjoining HORN.

Page 18.   18 May 1789.   North Carolina Grant Henry BANNER 54¼ acres waters Buffalow Creek adjoining said

BANNER, Abraham MARTIN and BANNERS old line.

Page 19.   18 May 1789.   North Carolina Grant John DURHAM
          400 acres waters Deep Creek near Round Hill adjoin-
ing Abraham REESE, agreed line John CALTON, Thomas HEADLEY,
head spring on Strickling Branch and Big Branch.

Page 20.   18 May 1789.   North Carolina Grant John BOWLES
          300 acres Neatman Creek adjoining John FORGUSON
and James BOWLES.

Page 20.   18 May 1789.   North Carolina Grant John BOWLES
          200 acres adjoining James BOWLES West side Brushy
Fork.

Page 21.   18 May 1789.   North Carolina Grant Martha PITTS
          300 acres Deep River adjoining Guilford County line.

Page 21.   18 May 1789.   North Carolina Grant Nathan DILLON
          500 acres waters Muddy Creek and Abbits Creek
adjoining Rowan County line and Ashley JOHNSON.

Page 22.   18 May 1789.   North Carolina Grant Nathan DILLON
          400 acres Blews Creek adjoining Joseph NELSON,
HAMPTON and GRINER.

Page 22.   18 May 1789.   North Carolina Grant Nathan DILLON
          200 acres Blews Creek adjoining HUTCHINS.

Page 23.   18 May 1789.   North Carolina Grant Nathan DILLON
          100 acres Blews Creek adjoining HAMPTON, NELSON,
DRENNON, and HUTCHINS.

Page 23.   9 August 1789.   North Carolina Grant John CARTY
          150 acres Fishers River adjoining Edmund HODGES.

Page 24.   18 July 1788.   North Carolina Grant Justice
          REYNOLDS 150 acres North fork Forbis Creek.

Page 24.   18 May 1789.   North Carolina Grant James LEONARD
          400 acres waters Dutchman Creek in Rowan County
line and crossing said Creek.

Page 25.   18 May 1789.   North Carolina Grant Adam TATE 400
          acres Pinch Gut Creek.

Page 26.   18 May 1789.   North Carolina Grant Adam TATE 300
          acres Great Creek or Pinch Gut adjoining Joseph
TATES former corner.

Page 26.   18 May 1789.   North Carolina Grant Joseph JESSOP
          300 acres Pinch Gut or Big Creek of Dan River and
branches thereof adjoining Adam TATE.

Page 27.   18 May 1789.   North Carolina Grant Joseph JESSOP
          150 acres North side Big Creek of Dan River
adjoining MARTIN.

Page 27.   18 May 1789.   North Carolina Grant Moses GRIGG
           200 acres adjoining Tates fork of Big Creek.

Page 28.   18 May 1789.   North Carolina Grant Samuel JACKSON
           150 acres Big Creek of Dan River.

Page 28.   18 May 1789.   North Carolina Grant Curtis JACKSON
           100 acres waters Big Creek of Dan River adjoining
Samuel JACKSON.

Page 29.   18 May 1789.   North Carolina Grant Joseph HIETT
           400 acres waters Yadkin River and waters Dan River
adjoining said HIETTS land crossing Branch Toms Creek, Isaac
JONES, Joseph BANNER, and Micajah CLARK.

Page 29.   18 May 1789.   North Carolina Grant Joseph HIETT
           200 acres adjoining corner tract run out for Thomas
EVANS, branch Toms Creek and McKINNEYS line.

Page 30.   18 May 1789.   North Carolina Grant Zopher JAYNE
           300 acres Toms Creek, North side Bear Branch, a
draft of Toms Creek and crossing Pine Branch.

Page 30.   18 May 1789.   North Carolina Grant Samuel BOND
           100 acres branch Big Creek.

Page 30.   18 May 1789.   North Carolina Grant Samuel HAGGARD
           128 acres Boons Creek.

Page 31.   18 May 1789.   North Carolina Grant John SWIM 250
           acres waters Deep Creek spur Fox Knob in Frederick
MILLERS line adjoining Michael SWIM, Jordan MANNERING, top
of Fox Knob as it circles.

Page 31.   18 May 1789.   North Carolina Grant Zachariah
           SPURLING 100 acres top Fox Knobb West of Rock
House, spur said Knob.

Page 32.   18 May 1789.   North Carolina Grant Zachariah
           SPURLING 100 acres Greenberrys Mill Creek.

Page 32.   18 May 1789.   North Carolina Grant William ELLIS
           150 acres Henry WAGGONERS line.

Page 33.   18 May 1789.   North Carolina Grant Michael SWIM
           100 acres South side Fox Knobb adjoining David
MARTINS former survey (now Nathan HANES) below old meadow
improvement and adjoining John SWIM.

Page 33.   18 May 1789.   North Carolina Grant Barnabas HOWARD
           100 acres Dan River adjoining William JESSOP.

Page 34.   18 May 1789.   North Carolina Grant John NUNNS 150
           acres Beaver Dam Creek.

Page 34.   18 May 1789.   North Carolina Grant Peter BELLAR
           300 acres Richard NUNNS Northeast corner adjoining
Alexander MARTIN and Richard COX.

Page 35. 18 May 1789. North Carolina Grant Thomas AYERS
100 acres Yadkin River adjoining HAWKINS near
White Rock ford.

Page 35. 18 May 1789. North Carolina Grant Thomas AYRES 50
acres Yadkin River adjoining his former corner.

Page 36. 18 May 1789. North Carolina Grant James SISK 150
acres Swan Creek in Wilkes County line.

Page 36. 18 May 1789. North Carolina Grant Francis CLANTON
400 acres Gentrys line crossing Deep Creek adjoining agreed line with Richard PASSONS South side Brushy
Mountain near Hickory Cabbin.

Page 37. 3 November 1784. North Carolina Grant Amos
KILBOURN 150 acres Grassy Creek adjoining MARTIN.

Page 37. 10 July 1788. North Carolina Grant William T.
LEWIS 1,490 acres Western District, South fork
Forked Deer River adjoining Martin ARMSTRONG, Junr., William
HAWKINS, William HUGHLETT, and Henry RUTHERFORD.

Page 38. 18 May 1789. North Carolina Grant William T. LEWIS
1,500 acres Western District head Long fork of
Mississippi adjoining John Gray BLOUNT, Thomas BLOUNT, and
Alexander McKEE.

Page 38. 10 July. North Carolina Grant William T. LEWIS
1,000 acres Western District both sides South
fork Forked Deer River adjoining David SHELTON, William
POLK, and said LEWIS' land.

Page 39. 10 July 1788. North Carolina Grant William T.
LEWIS 1,000 acres Western District waters North
fork Forked Deer River adjoining said LEWIS and Ephraim
DAVIDSON.

Page 39. 10 July 1788. North Carolina Grant William T.
LEWIS 5,000 acres Middle District West side
Richland Creek adjoining Charles POLK.

Page 40. 18 May 1789. North Carolina Grant William T.
LEWIS 500 acres Hawkins County South side Clinch
River called Third bottom above mouth said river.

Page 40. 18 May 1789. North Carolina Grant William T.
LEWIS 500 acres Haskins County South side Clinch
River some distance above mouth adjoining another survey for
LEWIS.

Page 41. 18 May 1789. North Carolina Grant William JESSUP
300 acres Dan River.

Page 41. 9 August 1787. North Carolina Grant John PERSONS
200 acres Reed Creek adjoining Richard PERSON,
GENTRY and HARRELL.

Page 42.   9 August 1787. North Carolina Grant John WRIGHT
           640 acres Great Branch North fork Hunting Creek.

Page 42.   18 May 1789. North Carolina Grant William REYNOLDS
           100 acres Archers Creek adjoining his former
survey.

Page 43.   18 May 1789. North Carolina Grant James MARTIN
           100 acres North fork Big Creek.

Page 43.   18 May 1789. North Carolina Grant Jesse STANDLEY
           200 acres East side Neatman Creek adjoining John
BOLES.

Page 44.   18 May 1789. North Carolina Grant Henry SOUTHARD
           100 acres waters Camp Creek and crossing Grassy
fork.

Page 44.   9 August 1787. North Carolina Grant John BRANNON
           100 acres Morrisons Creek, South side Yadkin River
adjoining Benjamin WHEELESS.

Page 45.   18 May 1789. North Carolina Grant John LEGGETT
           100 acres Yadkin River below WHEELESS.

Page 45.   18 May 1789. North Carolina Grant Joshua FREEMAN
           200 acres South fork Codys Creek adjoining BRAY.

Page 46.   18 May 1789. North Carolina Grant Samuel HUMPHREYS
           100 acres Big Flat Shoals Creek.

Page 46.   18 May 1789. North Carolina Grant Samuel HUMPHREYS
           100 acres little Flat Shoals Creek.

Page 47.   18 May 1789. North Carolina Grant Samuel HUMPHREYS
           100 acres Stony Creek.

Page 47.   18 May 1789. North Carolina Grant Samuel FOX 100
           acres South side Standleys Branch, waters Townfork.

Page 48.   18 May 1789. North Carolina Grant William VENABLE
           200 acres South fork little Yadkin.

Page 48.   18 May 1789. North Carolina Grant David SPENCE
           200 acres Fall Creek between Fox Knobb and Brushy
Mountain including Nath'l MORRISONS old improvement and
adjoining Wm. T. LEWIS.

Page 49.   18 May 1789. North Carolina Grant Lott IVEY 250
           acres Tarrarat River.

Page 49.   18 May 1789. North Carolina Grant Reuben SHORES
           200 acres Deep Creek adjoining his own land and
William SPARKS.

Page 50.   18 May 1789. North Carolina Grant William
           STEELMAN 138 acres North fork Dutchmans Creek in
Rowan County line adjoining Thomas COCK and Jesse Reese.

Page 50.   18 May 1789.   North Carolina Grant Gayer MACEY
            133 acres Blews Creek adjoining Robert WALKER.

Page 51.   18 May 1789.   North Carolina Grant Joshua COOK
            215 acres North fork Deep Creek adjoining EASLEY.

Page 51.   18 May 1789.   North Carolina Grant Abraham CRESON
            225 acres South side Yadkin River adjoining Giles
HUDSPETH and CRESON.

Page 53.   18 May 1789.   North Carolina Grant Charles JOHNSON
            200 acres waters Osburns Creek adjoining John
RECTOR and County line that divides Wilkes and Surry Counties.

Page 53.   18 May 1789.   North Carolina Grant Andrew MARTIN
            200 acres waters Yadkin River, head Whitakers
Branch North side said Yadkin.

Page 54.   18 May 1789.   North Carolina Grant Andrew MARTIN
            150 acres North side Yadkin River adjoining Edward
WILBURN, crossing Mitchells River.

Page 54.   18 May 1789.   North Carolina Grant Philip HOWARD
            120 acres adjoining his own land and MOSBY.

Page 55.   9 August 1787.   North Carolina Grant Philip HOWARD
            5 acres being an Island in Yadkin River.

Page 55.   9 August 1787.   North Carolina Grant Henry AYRES
            100 acres waters Forbes Creek adjoining Robert
AYRES former survey.

Page 56.   10 July 1788.   North Carolina Grant William T.
            LEWIS 5,000 acres Middle District on Big Creek
North waters Elk River adjoining said LEWIS.

Page 56.   19 July 1788.   North Carolina Grant Joel LEWIS and
            Benjamin GOODIN 300 acres Green County on Big Gap
Creek adjoining conditional line between Benjamin CARTER
and Alexander GOODIN at foot Rays Mountain.

Page 57.   10 July 1788.   North Carolina Grant William T.
            LEWIS 2,500 acres Greene County adjoining Henderson
and Company and Robert G. HARPER.

Page 57.   10 July 1788.   North Carolina Grant William T.
            LEWIS 400 acres Hawkins County, North side Clinch
River including mouth first Creek above mouth Emry River.

Page 58.   10 July 1788.   North Carolina Grant William T.
            LEWIS 5,000 acres Middle District South side Duck
River on Globe Creek adjoining said LEWIS survey.

Page 58.   10 July 1788.   North Carolina Grant William T.
            LEWIS 5,000 acres Middle District both sides
Richland Creek, waters Elk River adjoining George DOHERTY
and Roby HAYS, and Thomas BUNCOMB.

Page 59. 10 July 1788. North Carolina Grant Micajah Green
          LEWIS 5,000 acres Middle District Richland Creek
adjoining John ARMSTRONG below his Southwest corner.

Page 59. 10 July 1788. North Carolina Grant Micajah Green
          LEWIS 1,000 acres Western District, waters South
fork Forkeddeer River adjoining David SHELTON and Wm. T.
LEWIS.

Page 60. 18 May 1789. North Carolina Grant Wm. T. LEWIS
          500 acres Hawkins County on Creek runs into Clinch
River North above mouth Emry River adjoining LEWIS'S 400
acre survey.

Page 60. 18 May 1789. North Carolina Grant William T.
          LEWIS 400 acres Hawkins County on Creek empties
into Clinch River, mouth Emry River adjoining LEWIS 500
acre survey.

Page 61. 9 August 1787. North Carolina Grant Curtis JACKSON
          200 acres both sides Toms Creek of Yadkin River
adjoining Lewis CONNER, Thomas EVANS and CLARK.

Page 61. 9 August 1787. North Carolina Grant Reuben
          PINION 100 acres North side Cane Brake Branch.

Page 62. 14 August 1793. Thomas HUDSPETH to James LOCKET,
          Fayette County, Kentucky, 100 pounds, 500 acres
Western District North fork Forkeddeer River adjoining
Anthony SHARPE, Martin ARMSTRONG, tract formerly granted to
William HUGHLETT 10 July 1788. Witnesses: John CARTER and
Aires HUDSPETH. Signed: Thomas HUDSPETH.

Page 63. 9 August 1787. North Carolina Grant Thomas
          BALKUM 200 acres both sides Red Bank Creek.

Page 63. 18 May 1789. North Carolina Grant Edmund WOOD
          100 acres little Beaver Dam Creek adjoining his
former line.

Page 64. 18 May 1793. North Carolina Grant Abner GREENWOOD
          100 acres both sides Yadkin River adjoining William
JOHNSON and BOHANNON.

Page 64. 18 May 1789. North Carolina Grant William MORRIS
          50 acres Red Bank Creek adjoining Hammond MORRIS.

Page 65. 18 May 1789. North Carolina Grant David REVES
          200 acres North side North fork Deep Creek adjoin-
ing James REVES and his own former tract.

Page 65. 16 May 1789. North Carolina Grant Nathaniel
          MORRIS 150 acres head Thomas Branch near Brushy
Mountain adjoining HEREMON.

Page 66. 20 December 1791. North Carolina Grant Samuel
          RIGGS 100 acres North side Mitchells River adjoin-
ing his own line.

Page 66.   20 December 1791.   North Carolina Grant Samuel
          RIGGS 50 acres waters Mitchells River adjoining
said RIGGS in Wilkes County line near Red Bank Spring.

Page 67.   20 December 1791.   North Carolina Grant Robert
          HARRIS 77 acres Tarrarat River including Richard
HILLS improvement.

Page 67.   20 December 1791.   North Carolina Grant George
          THOMPSON 150 acres Fishers River including John
MOBLEYS improvement.

Page 68.   18 May 1789.   North Carolina Grant Nicholas
          GENTRY 240 acres waters South fork Deep Creek
adjoining his former survey crossing Big Branch in HUDSPETH
old line.

Page 68.   18 May 1789.   North Carolina Grant Nicholas GENTRY
          150 acres waters Deep Creek.

Page 68.   18 May 1789.   North Carolina Grant John Thomas
          LONGINO 100 acres Bean Shole Creek adjoining
Frederick THOMPSON.

Page 69.   18 May 1789.   North Carolina Grant Matthew TAYLOR
          100 acres South side Yadkin River on Bean Shole
Creek.

Page 69.   20 December 1791.   North Carolina Grant Robert
          WALKER 300 acres Tesse HULINS line.

Page 70.   20 December 1791.   North Carolina Grant Robert
          WALKER 300 acres waters Abbits Creek adjoining
FIELDS, TEAGUE, UNTHANK, PAIN and including WHEELERS improvement.

Page 70.   24 December 1792.   North Carolina Grant William
          COOK 500 acres South side Yadkin River adjoining
CARTER and CRITCHFIELD.

Page 71.   24 December 1792.   North Carolina Grant Thomas
          BURCH 300 acres waters North fork Deep Creek,
HUFFS meadow adjoining James JONES.

Page 71.   20 December 1791.   North Carolina Grant Charles
          WORD 150 acres West side Middle Tarraraet River
named Bleckers Creek including the Schoolhouse and WORDS
former corner.

Page 72.   20 December 1791.   North Carolina Grant Edmund
          PACE 200 acres Fishers River adjoining Richmond
PACE including his own improvement.

Page 73.   10 December 1790.   North Carolina Grant Thomas
          WILLIAMS 300 acres Forbis Creek adjoining
DEVENPORT, SPEER, and COGBURN.

Page 73.   10 December 1790.   North Carolina Grant John WILLIA

200 acres Reedy fork including his improvement and Wilkes County line.

Page 74. 10 December 1790. North Carolina Grant John WILLIAMS 200 acres Forbis Creek adjoining Daniel ENGLAND and COGBURN.

Page 74. August 1787. North Carolina Grant Henry SPEER 200 acres little Fishers River adjoining Tuckers Spring and Garner TUCKER.

Page 75. 18 May 1789. North Carolina Grant Henry SPEER 400 acres North fork Deep Creek.

Page 75. 18 May 1789. North Carolina Grant Henry SPEER 250 acres North fork Harmons Creek adjoining HOLT.

Page 76. 9 August 1787. North Carolina Grant Joseph WILLIAMS 424 acres, Andersons corner on Yadkin River adjoining JONES, LIP, and BRIDGFARMER.

Page 76. 10 December 1790. North Carolina Grant Joseph WILLIAMS 14 acres South bank Yadkin River adjoining LEGETT (formerly known by WHEALESS) adjoining Reuben WHEALESS.

Page 77. 24 December 1792. North Carolina Grant John DULING, Junr. 43 acres Forbis Creek adjoining Joseph MURPHEY, DEVONPORT, widow BURK and VANDEVER.

Page 77. 24 December 1792. North Carolina Grant William DUELING 300 acres waters Forbis Creek adjoining William DEVENPORT.

Page 78. 1 January 1794. North Carolina Grant Benjamin KELLEY 200 acres on Brooks Ferry road adjoining MILLER, Guilford County line and YATES.

Page 78. 1 January 1794. North Carolina Grant Edmond WOOD 125 acres Beaver Dam Creek adjoining WOODS former line.

Page 79. 14 August 1790. Nathaniel STUART to Henry NORMAN 75 pounds Virginia Currency, 150 acres little Fish River. Witnesses: William NORMAN, George KEITH, and Joseph HOLDER. Signed: Nathaniel (X) STUART and Mary (X) STUART.

Page 80. 2 August 1790. Thomas NORMAN to Henry NORMAN, 50 pounds, 150 acres little Fishers River, conditional line between Thomas and Henry. Witnesses: Moses COCKERHAM and William HAWKS. Signed: Thomas NORMAN and Elizabeth (X) NORMAN.

Page 80. 2 August 1790. Thomas NORMAN to William NORMAN, 40 pounds, 150 acres little Fishers River adjoining George KEITH. Witnesses: Henry NORMAN, Moses COCKERHAM, and William Hawks. Signed: Thomas NORMAN and Elizabeth (X) NORMAN.

Page 81. 1 February 1790. Daniel PILCHER to Phebe PHILCHER
in compliance to his Father's Will, Daniel gives
his Mother, Phebe, 75 acres waters North fork Deep Creek,
East side said Daniels plantation near road, leads from
Scritchfields ford to the Shallowford road on the Yadkin
River. Witnesses: H(enry) SPEER, James GIBBINS, and Daniel
LIVERTON. Signed: Daniel (X) PILCHER.

Page 82. 8 August 1789. Ninian RILEY, Senr. to Ninian
RILEY, Junr. for love, 267 acres, waters Hunting
Creek adjoining Original tract. Witnesses: Stephen WOOD,
and Gerrard RILEY. Signed: Ninian RILEY.

Page 83. 14 November 1789. Thomas WILLIAMS and wife, Sarah,
to John JOHNSON, 100 pounds, 100 acres South fork
Forbush Creek adjoining JONES, being State Granted to Aaron
SPEER. Witnesses: H(enry) SPEER, Benjamin HUTCHENS, and
Jonas REYNOLDS. Signed: Thomas WILLIAMS and Sarah (X)
WILLIAMS.

Page 84. 24 December 1792. North Carolina Grant Gabriel
FENDER 170 acres waters Waggoners Creek adjoining
ELLIS & WAGGONER.

Page 84. 24 December 1792. North Carolina Grant Andrew
CORNELIUS 100 acres top of one of the Brushy
Mountains adjoining John HILL.

Page 85. 24 December 1792. North Carolina Grant Jeremiah
REYLA 200 acres waters Hunting Creek adjoining
William BURNSIDE, Ninian REYLA, Mary DOLLASON, Rowan County
line.

Page 85. 24 December 1792. North Carolina Grant Stephen
HOBSON 150 acres Forbis Creek adjoining his line.

Page 86. 24 December 1792. North Carolina Grant William
WHITEFIELD 100 acres South side Brushy Mountain
adjoining George SPARKS, Shore and North side Deep Creek.

Page 86. 24 December 1792. North Carolina Grant Moses
AYRES 50 acres North side Yadkin River adjoining
Amos LONDON.

Page 87. 24 December 1792. North Carolina Grant Richard
JACKS 400 acres Deep Creek adjoining William
ELLIOTT, Frederick LONG and WAGGONER.

Page 88. 24 December 1792. North Carolina Grant John MASH
200 acres Bar Branch, North side Yadkin River.

Page 88. 24 December 1792. North Carolina Grant Aaron
MOORE 100 acres waters Double Creek.

Page 89. 24 December 1792. North Carolina Grant William
ADAMS 54 acres waters Forbis Creek.

Page 90. 24 December 1792. North Carolina Grant William

ADAMS 187 acres Forbis Creek adjoining JONES and John MARSHALL.

Page 90. 24 December 1792. North Carolina Grant William RUTLEDGE 640 acres Deep Creek.

Page 91. 24 December 1792. North Carolina Grant Samuel BRICKNELL 50 acres Yadkin River adjoining Reuben SHORE and Wilkes County line.

Page 91. 24 December 1792. North Carolina Grant Moses RUTLEDGE 300 acres head Fishers Creek adjoining the Rowan County line.

Page 92. 24 December 1792. North Carolina Grant John LANTRUPE 200 acres Fishers River adjoining Jarvis Branch dividing branch between said LANTRUPE and JARVIS.

Page 93. 24 December 1792. North Carolina Grant John BYRSON, Senr. 50 acres Lovings Creek adjoining his former line.

Page 93. 24 December 1792. North Carolina Grant Benjamin WIGFIELD 100 acres North fork Hunting Creek adjoining his own land.

Page 94. 24 December 1792. North Carolina Grant James WELLS 100 acres waters Deep Creek adjoining his old corner, WINSTON and SHORE.

Page 94. 24 December 1792. North Carolina Grant Nathaniel MOXLEY 150 acres beside Iron Work near fork Enyarts road.

Page 95. 24 December 1792. North Carolina Grant Ann WHITEHEAD 100 acres Fasen Branch.

Page 95. 24 December 1792. North Carolina Grant John RIDENS 600 acres waters Forbis Creek adjoining GLEN, Brooks old Ferry road, dividing line between said RIDINS and James GLEN'S Orphans, STEWART, WINSCHOT, GENTRY, and BROOKS.

Page 96. 24 December 1792. North Carolina Grant Moses AYERS 50 acres North side Yadkin River, mouth Fall Creek.

Page 97. 24 December 1792. North Carolina Grant Hugh LOGAN 89½ acres waters Josephs Creek adjoining Andrew SPEER.

Page 97. 24 December 1792. North Carolina Grant Andrew MANNING 200 acres Deep Creek adjoining Moses SWIM, Nathaniel HAINES, MACKLYEAS, and ELLIS.

Page 98. 24 December 1792. North Carolina Grant Jacob HUTTS 240 acres South side Hammons Creek adjoining George BATES.

Page 99.   24 December 1792.   North Carolina Grant Grimes
        HOLCOMB 200 acres Fall Creek adjoining 200 acres
surveyed for Henry SPEER and Henry HOLCOMBS land.

Page 99.   24 December 1792.   North Carolina Grant Henry
        WINTEL 100 acres waters Deep Creek adjoining William
BATES.

Page 100.   24 December 1792.   North Carolina Grant John
        BOHANNON 100 acres waters Cranverry adjoining
Bennett SMITH.

Page 100.   24 December 1792.   North Carolina Grant Hugh
        ARMSTRONG 200 acres Brushy Fork Pauls Creek
adjoining Collins HAMPTON, Clabun LAURANCE, his own former
line.

Page 101.   24 December 1792.   North Carolina Grant John
        BOHANNON 100 acres waters North fork Deep Creek
adjoining BRAMBLET, head Racoon Branch and Greensberry
PATTERSON.

Page 101.   24 December 1792.   North Carolina Grant Labon
        HICKS 200 acres waters Deep Creek adjoining Wm.
WOOLDRIDGE, Richard BLALOCK, Wm. Terrel LEWIS (RAYNES old
place), and Piney Knobbs.

Page 102.   24 December 1792.   North Carolina Grant George
        LOGAN and Henry SPEER 100 acres Big Branch
Forbis Creek adjoining Thomas CARSON, John LOGANS Mill Seat,
and James GRAHAM.

Page 102.   24 December 1792.   North Carolina Grant James
        MATTHEWS 250 acres North fork Forbes Creek
adjoining MURPHEY.

Page 103.   24 December 1792.   North Carolina Grant John
        SUMMERS 200 acres waters North side Yadkin River
adjoining Moses AYRES.

Page 104.   24 December 1792.   North Carolina Grant Lewis
        ELLIOTT 150 acres waters Deep Creek adjoining
Sam'l ARNOLD and Wheatens path.

Page 104.   24 December 1792.   North Carolina Grant William
        JOHNSON 129 acres waters Forbis Creek adjoining
his own land.

Page 105.   24 December 1792.   North Carolina Grant John
        WILLIAMS 55 acres waters Forbis Creek adjoining
corner his 100 acre tract, Ridge Road, agreed line with
Joseph ENGLAND.

Page 105.   24 December 1792.   North Carolina Grant John
        WILLIAMS 100 acres waters Forbis Creek adjoining
his former corner.

Page 106.   24 December 1792.   North Carolina Grant Matthias

CARPENTER 150 acres Rocky Branch waters, North fork Hunting Creek adjoining old road, WOOD and JOHNSON.

Page 106. 24 Dec. 1792. N.C. Grant Thomas VESTAL 24 acres waters Forbis Creek adjoining William JOHNSON, the old line and John JOHNSON.

Page 107. 2 May 1790. Isaac STUBBS to George HOBSON, Chatham County, North Carolina, 150 pounds, 100 acres Forbis Creek part State Grant ot William JOHNSON. Witnesses: Thomas VESTAL, Stephen HOBSON, and Rachel HOBSON. Signed: Isaac STUBBS and Margaret STUBBS.

Page 108. 24 Dec. N.C. Grant Isaac STUBBS 25 acres waters Forbis Creek adjoining his own corner.

Page 108. 24 Dec. 1792. N.C. Grant Joseph HUDSPETH 100 acres North fork Deep Creek adj. Joshua BROWN and ELMORE.

Page 109. 24 December 1792. North Carolina Grant Justice RENDELS 250 acres waters North fork Deep Creek near Round Hill, adjoining said REYNOLDS 100 acre entry made by Edmon Balley adjoining Thomas HEADLEY and John DURRUM.

Page 109. 24 December 1792. North Carolina Grant John PENRIGHT 200 acres Fishers Creek adjoining Mosleys road, agreed line of George DEBOARD.

Page 110. 24 December 1792. North Carolina Grant Henry SPEER 500 acres waters Forbis Creek adjoining Thos. ELLIOTT, DEULING, HARDGROVE, and Joseph MURPHEY.

Page 110. 24 December 1792. North Carolina Grant Henry SPEER 100 acres waters Hunting Creek near Knob adjoining HICKS and CAHOON.

Page 111. 2 April 1788. John MOLER and wife, Susannah, to Lewis BEARD, 100 pounds, 100 acres head waters Deep Creek, agreed line said MOLER and John PARSONS, Spring Branch adjoining Adam SHEEKS; being part 200 acres from Wm. Terrell LEWIS and Mary LEWIS to said MOLER. Witness: Adam (X) SHEEK. Signed: John MOLER and Susanna (X) MOLER.

Page 112. 20 December 1790. John WRIGHT and wife, Cathan, Rowan County, to William WRIGHT, 100 pounds, 280 acres in Surry and Rowan Counties, South side Yadkin River below mouth Coats Branch; GRANVILLE Granted Samuel BRYAN 31 December 1760; by BRYAN to Elizabeth ANDERSON, wife of Timothy ANDERSON 24 September 1762; by Timothy to WRIGHT. Witnesses: Joseph BOWEN, Samuel HARPER, and Rachel BOWEN. Signed: John WRIGHT and Cathan WRIGHT.

Page 113. 22 January 1790. Joseph MURPHEY to Moses BAKER 100 pounds, 218 acres Forbis Creek being part 640 acres Granted Joseph MURPHEY 4 November 1779. Witnesses: H(enry) SPEER AND Damuel (X) HICKS. Signed: Joseph (X) MURPHEY.

Page 115. 5 February 1791. Joseph JESSOP, Stokes County, to Isaac JONES 6 pounds, 4 shillings Specie, 100

60

acres both sides Grassy fork, Big Creek of Dan River; Granted
LEWIS 3 April 1780. Witnesses: Joseph JACKSON and Jacob
JESSOP. Signed: Lewis CONNER (Phebe did not sign).

Page 117. 29 May 1790. Arge GARNER to Charles VANDEVER,
100 pounds, 73 acres waters Turners Creek adjoining
Andrew SPEER and Benjamin SPEER. Witnesses: Thomas DONNILY,
Wm. COLVARD, and Jacob SPEER, Junr. Signed: Arge GARNER.

Page 118. 12 August 1789. Joseph ASHLEY to Jesse BUMPS,
100 pounds, 200 acres North side Flat Shole Creek
where John HEARD now lives. Witnesses: John HEARD and Rezia
JARVIS. Signed: Joseph ASHLEY.

Page 119. 1 December 1791. Stephen HIDE to William JOHNSON,
100 pounds, 200 acres waters Fall Creek adjoining
Ellis FOULER and Geo. HOLCOMB; Granted Jesse STAMFORD 9
November 1787. Witnesses: John Thomas LONGINO and James
DURHAM. Signed: Stephen (X) HIDE.

Page 120. 12 October 1790. John BRANHAM, Wilkes County,
North Carolina, to James DURHAM, 200 pounds, 100
acres South side Yadkin River, Morrises Creek adjoining
Benj. WHELESS; Granted BRAHAM 1787. Witnesses: Joseph
LASSWELL and Allen WHELESS. Signed: John (X) BRANHAM.

Page 121. 27 November 1790. Thomas POINDEXTER and wife,
Elizabeth, Stokes County, North Carolina, to
Daniel SCOTT, 640 pounds, 640 acres South side Yadkin River
above Job MARTINS. Witnesses: Job MARTIN, Alexander KERR,
and Arthur SCOTT. Signed: Thomas POINDEXTER and Elizabeth
POINDEXTER.

Page 121. 29 November 1790. Daniel SCOTT to Alexander
KERR, 100 pounds, 100 acres South side Yadkin
River. Witnesses: Bartlet EADS and John KERR. Signed:
Daniel (X) SCOTT.

Page 122. 18 November 1790. Thomas COOK, Wilkes County,
North Carolina, to John WILES, 400 pounds North
Carolina Currency, 215 acres South fork Deep Creek adjoining
EASLEY, purchased by Joshua COOK from the Land Office 9
August 1787. Witnesses: William DAVIS and Thomas (X) CLANTON.
Signed: Thomas (X) COOK.

Page 123. 20 February 1790. Lindsey CARLTON to John DAVIS,
Junr., Chatham County, North Carolina, 50 pounds,
100 acres Round Hill, waters North fork Deep Creek. Witnesses: John MARSHALL, Joseph DAVIS, and William DAVIS. Signed:
LINDSEY (X) CALTON.

Page 124. 24 December 1792. North Carolina Grant Justice
RANDELS (REYNOLDS) 100 acres Baleys Branch
adjoining Thomas HADLEY and HOLCOMB.

Page 124. 20 December 1791. North Carolina Grant Thomas
COOK 100 acres Dutchmans Creek adjoining Rowan

County line.

Page 125.   24 December 1792.   North Carolina Grant William
            ELLIOTT 300 acres Deep Creek near Piney Knobb.

Page 125.   24 December 1792.   North Carolina Grant Thomas
            FLOYD 300 acres South side Yadkin River on Baleys
Creek.

Page 126.   10 December 1790.   North Carolina Grant Jacob
            McCRAW 200 acres waters Pauls Creek adjoining
James BROWN.

Page 126.   10 December 1790.   North Carolina Grant Jacob
            McCRAW 100 acres Ozburns Creek including Jane
COYLES improvement.

Page 127.   20 December 1791.   North Carolina Grant Abijah
            ELMORE 200 acres Forbis Creek adjoining said
ELMORE, BOREN, John WILLIAMS, RAMEY and PILCHER.

Page 128.   18 May 1789.   North Carolina Grant William MUNKES
            100 acres Beaver Dam Creek, waters Fishers River.

Page 128.   20 December 1791.   North Carolina Grant Richard
            LAURANCE 200 acres Sead Kain, waters Tarrarat
River.

Page 129.   15 October 1792.   William HOLAMAN, Stokes County,
            North Carolina, to John NEALEY, 90 pounds, 200
acres North side Yadkin River, branches Bishops Creek adjoining Charles PARKER.   Witnesses: Pleasant KERBY and William
HOLAMAN, Junr.   Signed: William (X) HOLLAMAN.

Page 130.   26 December 1789.   Harris REAVIS, Rutherford
            County, to Jesse REAVIS, 50 pounds, 540 acres
waters Hammons Creek adjoining George MOORE.   Witnesses:
Joseph REAVIS and John REAVIS.   Signed: Harris (X) REAVIS.

Page 131.   20 July 1789.   Harris REAVIS, Rutherford County,
            to George MOORE, 10 pounds, 100 acres waters
Dutchmans Creek.   Witnesses: Joseph REAVIS and John REAVIS.
Signed: Harris (X) REAVIS.

Page 133.   1 August 1790.   Samuel HUMPHREYS to John HURD,
            20 pounds, 100 acres little Flat Shole Creek.
Witnesses: Andrew KINCANNON and Jesse LESTER.   Signed:
Samuel HUMPHREYS.

Page 133.   9 May 1791.   Jesse BUMP to John HEARD, 100 pounds,
            200 acres Flat Shole Creek including the Mill
Seat and including plantation where said HEARD now lives.
Witnesses: Edward LOVELL and Sarah (X) PEACOCK.   Signed:
Jesse BUMP.

Page 134.   26 February 1791.   Joel LEWIS to William SPARKS,
            Senr., 15 pounds, 100 acres adjoining James PARSONS

and said SPARKS. Witnesses: Wm. T. LEWIS and William SPARKS, Junr. Signed: Joel LEWIS.

Page 135.   24 December 1792.   North Carolina Grant Henry COGBOURN 100 acres Forbis Creek.

Page 136.   11 August 1790.   Reuben SHORES to David HARVILL, 50 pounds, 200 acres waters Deep Creek adjoining the Hickory Cabbin, CLATON, George SPARKS, Charles JOHNSON, and Chesnut Ridge Mountain. Witnesses: John PERSONS and Charles (X) JOHNSON. Signed: Reuben SHORE.

Page 137.   15 February 1791.   Isham ROYALTY to Joel MACKEY, 4 pounds, 100 acres Beaver Dam Creek, branch Fishers River adjoining said MACKEY and his Mill. Witnesses: James BRYSON, Sterling HUDSON, and Archibel (X) McKEVER. Signed: Isham ROYALTY.

Page 138.   18 February 1786.   John LYON to Daniel PILCHER, 60 pounds, 200 acres waters Deep Creek adjoining Jacob GALLION. Witnesses: James THOMAS, John (X) BOLETJACK, and James (X) PILCHER. Signed: John (X) LYON and Sarah (X) LYON.

Page 139.   10 May 1790.   Eliphalet JARVIS to Ephraim PHILLIPS, 150 pounds, 100 acres on Fishers River adjoining said JARVIS. Witnesses: John HUGHES, Justice REYNOLDS, and Edward SMITH. Signed: Eliphalet JARVIS.

Page 140.   3 January 1791.   Ambrose BRAMLETT to James VESTAL, 82 pounds, 10 shillings, 165 acres both sides North fork Deep Creek adjoining mouth Mill Creek adjoining Greenberry PATTERSON, Simon HADLEY and the Iron Works Road. Witnesses: Daniel VESTAL, David (X) VESTAL and James (X) VESTAL. Signed: Ambrose BRAMLETT.

Page 141.   12 May 1791.   Henry PATTILLO to Daniel WAGGONER, 200 pounds, 200 acres waters Deep Creek adjoining HUTCHENS. Witnesses: H(enry) SPEER and Aires HUDSPETH. Signed: Henry PATTILLO.

Page 142.   4 July 1788.   Leander HUGHES to Samuel KIRBY, 200 pounds North Carolina money, 93 acres North side Yadkin River, both sides Swan Creek adjoining John SATER: being part land that belonged to Samuel STEWART. Witnesses: Robert MATTHEWS and James (X) MARTIN. Signed: Leander HUGHES.

Page 143.   6 August 1791.   William COOK, guardian to orphans of William RIDGE, deceased, to William and Thomas RIDGE, two of said orphans, 150 pounds, 200 acres South side Yadkin River opposite mouth Fishers River; land formerly belonging to Nathaniel WOODRUFF. Acknowledged. Signed: William COOK.

Page 144.   10 August 1790.   John TALIAFERRO to Gidion EDWARDS, 300 pounds Virginia money, 300 acres both sides Fishers River. Witnesses: Benjamin TALIAFERRO, Thomas NORMAND, and Charles TALIAFERRO. Signed: John TALIAFERRO.

Page 144.   31 August 1790.   Jacob JONES and wife, Martha, to Samuel WILSON, 50 pounds North Carolina Currency, 100 acres East side Canada Creek. Witnesses: Reuben DEBORD and John COPELAND. Signed: Jacob (X) JONES and Martha (X) JONES.

Page 146.   4 May 1791.   Samuel HUMPHREYS to Thomas BALL, 65 pounds, 100 acres Big Flat Shoal Creek. Acknowledged. Signed: Samuel HUMPHREYS.

Page 147.   1 January 1791.   Joseph PHILLIPS, Stokes County, to Minor MARSH, 4 horses, 1 cow actually delivered and 150 acres; part 300 acre Fisher River, West side originally granted Elijah THOMPSON 3 November 1784. Witnesses: Benjamin BLEDSOE, (a signature in German), and Thomas (X) RANSON. Signed: Joseph PHILLIPS.

Page 147.   11 November 1789.   Richard GOODE, Esq., late Sheriff, to David HUDSPETH (land lost by Executors of estate of John HUDSPETH, deceased, to satisfy Jacob RIGOR), 20 pounds, 11 shillings, 8 pence for 600 acres and all estate rights, etc. of said Executors and all rights of Mary HUDSPETH, widow and relict of John HUDSPETH, deceased. Witnesses: William THORNTON and John Thomas LONGINO. Signed: Richard GOODE.

Page 148.   15 January 1791.   Henry SPEER to Strangeman HUTCHENS, 25 pounds, 75 acres waters South fork Forbis Creek adjoining Benajamin HUTCHENS: land granted Henry SPEER. Witnesses: John JOHNSON, John MACKIE, and Thomas VESTAL. Signed: H. SPEER.

Page 149.   26 August 1791.   George CARTER and wife, Mary, of Wythe County Virginia, to Charles SMITH, 150 pounds money of Virginia, 350 acres Tararat River adjoining upper end Richard LAURENCES land on Mounts Branch. Witnesses: John JENKINS and Dannial (X) COLLINS. Signed: George CARTER and Mary CARTER.

Page 151.   10 November 1791.   Eliphalet JARVIS to Thomas RAIBON, 500 pounds, 100 acres waters Fishers River adjoining Wootons Branch and the old line. Witnesses: Thomas NORMAND and Benjamin SNEED. Signed: Eliphalet (X) JARVIS.

Page 152.   17 November 1791.   David REAVES, Reatherford County, North Carolina, to Thomas HUTCHENS, 100 pounds, 119 acres waters North fork Deep Creek adjoining James REAVES on Bigg Branch said Creek that Thomas GALLION lived on adjoining John STANFIELD; part 200 acres granted David REAVES 16 March 1784. Witnesses: H(enry) SPEER, John STANFIELD, and James (X) CAIN. Signed: David REAVES.

Page 153.   23 November 1790.   Abraham REESE to Joseph MARSHILL, 40 pounds, 100 acres North fork Deep Creek. Witnesses: Thomas BURCH and Joseph KEYS, Junr. Signed: Abraham (X) REESE.

Page 154. 15 May 1790. Henry SPEER to John MILLER, 20
          pounds, 125 acres North fork Hammons Creek.
Witnesses: Henry PATTILLO, Thomas MASON, and David WELCH.
Signed: H. SPEER.

Page 154. 12 November 1791. Henry SPEER to Jacob MILLER,
          50 pounds, 125 acres waters Hammons Creek adjoin-
ing John MILLER and HOOTS. Witnesses: Henry PATTILLO, Daniel
KELLER, and James CAMPBELL. Signed: H. SPEER.

Page 155. 27 February 1783. Zachariah RAY to William
          GIBBONS, 5 pounds (no acres), waters Deep Creek
in Iron Works road and adjoining TANNER. Witnesses: Robert
LANIER and Henry SPEER. Signed: Zachariah RAY.

Page 156. 15 March 1790. John JOHNSON, Rowan County, to
          James PHARES, 50 pounds Specie, 200 acres North
Hunting Creek adjoining MOSBY and MOLER. Witnesses: Stephen
WOOD and Ann WOOD. Signed: John JOHNSON.

Page 157. 3 January 1791. Matthew Jouet WILIAMS to John
          BRUCE, 50 pounds, 100 acres Deep Creek adjoining
said BRUCE, KIMBROUGH, SKIDMORE: land granted Matthew J.
WILLIAMS 13 October 1783. Witnesses: Jo WILLIAMS and
William THORNTON. Signed: Matt J. WILLIAMS.

Page 158. 8 July 1793. Abraham REESE to John HUFF, 5
          shillings, 100 acres waters North fork Deep Creek,
West Cows Branch to Northwest corner 500 acres surveyed to
said RESSE 24 February 1780 adjoining Thomas HOLCOMB below
Reeses Mill. Witnesses: John BOND and William BOND. Signed:
Abraham (X) REESE.

Page 159. 5 March 1791. Benjamin SPEER to David HOWELL,
          5 pounds, 120 acres Turners Creek adjoining
STEELMAN. Witnesses: H(enry) SPEER, William HAGANS, and
Samuel SPEER. Signed: Benjamin SPEER.

Page 160. 5 March 1791. Benjamin SPEER to David HOWELL,
          10 pounds, 50 acres Piney Knob Branch; land
granted Benjamin SPEER. Witnesses: H(enry) SPEER, William
HAGANS, and Samuel SPEER.

Page 161. 28 May 1791. Joshua BROWN to Henry SPEER, 100
          pounds, 150 acres waters North fork Deep Creek
adjoining ELMORE: land granted Joshua BROWN. Witnesses:
Samuel CROCKET, Moses BAKER, and Benjamin HICKS. Signed:
Joshua (X) BROWN.

Page 162. 8 February 1789. Henry PATTILLO to Daniel
          WAGGONER, Rowan County, 100 pounds, 200 acres
waters North fork Deep Creek adjoining HUTCHENS. Witnesses:
John ALLEN, H(enry) SPEER, and Stephen ALFRED. Signed:
Henry PATTILLO.

Page 163. 15 March 1790. Robert DOAK, Guilford County, to
          Henry HERRING, 100 pounds, 47 acres Stuarts Creek

in the Hollow in said Doaks beginning line; part tract 640 acres said DOAK obtained by deed from Andrew BAILEY to Quintin POOLER. Witnesses: Bennett CREED, James MATTHEWS, and John HANNA. Signed: Robert DOAK.

Page 164. 14 November 1791. George HOLCOMB to Benjamin CLANTON, 140 pounds, 250 acres waters North fork Deep Creek adjoining John WILLIAMS and agreed line between Geo. HOLCOMB and Grimes HOLCOMB; being part tract granted George HOLCOMB 24 October 1782. Witnesses: John Thomas LONGINO, George SMITH, and Frederick LONG. Signed: George (X) HOLCOMB.

Page 165. 1 August 1791. James COFFEY, Stokes County, to Job MARTIN, 25 pounds, 200 acres South side Yadkin River adjoining Job MARTIN, crossing Baileys Creek; land granted Mary NAWLIN 24 October 1782; by Mary to said COFFEY. Witnesses: Valentine MARTIN, John CONRAD, and Leonard SCOTT. Signed: James COFFEY.

Page 166. 18 May 1789. North Carolina Grant Pilgrim POPE 640 acres waters North and South forks Deep Creek adjoining LURGENER and the widow WHITEFIELD.

Page 166. 3 January 1792. Simon HADLEY to Richard BROWN, 30 pounds, 100 acres waters North fork Deep Creek adjoining Thomas HADLEY and said Simon HADLEY. Witnesses: William ADAMS and Joseph HINSHAW. Signed: Simon HADLEY.

Page 167. 10 August 1790. Robert MATTHEWS, Iredell County, to Jonathan ADAMS, 30 pounds, 50 acres waters South fork Forbis Creek. Witnesses: John MARSHALL and William ADAMS, Junr. Signed: Robert MATTHEWS.

Page 168. 2 March 1791. John JACKSON, Stokes County, to Benjamin HIATT, 70 pounds, 93 acres both sides Chinquemin Creek. Witnesses: Jacob WORLEY, Benjamin CARR, and William STOW. Signed: John JACKSON.

Page 169. 13 June 1791. John BRUCE to Henry SPEER, 160 pounds, 100 acres adjoining said BRUCE, KIMBROUGH, SKIDMORE, crossing Deep Creek and including land granted Matthew Jouet WILLIAMS 13 October 1783; by WILLIAMS to John BRUCE 3 January 1791. Witnesses: William THORNTON and H(enry) PATTILLO. Signed: John BRUCE.

Page 170. 24 March 1791. John KIMBROUGH, Montgomery County, North Carolina, to Goldman KIMBROUGH, 150 pounds, 191½ acres; part tract sold by Thos. TURNER to Marmaduke KIMBROUGH 4 March 1768; by KIMBROUGH to John KIMBROUGH. Witnesses: Robert WILLIAMS, Constantine LADD, and Will CUPPLES. Signed: John KIMBROUGH.

Page 171. 31 December 1791. James CAMPBELL to Goldman KIMBROUGH, 50 pounds, 70 acres waters Yadkin River adjoining said KIMBROUGH and John HUNT. Witnesses: H(enry) SPEER, James TODD, and Daniel LIVERTON. Signed: James CAMPBELL.

Page 172.   10 December 1791.   Grimes HOLCOMB to Thomas ARNAL
            5 pounds, 200 acres Haw Branch; being part 300
acres granted John WILLIAMS.   Witnesses: Airs HUDSPETH and
John WILLIAMS.   Signed: Grimes (X) HOLCOMB.

Page 173.   20 October 1791.   John HAMON to Samuel HAGGARD,
            60 pounds, 140 acres South side Yadkin River
above Thomas FREEMANS plantation.   Witnesses: James BADGETT,
Joseph KERBY, and Joshua FREMAN.   Signed: John (X) HAMON.

Page 173.   16 August 1791.   Peter ELDER, Spartanburg County,
            South Carolina, to Leven SPEER, 35 pounds North
Carolina money, 200 acres waters Yadkin River called Josephs
Branch adjoining his former corner.   Witnesses: Thomas
ROBINSON and Nancy (X) ROBINSON.   Signed: Peter (X) ELDER
and Elizabeth (X) ELDER.

Page 174.   16 October 1789.   William LAFOON to John COX "for
            good and lawful money of North Carolina", a tract
of land purchased of Gilbert CERNEY in the Hollow on Stony
Creek.   Witnesses: Alexander BRYSON, Thomas NORMAND, and
FROST & SNOW.   Signed: William LAFOON.

Page 175.   1 December 1791.   Peter DOWNEY to William COOK,
            Junr., 200 pounds, 140 acres mouth Pipes Creek,
South side Yadkin River to place agreed on by John PIPES,
the elder and Humphrey COCKERHAM between Yadkin River and
Pipes Creek in said PIPES original survey adjoining John
PARKS including plantation Wm. COOK, Junr. now lives on and
his river plantation.   Witnesses: James DOWNEY, Wm. T. LEWIS,
and William COOK, Senr.   Signed: Peter (X) DOWNEY.

Page 177.   24 December 1792.   North Carolina Grant Henry
            HAMBRICK 320 acres Camps Branch adjoining SPURLING.

Page 177.   23 January 1793.   William ELLIS, Wilkes County,
            North Carolina, to Gabriel FENDER, 40 pounds,
150 acres granted said ELLIS adjoining Henry WAGGONER.
Witnesses: Aires HUDSPETH, Amariah FENDER, and Richard
GENTRY.   Signed: William ELLIS.

Page 178.   15 May 1792.   John Thomas LONGINO, Yeoman, to
            Edward BOND, planter, Guilford County, 150 pounds,
440 acres waters Yadkin River, creek called Seven Island
road leads from Round Hill to Critchfields ford adjoining
John BIDDICK; part entry James LINDSAY and since taken from
him by execution and sold at public auction to discharge of
forfeited recognizance Superior Court.   Witnesses: William
HOUGH and Thomas HADLEY.   Signed: John Thomas LONGINO.

Page 179.   6 August 1791.   Gideon EDWARDS to Charles
            TALIAFERRO, 300 pounds Virginia Currency, 300
acres both sides Fishers River.   Witnesses: Benjamin TALIA-
FERRO, Sarah TALIAFERRO, and Anna TALIAFERRO.   Signed:
Gideon EDDARDS.

Page 180.   26 November 1791.   John TALIAFERRO to Philip
            PRICHARD, 100 pounds, 540 acres on a branch

adjoining Zachariah SENTER and William MUNSKEES. Witnesses:
Charles TALIAFERRO, James (X) TUCKER, and Zachariah SENTER.
Signed: John TALIAFERRO.

Page 180.   21 March 1792.   John HUTCHENS to Joseph HUDSPETH,
          40 pounds, 42 acres North side Deep Creek; part
tract 640 acres granted James REAVIS, Senr. 20 September
1779 adjoining John HUTCHENS and John STANFIELD. Witnesses:
Frederick TANNER and Daniel (X) CAIN. Signed: John HUTCHENS.

Page 181.   15 March 1790.   Ratliff BOON to Charles SIMMONS,
          100 pounds, 200 acres Rutledge Creek; granted
said BOON 3 November 1784. Witnesses: William HARRIS, John
JACKSON, and Ryals SIMMONS. Signed: Ratliff BOON and Daniel
BOON.

Page 182.   24 December 1792.   North Carolina Grant Valentine
          MARTN 620 acres head branches Baileys Creek
adjoining Thomas FLOYD.

Page 183.   13 October 1783.   North Carolina Grant Jacob
          SALLEY 135 acres Northeast corner his other survey
adjoining Jacob CAMPERLIN and Daniel WEAVER including a
small improvement.

Page 184.   13 November 1792.   John HORN, Senr. to Adonijah
          HARBOUR, 100 pounds, 100 acres; tract whereon
said HORN formerly resided North side Yadkin River adjoining
said HARBOUR, agreed line William LAYN and said HORN and
agreed line Reubin JACKSON and said HARBOUR adjoining ridge
path leads to Bean Sholes. Acknowledged. Signed: John HORN.

Page 185.   1792.   Airs HUDSPETH to Thomas HOLCOMB, 60 pounds,
          100 acres waters South fork Deep Creek; part
tract sold to said HUDSPETH by Gibson WOOLDRIDGE 13 July
1784. Witnesses: Moses AYERS and John Thomas LONGINO.
Signed: Airs HUDSPETH.

Page 186.   1 January 1794.   North Carolina Grant John
          WILLIAMS 30 acres waters North fork Deep Creek
adjoining Jonas REYNOLDS, John PETYJOHN, BOND and his own
land.

Page 186.   30 April 1792.   Jacob PETTIJOHN to George HOLCOMB,
          50 pounds, 140 acres waters Deep Creek adjoining
Peter SUMMERS, Peter SPRINKLE. Witnesses: Mary (X) CROCKETT,
and H(enry) SPEER. Signed: Jacob (X) PETTIJOHN.

Page 187.   5 January 1793.   Peter MIERS and wife, Mary, to
          John WILLIAMS, 70 pounds, 100 acres North fork
Deep Creek; part 160 acres granted MIERS 3 November 1784
adjoining Charles RUSSELL and PETTIJOHN. Witnesses: H(enry)
SPEER, Abner GREENWOOD, and Abijah ELMORE. Signed: Peter
(X) MIERS and Mary (X) MIERS. . . .13 February 1793. Mary
MIERS came before Henry SPEER, J.P. and relinquished her
dower in above land.

Page 188.   16 March 1793.   Charles HUNT, Town of Salisbury,

Rowan County, to Christian SHEEKS, 13 pounds, lot #34, town Huntsville on High Street. Witnesses: William THORNTON and Thomas ANDERSON. Signed: Chas. HUNT.

Page 189. 17 May 1792. William T. LEWIS to Thomas CLANTON, 2,000 pounds Specie, 1,000 acres Western District, waters North fork Forkeddeer River adjoining Ephraim DAVIDSON. Witnesses: Thomas WRIGHT and James DEFREY. Signed: Wm. T. LEWIS.

Page 190. 20 December 1791. North Carolina Grant Bartholomew RAMEY 188 acres Stony Creek waters, Tarrarat River including Richard HILLS improvement.

Page 191. 20 December 1791. North Carolina Grant Thomas PUCKETT 200 acres Flat Shoal Creek.

Page 191. 8 August 1791. Minor MARSH to John MARSH, Junr., 50 pounds, 75 acres Fishers River. Witnesses: Thomas MARSH, William BLEDSOE, and Daniel MARSH. Signed: Minor MARSH.

Page 192. 9 February 1793. Christian SMITH, Executor, Abraham LYMBACK, deceased, in right his wife, to Daniel LINEBACK, 60 pounds, 240 acres waters branch empties into Yadkin River, South side through Thompson GLENS plantation adjoining said GLEN, Andrew SPEER, Geo. RIDINGS, and John Thos. LONGINO; land sold by LONGINO to Hugh MORRIS; by MORRIS to Abraham LYMBACK. Witnesses: Oswell PHILLIPS and Matthew BROOKS. Signed: Christian SMITH.

Page 193. 20 December 1791. North Carolina Grant Joseph JESSOP 50 acres Toms Creek adjoining his Mill tract former CLARKS and adjoining the Mill Pond.

Page 193. 9 August 1787. North Carolina Grant Isaac ELSBERRY 100 acres North fork Hunting Creek adjoining his former corner.

Page 194. 20 December 1791. North Carolina Grant Henry SPEER 240 acres North fork Hunting Creek adjoining Thomas WOOLDRIDGE, Matthew SPARKS and KEEL.

Page 194. 22 February 1794. Henry SPEER to Joseph SMITH, 200 pounds, 240 acres North fork Hunting Creek adjoining Thos. WOOLDRIDGE, Matt SPARKS, ROTEN; granted H. SPEER 20 December 1791. Acknowledged. Signed: H. SPEER.

Page 195. 24 December 1792. North Carolina Grant Samuel GENTRY 400 acres head waters, Deep Creek North side Fox Knob Mountain adjoining Michael HENDERSON, Moses WOODRUFF, top said Mountain.

Page 196. 18 May 1789. North Carolina Grant William ALNUTT 500 acres Buck Shoal Branch, waters Hunting Creek adjoining WARD, WINDSOR and GLOVER.

Page 197.   10 December 1790.   North Carolina Grant James
          BURNSIDES 540 acres waters Hunting Creek adjoining
Isaac MIZE, Henry SPEER and COOK.

Page 198.   24 December 1792.   North Carolina Grant John WARD
          300 acres waters South fork Deep Creek adjoining
ELLIOT and Airs HUDSPETH.

Page 198.   30 January 1792.   James SANDERS to Jeremiah RILEY,
          20 pounds, 300 acres waters Hunting Creek head of
draft Buck Shoal branch adjoining Joshiah WILSON. Witnesses:
Thomas WRIGHT and Isaac JOHNSON. Signed: James (X) SANDERS.

Page 199.   17 August 1789.   John Neidy ANDERSON to Gerard
          RILEY, Wilkes County, North Carolina, 100 pounds,
200 acres waters Hunting Creek being place ANDERSON now
lives on. Witnesses: Stephen WOOD and Elisha CAST. Signed:
John Neidy (X) ANDERSON and Sarah (X) ANDERSON.

Page 200.   1791.   North Carolina Grant Zopher JAYENE 640
          acres waters Forbis Creek adjoining Henry JAYNE
and MATHIS.

Page 201.   24 December 1792.   North Carolina Grant Millington
          BLALOCK 640 acres waters Deep Creek near Brushy
Mountain on Camp Branch.

Page 202.   21 May 1792.   John LYNCH, Stokes County, to
          Thompson GLEN, 100 pounds, 230 acres waters
Yadkin River, Joseph Branch adjoining LOGAN, FORBIS, Moses
BAKER; part 341 acres State granted Timothy COE 3 April
1780; by Sheriff to LYNCH 1789. Witnesses: William THORNTON,
Bomas TRUDAKER, and Frederick MILLER. Signed: John LYNCH.

Page 203.   15 May 1792.   John DUNNAGAN, Senr. to Andrew
          KINCANNON, 60 pounds, 100 acres both sides Toms
Creek; part tract said DUNNAGAN now lives on, formerly
taken up by Philip SHORE and sold to DUNNAGAN. Witnesses:
James DUNNAGAN, John HARRIS, and James KINCANNON. Signed:
John DUNNAGAN.

Page 204.   17 May 1792.   Joel LEWIS to Reuben SHORES, 12
          pounds, 300 acres waters South side Yadkin River
adjoining William Terrel LEWIS, said SHORE, SWIM, COBB;
being granted Joel LEWIS 10 May 1789. Witnesses: Thomas
WRIGHT and Charles HUDSPETH. Signed: Joel LEWIS.

Page 204.   27 June 1789.   William COOK, Junr. to James
          HALHORN of Virginia, 80 pounds North Carolina
money, 300 acres, draft Roberts Branch South side Yadkin
River adjoining McBRIDE. Witnesses: William COOK, Reuben
SHORE, Junr., and Francis (X) KEATON. Signed: William
COOK, Junr.

Page 205.   1 December 1791.   William Terrel LEWIS to William
          COOK, Senr, 400 pounds, 200 acres South side
Yadkin River, Iron road adjoining LEWIS own line, formerly
Peter SALLEYS adjoining Richard Henry DENNIS. Witnesses:

John BURCH, Joel LEWIS, William COOK, Jurn., and Zenas
BALDWIN. Signed: Wm. T. LEWIS.

Page 206. 1 December 1791. William T. LEWIS to William
            COOK, Senr., 500 pounds, 200 acres South side
Yadkin River above the Fish Pot adjoining LEWIS old line.
Witnesses: John BURCH, Joel LEWIS, William COOK, Junr., and
Zenus BALDWIN. Signed: Wm. T. LEWIS.

Page 207. 14 April 1792. Edward LOVELL and wife, Rebeckah,
            to Joseph JACKSON, 600 pounds, 400 acres both
sides Toms Creek being land said LOVELL now lives on.
Witnesses: Bowater SUMNER and John JACKSON. Signed: Edward
LOVELL and Rebeckah (X) LOVELL.

Page 208. 2 May 1792. Thomas GREEN to John WOOLFINSPERGO,
            300 pounds, 200 acres each side Forkners Creek
adjoining FORKNER. Witnesses: William SMITH, Mallory SMITH,
and Charles SMITH. Signed: Thomas GREEN.

Page 209. 10 February 1791. Henry HERRIN to Bennet CREED,
            100 pounds North Carolina Currency, 150 acres
Beach Creek. Witnesses: James BRYSON, John DAVIS, and Colby
CREED. Signed: Henry HERRING.

Page 209. 23 January 1792. John Thomas LONGINO to Robert
            FERGUSON, Junr., 16 pounds, 200 acres waters
Dills Creek adjoining William ROBERTSON, land surveyed for
Rachel LANDERS 12 May 1779. Witnesses: Thomas LONGINO and
George SMITH. Signed: John Thomas LONGINO.

Page 210. 10 August 1790. Robert MATTHEWS, Iredell County,
            to George ADAMS, 60 pounds, 92 acres waters South
fork Forbis Creek adjoining John ADAMS. Witnesses: John
MARSHILL and William ADAMS, Junr. Signed: Robert MATTHEWS.

Page 211. 10 August 1790. Robert MATTHEWS, Iredell County,
            to William ADAMS, Junr., 60 pounds, 66 acres South
fork Forbis Creek adjoining Jonathan ADAMS. Witnesses: John
MARSHILL and Jonathan ADAMS. Signed: Robert MATTHEWS.

Page 212. 10 August 1790. Robert MATTHEWS, Iredell County,
            to John ADAMS, 60 pounds, 92 acres, waters Forbis
Creek adjoining William ADAMS, State granted said MATTHEWS
18 May 1789. Witnesses: John MARSHILL and Jonathan ADAMS.
Signed: Robert MATTHEWS.

Page 213. 2 September 1791. William T. LEWIS to Dugal
            McMIKLE, 100 pounds, 80 acres South side Yadkin
River, part 200 acres granted Olive ROBERTS, laid off by H.
SPEER, County surveyor. Witnesses: Joel LEWIS, Aaron MOSER,
and James JANE (JAYNE). Signed: Wm. T. LEWIS.

Page 214. 6 August 1791. Thomas GARNER to John CONNILY, 40
            pounds, 24 3/4 acres waters Turners Creek adjoin-
ing PRIDDY, Jacob SPEER, his old former corner. Witnesses:
James CONNELY and Edward SCOTT. Signed: Thomas GARNER and
Lewis GARNER.

Page 215. 6 August 1791. Thomas GARNER to John DONNILY, Senr., 100 pounds, 144 3/4 acres waters Turners Creek. Witnesses: James DONNILY and Edward SCOTT. Signed: Thomas GARNER and Lewis GARNER. . . .The said James DONNILY saw Lewis GARNER sign same for himself and also for his Father, Thomas GARNER.

Page 216. 19 March 1790. Arge GARNER to James DONNILY, 50 pounds, 73 acres waters Elrod Creek adjoining Jacob SPEER, Andrew SPEER, and PRIDDY. Witnesses: Thomas DONNILY and William HAGIN. Signed: Arge GARNER.

Page 216. 21 April 1792. Philip HOWARD to Thomas MOSBY, 50 pounds, 60 acres Surry County, being part 60 acres State granted Philip HOWARD 8 May 1789. Witnesses: Samuel MOSBY and John WINSTON. Signed: Philip HOWARD.

Page 217. 1 December 1791. William T. LEWIS to William COOK, Senr., 386 pounds, 386 acres South side Yadkin River, mouth Cobbs Creek adjoining LEWIS and Peter SALLA. Witnesses: Joel HURT (or HUNT) and Isaac (X) EMANUEL. Signed: Wm. T. LEWIS.

Page 218. 1 December 1791. Wm. T. LEWIS to William COOK, Senr., 175 pounds, 175 acres waters Falls Creek, West side Peach Bottom Creek, conditional line between LEWIS and James DOWNEY adjoining Peter SALLA and crossing Cobbs Creek. Witnesses: Robert H. DYER, Joel HURT, Polly BALDWIN, and Isaac (X) EMANUEL. Signed: Wm. T. LEWIS.

Page 219. 28 November 1791. John TALIAFERRO to James TUCKER, 100 pounds Virginia Currency, 230 acres waters Little Fish River. Witnesses: Charles TALIAFERRO, Philip (X) PRICHARD, and Zachariah SENTER. Signed: John TALIAFERRO.

Page 220. 28 July 1792. Zenas BALDWIN to John BARR, 100 pounds, 150 acres Cobbs Creek adjoining COBB, Beaver dam Creek and Gilbert HAN (or HAM). Witnesses: William COOK, John BURCH, and William BURCH. Signed: Zenas BALDWIN.

Page 221. 6 July 1790. Peter SALLEY to William COOK, Senr., 7 pounds, 14 acres South side Yadkin River known as Peter SALLEYS old plantation. Witnesses: Airs HUDSPETH, Obediah MARTIN, and Cornelius PHILLIPS. Signed: Peter SALLE.

Page 221. 22 October 1791. James CAMPBELL to George KIMBROUGH, 40 pounds, 100 acres waters Yadkin River adjoining Goldman KIMBROUGH and Leonard RICHARD(S). Witnesses: J.S. FROHOCK, Augustine (X) WILLARD, and John HUNT. Signed: James CAMPBELL.

Page 222. 14 August 1792. George KIMBROUGH to Isaac SESSIONS, 50 pounds, 100 acres adjoining corner 300 acres surveyed Abraham CRESON adjoining Goldman KIMBROUGH and Leon. RICHARDS. Witness: John HUNT. Signed: George KIMBROUGH.

Page 223. 22 October 1791. James CAMPBELL to John HUNT, 50

pounds, 100 acres some branches Turners and Lick
Run Creeks, waters Yadkin River adjoining George KIMBROUGH
land sold him by James CAMPBELL, Matthias STEELMAN and Leonard
RICHARDS. Witnesses: Joshua HARBIN and Richard HOLLAND.
Signed: James CAMPBELL.

Page 224. 29 May 1792. Joshua CRESON, Executor, Will of
Abraham CRESON, deceased, to Chas. HUNT, merchant,
Salisbury, Rowan County, 150 pounds, 158 acres South side
Yadkin River being State granted Abraham CRESON 9 August
1787. Witnesses: John HUNT and Isham FROHOCK. Signed:
Joshua CRESON.

Page 225. 15 August 1792. Hugh ARMSTRONG, Esq., Sheriff,
to Thomas HEADLEY, Yeoman, (land lost by Wm. RAMEY
and land seized by Deputy Sheriff John Thomas LONGINO), 2
tracts, 350 acres waters North fork Deep Creek adjoining
Thomas HEADLEY, John DURAM, Justice REYNOLDS. Witnesses:
H(enry) SPEER, James JONES, and Airs HUDSPETH. Signed: Hugh
ARMSTRONG.

Page 226. 27 July 1792. Abiel COBB, farmer, Pendleton
County, South Carolina, to Daniel MORRIS, farmer,
60 pounds, 300 acres Cobbs Creek adjoining Josiah KEEN, State
granted to COBB 3 April 1781. Witnesses: Joel LEWIS, Gibson
WOOLDRIDGE, and Nathaniel MORRIS. Signed: Abiel COBB.

Page 227. 10 October 1791. William T. LEWIS to William
COCKERHAM, 100 pounds, 120 acres back line formerly
State granted Oliver ROBERTS, 200 acres Yadkin River adjoining Dugal McMICKLE. Witnesses: James DOWNEY, State COOK,
and Obediah MARTIN. Signed: Wm. T. LEWIS.

Page 228. 14 January 1792. William PETTY, Senr. to Christian
FENDER, 32 pounds North Carolina Currency, 300
acres waters Deep Creek adjoining Henry HAMBRICK, William
BLALOCK, Richard BLALOCK; land entered by George PHILIPS
and surveyed 26 May 1786. Witnesses: William ELLIOTT and
Nimrod (X) FENDER. Signed: William PETTY.

Page 229. 16 February 1792. Mortgage Deed, Jacob WEAVER to
Aaron SPEER, Senr., 300 acres head branch McFees
Creek adjoining James JONES, William MOORE, Simeon CARTER
(said Jacob Bound unto said SPEER 50 pounds; if said
obligation paid, this deed be null and void.) Witnesses:
William COOK and William JOHNSON. Signed: Jacob (X) WEAVER.

Page 229. 11 August 1792. Richard GOODE to Reuben SPARKS,
50 pounds, 340 acres Brushy Mountain County line,
crossing branch Hunting Creek to dividing line between Surry
and Wilkes Counties. Witnesses: John COOLEY, Senr., John
COOLEY, Junr., and Hannah COOLEY. Signed: Richard GOODE.

Page 230. 2 September 1786. Henry SPEER to Charles RUSSELL,
20 pounds, 121 acres waters North fork Deep Creek
adjoining John WILLIAMS, George HOLCOMB and HUDSPETH.
Witnesses: William HOUGH, Peter (X) MIERS, and Levi (X)
SHINN. Signed: H. SPEER.

Page 231.   28 May 1789.   Thomas JACKS to Edward JAMES, 50
          pounds, 100 acres head waters Deep Creek adjoining
COLLINS, being part 250 acre tract. Witnesses: Thomas WRIGHT,
and Airs HUDSPETH. Signed: Thomas (X) JACKS.

Page 232.   12 April 1788.   William T. LEWIS to Joel LEWIS,
          100 pounds, 250 acres South side Yadkin River
against Tumbling Falls. Witnesses: William COOK, Junr.,
Thomas JOHNSON, and J.M. LEWIS. Signed: Wm. T. LEWIS.

Page 233.   15 June 1792.   Joel LEWIS to James DEFREES, 250
          pounds, 250 acres South side Yadkin River against
Tumbling Falls. Witnesses: John HUNT, Wm. T. LEWIS, and J.
FROHOCK. Signed: Joel LEWIS.

Page 234.   26 October 1792.   John CHESNUTT, Camden, South
          Carolina, surviving Executor, Will of Ely KERSHAW,
deceased, (said Will bearing date 1 August 1780 and recorded
office Secretary State of South Carolina, stating residue his
estate be divided equally among his 3 children) to Richard
LAURANCE, 200 Mexican Dollars, 120 acres both sides Renfroes
Creek, East fork Tarrarat River on an Island in said River;
being land William DALTON sold Martin ARMSTRONG 24 January
1775; by ARMSTRONG to Joseph KERSHAW, William ANCRUM, John
CHESNUTT, Ely KERSHAW and Aaron LOVCOCK, merchants and co-
partners then existing at Camden, South Carolina; then to
Ely KERSHAW at disolution said co-partnership. Witnesses:
James LAURANCE, Richard LAURANCE, Junr., and John CRAVEN.
Signed: John CHESNUTT. . . .Received of Richard LAURANCE,
200 dollars or 46 pounds, 13 shillings, 4 pense in South
Carolina Sterling. Witnesses: James LAURANCE and Richard
LAURANCE, Junr. Signed: John CHESNUTT.

Page 236.   22 November 1790.   Abraham SKIDMORE to Henry SPEER,
          100 pounds, 20 acres both sides Deep Creek adjoin-
ing said SPEER below Fish Trap at foot hill adjoining John
SKIDMORE, South side Creek at the Bridge Place. Witnesses:
William SPILMAN, Thomas MASON, and William DOWLING. Signed:
Abraham (X) SKIDMORE.

Page 237.   22 September 1792.   Airs HUDSPETH to John
          HUDSPETH, 100 pounds North Carolina Currency, 400
acres North side South fork Deep Creek, North of the Swisher,
a draft of Deep Creek adjoining John BLALOCK and John HUDSPETH.
Witness: Joseph HILL. Signed: Airs HUDSPETH.

Page 238.   11 October 1792.   Arthur SCOTT to Edward LOVELL,
          Arthur SCOTT, Jean THOMPSON, Executrix and Joseph
ASHLEY, Executor, Will of Samuel THOMPSON, deceased, 500
pounds, 640 acres in Surry and Stokes Counties on Yadkin
River adjoining tract formerly claimed by Gideon WRIGHT,
below mouth little Yadkin (excepting the saw and grist mills
and seats on which they stand, which is hereby conveyed by
Arthur SCOTT to Edward LOVILL and Arthur SCOTT, separate and
apart from co-partnership of SCOTT, LOVELL and THOMPSON.
Witnesses: Jeremiah EARLEY, Nathan HAINES, and Samuel
THOMPSON. Signed: Arthur SCOTT.

Page 239. 14 September 1789. William HICKMAN to Joseph
          WELCH, 50 pounds, 150 acres branch Snow Creek that
makes in near Reuben DODSONS. Witnesses: John HUGHES and
Reuben DODSON. Signed: William HICKMAN.

Page 240. 13 January 1791. John SANDERS, Burbon County,
          Virginia, to Samuel ELLIS, Iredell County, North
Carolina, 100 pounds, 317 acres in Surry County on North
Hunting Creek adjoining James SANDERS. Witnesses: Stephen
WOOD and Brittain SANDERS. Signed: John SANDERS.

Page 241. 6 February 1793. John ALLEN to Peter HAMLEN, 50
          pounds, 100 acres, the plantation where John ALLEN
has lately lived, East side Fishers River where Howards road
crosses said river adjoining said ALLEN to waggon road ajoin-
ing John RICHARDS. Witnesses: David BRAY and William BRAY.
Signed: John (X) ALLEN and Elenor (X) ALLEN.

Page 242. 18 November 1791. James REAVIS to Thomas HUTCHENS,
          40 pounds, 40 acres North side Deep Creek adjoining
Northwest corner, 640 acres surveyed to said James REAVES 12
January 1779; part said 640 acres. Witnesses: Joseph REAVIS,
John REAVIS, and David REAVIS. Signed: James REAVIS.

Page 242. 18 November 1791. James REAVIS to John STANDFIELD,
          100 pounds, 200 acres North fork Deep Creek adjoin-
ing Frederick SHORE, part 640 acres granted said REAVIS.
Witnesses: Joseph REAVIS, John REAVIS, and David REAVIS.
Signed: James REAVIS.

Page 243. 17 November 1791. David REAVIS, Rutherford County,
          North Carolina, to John STANDFIELD, 60 pounds, 81
acres, waters North fork Deep Creek adjoining corner, 200
acres granted David REAVIS 16th March 1784 adjoining Thomas
HUTCHENS, Big Branch where Thomas GALLION lived. Witnesses:
H(enry) SPEER, Thomas HINCHEY, and Thomas HUTCHENS. Signed:
David REAVIS.

Page 244. 10 February 1793. Amos SCRITCHFIELD, Spartanburg
          County, South Carolina, to Sherod BROCK, 20 pounds,
100 acres waters Fishers River adjoining land where John
ALLEN, Junr. now lives. Witnesses: William MEREDITH, Rezia
JARVIS, and John SHORE. Signed: Amos SCRITCHFIELD.

Page 245. 26 December 1790. Jane TALIAFERRO, Heir Richard
          TALIAFERRO, deceased, to John TALIAFERRO, 50
pounds, 100 acres adjoining said John. Witnesses: Joseph
PORTER, Elizabeth RICHARDS, and Rachel RICHARDS. Signed:
Jane TALIAFERRO.

Page 246. 3 December 1791. John TALIAFERRO to William
          BAKER, 100 pounds, 307 acres waters (?) Creek
adjoining said TALIAFERRO and adjoining TUCKER. Witnesses:
Charles TALIAFERRO, Philip PRICHARD, and Joseph PORTER.
Signed: John TALIAFERRO.

Page 246. 29 December 1791. James SANDERS to Edward
          WILLIAMS, 300 pounds, _788_ acres waters Hunting

Creek in Iredell County from Surry County line adjoining
Samuel ELLIS, Isaac JOHNSON, being part 640 acres granted
James SANDERS 20 September 1779 and 200 acres granted James
SANDERS 9 August 1789. Witnesses: H(enry) SPEER and Jonathan
SANDERS. Signed: James (X) SANDERS.

Page 247. 20 December 1791. North Carolina Grant Robert
            JOHNSON, 280 acres adjoining RANDLEMAN and said
JOHNSON.

Page 248. 29 October 1792. Abijah ELMORE to Pearra CHIN,
            80 pounds, 190 acres waters Forbis Creek adjoining
ASHLEY on South side road leading from the Shallowford to
James PILCHERS old place, adjoining corner 320 acres granted
Jacob GALLION; by GALLION to Abijah ELMORE: being part said
GALLION granted and part 200 acres granted Abijah ELMORE.
Witnesses: H(enry) SPEER, William (X) HARDEN and Israel
NORDYKE. Signed: Abijah (X) ELMORE. . . .On 31 October 1792,
Elizabeth ELMORE, wife of Abijah relinquished her right of
dower in said land before Henry SPEER, J.P. Signed: Elizabeth
(X) ELMORE.

Page 249. 29 October 1791. Abijah ELMORE to Halifax ASHLEY,
            80 pounds, 180 acres waters Forbis Creek adjoining
Jacob GALLION, John STANDLEY and PILCHER: part land granted
said ELMORE and part granted GALLION. Witnesses: H(enry)
SPEER, William (X) HARDEN, and Israel NORDYKE. Signed:
Abijah ELMORE. . . .On 31 October 1792, Elizabeth ELMORE,
wife of Abijah relinquished her right of dower in said land
before Henry SPEER, J.P. Signed: Elizabeth (X) ELMORE.

Page 250. 26 November 1792. William WRIGHT to Mark HOLAMAN,
            315 pounds, 180 acres in Surry and Stokes Counties,
South side Yadkin River near fishing place above mouth Cates
Branch adjoining Henry MOCK, part 280 Granville granted
Samuel BRYSON 3 December 1760; by BRYSON to Elisabeth SLONE,
afterwards Elizabeth ANDERSON, wife Timothy ANDERSON; by said
ANDERSON to John WRIGHT 4 August 1778; by said John to
William WRIGHT. Witnesses: William THORNTON, William HOLAMAN,
and Rezia HARBIN. Signed: William WRIGHT.

Page 251. 5 November 1792. Henry SPEER to Sapphira REYNARD,
            200 pounds, 200 acres waters Logans and Josephs
Creeks adjoining John JOINER, Thompson GLEN, John COE.
Witnesses: George HEAD, John BARNS, and Charles (X) Vandever.
Signed: H. SPEER. . . .11 February 1793, Rachel SPEER, wife
of Henry relinquished her right of dower in above land before
John WILLIAMS and Samuel MOSBY, J.P.'S.

Page 252. 2 November 1792. Henry SPEER to John JOINER, 300
            pounds, 190 acres, waters Joseph and Logans Creek
adjoining John CARTER and the widow REYNARD. Witnesses:
George HEAD, J. JOINER, and John CARTER. Signed: H. SPEER.
. . . .11 February 1793, Rachel SPEER, wife of Henry SPEER
relinquished her right of dower in above land before John
WILLIAMS and Samuel MOSBY, J.P.'S.

Page 253. 7 May 1792. Henry SPEER to Benjamin GARRISH, 50

pounds, 112 acres waters Swisher Creek adjoining corner, 640 acres granted Edmond REAVIS and conveyed to H. SPEER. Witnesses: Nathaniel GWIN and David WELCH. Signed: H. SPEER.

Page 254. 29 December 1792. Benjamin GARRISH to William ZACHARY, 60 pounds, 112 acres waters Swishers Creek adjoining 640 acres granted Edmond REAVIS; by REAVIS to H. SPEER; by SPEER to Benjamin GARRISH. Witnesses: John JOHNSON and Jonas REYNOLDS. Signed: Benjamin GARRISH.

Page 255. 22 May 1792. George BROOKS and wife to Benjamin CAIN, 80 pounds, 150 acres Hermand Creek, South side of Yadkin River adjoining John HUMPHREY; land granted Thomas CAIN; by CAIN to George BROOKS 5 September 1787. Witnesses: Aquilla BECK and James (X) BIDWELL. Signed: George (X) BROOKS and Leah (X) BROOKS.

Page 256. 24 November 1792. Henry SPEER to Matthew BROOKS, Stokes County, 100 pounds, 148 acres adjoining Joseph MURPHEY and Robert FORBIS (now John CARTERS) being corner tract surveyed for William Hargus GRAY. Witnesses: Thompson GLEN, John CARTER, and James TODD. Signed: H. SPEER.

Page 257. 18 September 1794. Henry SPEER to Joseph WILLIAMS (amount blank), 392 acres Deep Creek adjoining CRESON, the cane brake, Wyatt GARNER; being tract sold SPEER by Silas ENYART and Sarah ENYART, his wife, 7 December 1786. Witnesses: William THORNTON and Robert WILLIAMS, Junr. Signed: H. SPEER.

Page 258. 18 September 1794. Henry SPEER to Joseph WILLIAMS, 100 pounds, 113½ acres waters Deep Creek adjoining Thomas SKIDMORE; being land sold SPEER by said SKIDMORE 23 May 1784. Witnesses: William THORNTON and Robert WILLIAMS, Junr. Signed: H. SPEER.

Page 259. 9 August 1787. Richard COOK, Rowan County, to James REAVIS, 200 pounds North Carolina Currency, 175 acres mouth Thomas CLANTONS spring branch adjoining said COOK and FRAZIERS field. Witnesses: David REAVIS and Charles (X) PEARSON. Signed: Richard (X) COOK.

Page 260. 16 March 1793. Charles HUNT, Salisbury, Rowan County, to David WELCH, 8 pounds, town lot No. 48, Huntsville. Witnesses: William THORNTON and John HUNT. Signed: Charles HUNT.

Page 261. 16 March 1793. Charles HUNT, Salisbury, Rowan County, to David WELCH, 5 pounds 12 shillings, lot No. 47, Huntsville on Arch and Second Streets. Witnesses: William THORNTON and John HUNT. Signed: Charles HUNT.

Page 261. 16 March 1793. Charles HUNT, Salisbury, Rowan County, to William MARTIN, 9 pounds, 2 shillings, lot No. 5, Huntsville High and Pine Streets. Witnesses: William THORNTON and John HUNT. Signed: Charles HUNT.

Page 262.   16 March 1793.   Charles HUNT, Salisbury, Rowan
          County, to William COOK, 8 pounds, 10 shillings,
6 pense, lot No. 32, town of Huntsville, High and First
Streets.   Witnesses: William THORNTON and J. FROHOCK.
Signed: Charles HUNT.

Page 263.   16 March 1793.   Charles HUNT, Salisbury, Rowan
          County, to William COOK, 5 pounds, lot No. 31,
Huntsville, First and Arch Streets.   Witnesses: William
THORNTON and John HUNT.   Signed: Charles HUNT.

Page 263.   16 March 1793.   Charles HUNT, Salisbury, Rowan
          County, to Thomas YOUNG, Iredell County, 8 pounds,
7 pense, lot No. 41, High and Third Streets, Huntsville.
Witnesses: William THORNTON and J(ohn) HUNT.   Signed:
Charles HUNT.

Page 264.   16 March 1793.   Charles HUNT, Salisbury, Rowan
          County, to Thomas YOUNG, Iredell County, 10 pounds,
lot No. 43, Huntsville.   Witnesses: William THORNTON and
J(ohn) HUNT.   Signed: Charles HUNT.

Page 265.   16 March 1793.   Charles HUNT, Salisbury, Rowan
          County, to Robert HORN, 9 pounds, 1 penny, lot
No. 13, Huntsville, corner High and Pine Streets.   Witnesses:
William THORNTON and J. FROHOCK.   Signed: Charles HUNT.

Page 266.   6 March 1793.   John WILLIAMS to John JOHNSON, 100
          pounds, 100 acres waters North fork Deep Creek
adjoining William HOUGH: part 300 acres granted said
WILLIAMS 18th May 1789.   Witnesses: William HOUGH and
Samuel SPEER.   Signed: John WILLIAMS.

Page 266.   7 October 1793.   John JOHNSON to Jesse VESTAL,
          Chatham County, North Carolina, 8 pounds, 2
shillings, 6 pence for 100 acres waters North fork Deep
Creek; part 300 acres granted John WILLIAMS 18th May 1789;
by said WILLIAMS to John JOHNSON 6 March 1793 and adjoining
William HOUGH.   Witnesses: John VESTAL and David VESTAL.
Signed: John JOHNSON.

Page 267.   15 May 1792.   John Thomas LONGINO, Yeoman, to
          Thomas WILES, planter, 90 pounds (no acreage),
South bank Swisher or Reeses Creek opposite Benjamin
GARRISH adjoining William RUTLEDGE, crossing Deep Creek
being part 540 acres lately the property of James LINDSEY.
Acknowledged.   Signed: John Thomas LONGINO.

Page 268.   24 December 1792.   North Carolina Grant John
          HANN 280 acres North fork Hunting Creek adjoining
Henry SPEER and Samuel MOSBY.

Page 269.   9 July 1794.   North Carolina Grant George LONG
          300 acres Smiths Branch adjoining Edward CHANDLER,
HOPPIS, Thomas EVERTON, PENRY on Mosbys Ridge and adjoining
ALSTON.

Page 269.   24 December 1792.   North Carolina Grant William

RICH, 200 acres waters Dills Creek, South side
Yadkin River adjoining William PHILLIPS.

Page 270.   10 February 1792.   Simon HADLEY to Moses ADAMS,
            30 pounds, 100 acres waters North fork Deep Creek
adjoining John HINSHAW land granted HADLEY 9 August 1787.
Witnesses: Joseph FINNEY and John (X) VESTAL.   Signed: Simon
HADLEY.

Page 271.   20 December 1791.   North Carolina Grant John
            MARSHALL 200 acres adjoining said MARSHALL, ADAMS,
and crossing Oldfield Branch.

Page 272.   20 December 1791.   North Carolina Grant John
            MARSHALL 110 acres adjoining Thomas VESTAL, ADAMS,
and crossing Forbis Creek.

Page 272.   24 March 1791.   John KIMBROUGH, Montgomery County,
            North Carolina, to Joseph WILLIAMS, 200 pounds,
191 acres adjoining CRESON, SPEER: being part tract sold by
Thomas TURNER to Marmaduke KIMBROUGH 4 March 1768; by M.
KIMBROUGH to John KIMBROUGH.   Witnesses: Robert WILLIAMS,
Constantine LADD, and Will CUPPLES.   Signed: John KIMBROUGH.

Page 273.   16 February 1788.   Richard GOODE, Esq., Sheriff,
            to Robert HARRIS (land lost by Norman MORGAN to
satisfy Robert HARRIS), 60 acres waters Tarrarat River
adjoining John McKINNEY and Robert HARRIS.   Witnesses:
A(ndrew) ROBINSON, Basel (X) RIDDLE, Hugh ARMSTRONG, and
Andrew KINCANNON.   Signed: Richard GOODE, Sheriff.

Page 274.   16 March 1790.   John JOHNSON to Valentine MOLER,
            300 pounds Specie, 248 acres North Hunting
Creek adjoining SANDERS and FORTIN(?).   Witnesses: S. WOOD
and Preshea WOOD.   Signed: John JOHNSON.

Page 275.   14 February 1790.   Wm. T. LEWIS to John FIELDER,
            Senr., 10 pounds, (no acreage), South side Camp
Branch waters Mitchells River above John FIELDERS.   Witnesses: Airs HUDSPETH and Zenas BALDWIN.   Signed: Wm. T. LEWIS.

END DEED BOOK E

Page 1. 13 May 1793. John WILLIAMS to Thomas GALLION, 20
pounds, 85 acres waters Deep Creek adjoining said
WILLIAMS' home tract of 340 acres. Witnesses: H(enry) SPEER,
David WELCH, and James TODD. Signed: John WILLIAMS.

Page 1. 1790. North Carolina Grant Daniel BILLS 250 acres
Forbis Creek adjoining Jonas REYNOLDS, Benj. HUTCHENS,
BASS, GIVENS and John MARTIN.

Page 2. 17 August 1793. Charles HUNT, Salisbury, Rowan
County, to Henry YOUNG, 15 pounds Specie, town lot
#33, Huntsville, on High and Second Streets. Witnesses:
Enoch POOR, Thomas ASHLEY, and J(ohn) HUNT. Signed: Chs.
HUNT.

Page 3. 20 December 1791. North Carolina Grant Henry SPEER,
600 acres big Long branch Hunting Creek adjoining
ROARD, MEHAFFEE and MARSHALL.

Page 4. 11 May 1793. Shelton GENTRY to Benjamin POTTER,
60 pounds, 100 acres both sides Fishers River.
Witnesses: John HUGHES, H. EDWARDS, and Gideon EDWARDS.
Signed: Shelton GENTRY.

Page 4. 24 December 1792. North Carolina Grant Samuel
ELLIS 200 acres waters North fork Hunting Creek
adjoining Mathias STEELMAN and Rowan County line.

Page 5. 13 May 1793. Henry SPEER to Charles RUSSELL, 30
pounds, 60 acres North fork Deep Creek adjoining
HUDSPETH, John WILLIAMS; to SPEER by Peter MIERS 4 May 1790.
Acknowledged. Signed: H. SPEER.

Page 6. 4 May 1790. Peter MIERS and Mary MIERS to Henry
SPEER, 30 pounds, 60 acres North fork Deep Creek
adjoining HUDSPETH and John WILLIAMS. Witnesses: Thomas
MASON, Sam CROCKET, and Joseph HENDERSON. Signed: Peter
(X) MIERS, (Mary does not sign).

Page 7. 6 April 1793. James JONES to Thomas THORNTON, 16
pounds, 200 acres McAfees Creek adjoining Aaron
SPEER and MOORE. Witnesses: Drury HOLCOMB and Simon HADLEY,
Junr. Signed: James JONES.

Page 7. 3 March 1792. Benjamin GRIFFITH to Thomas PATTERSON,
150 pounds North Carolina money, 200 acres; part
original property John GRIFFITH, deceased, both sides Stewarts
Creek and Arrarat River adjoining branch John McKINNEY, Junr.
lives on. Witnesses: David HUMPHREYS, Catheron HUMPHREYS,
and John HUMPHREYS. Signed: Benjamin (X) GRIFFITH.

Page 8. 27 July 1792. Benjamin CADLE to Thomas BRYAN, 60
pounds, 100 acres South side Tarrarat River,
conditional line between Daniel SMITH and BRYAN. Witnesses:
Daniel SMITH, Christopher AMBER, and Peter (X) BRYAN.

Signed: Benjamin (X) CADLE.

Page 9. 19 May 1792. John WILLIAMS, Blacksmith, Wilkes
County, North Carolina, to Moses WILLIAMS, 10 pounds,
100 acres adjoining Wilkes County line, little Reedy fork;
land granted said John by State of North Carolina 10 December
1790. Witnesses: Zadock RIGGS and Daniel BENCH. Signed:
John WILLIAMS.

Page 10. 14 November 1787. Nathaniel WILLIAMS to Henry
TILLEY, 60 pounds, 170 acres waters Tarrarat River,
conditional line between WILLIAMS and TILLEY; part 400 acres
granted Charles DUDLEY. Witnesses: George JOYCE, A(ndrew)
ROBINSON, and John (X) TILLEY. Signed: Nathaniel (X) WILLIAMS.

Page 11. 10 May 1793. John HAMMONDS to Joel APPLING, 50
pounds, 90 acres both sides Johnsons Creek adjoining
County line and BAKER. Witness: Robert WILLIAMS. Signed:
John (X) HAMMOND and Mary (X) HAMMOND.

Page 12. 24 December 1792. Benjamin BENSON to John BURK,
8 pounds, 34 acres branch Stewarts Creek called
Doctors branch; granted William WHORTON 3 April 1780.
Witnesses: Matthew DAVIS and Bennett CREED. Signed: Benjamin
BENSON and Peggy (X) BENSON.

Page 13. 6 July 1793. Henry SPEER to Peter SHERMER, Jr.,
20 pounds, 78 acres waters Deep Creek, part 200
acres surveyed for SPEER 11 January 1786 and adjoining
SHERMER. Witnesses: James LOVE, James TODD, and Samuel
SPEER. Signed: H. SPEER.

Page 14. 13 August 1792. Henry SPEER to Benjamin NICKOLS,
50 pounds, 100 acres waters North fork Deep Creek
adjoining Chas. RUSSELL; part 400 acres granted SPEER 13
April 1786. Witnesses: Jacob (X) PETTEJOHN and James (X)
McCOLLUM. Signed: H. SPEER.

Page 14. 4 August 1793. John JENKINS, Wythe County, Virginia,
to James SMITH, 1 pound, 200 acres both sides
Mounts Branch. Witnesses: Christopher ROWLES, Charles SMITH,
and Mallory SMITH. Signed: John JENKINS.

Page 15. 8 January 1793. Richard WOOTEN to Samuel WELCH
"value received", 150 acres West of North fork
Hunting Creek adjoining James SANDERS and line divides
Iredell and Surry. Witnesses: John B. HOY, Isaac JOHNSON,
Edward (X) WILLIAMS, James WILLIAMS, and John TEMPLER.
Signed: Richard WOOTEN and Mary (X) WOOTEN.

Page 16. 23 January 1792. Elizabeth JAYNE, widow, and
Executrix, Zopher JAYNE, deceased, of Montgomery
County, Virginia, to Joseph JESSOP, Stokes County, 100 pounds,
200 acres head Forbis Creek waters Yadkin River adjoining
William ADAMS. Witnesses: Samuel PARKER and Stephen JAYNE.
Signed: Elizabeth (X) JAYNE.

Page 17. 26 November 1787. William T. LEWIS, Heir at law

to Micajah LEWIS, deceased, to Laughlin McALYEA, 60 pounds Specie, 200 acres waters Deep Creek adjoining David MARTIN. Witnesses: Thomas SPENCE and Thomas JOHNSON. Signed: William T. LEWIS.

Page 17.   22 July 1785.   John CAIN to William McALYEA, 20 pounds, 200 acres head Cobbs Creek. Witnesses: Richard JACKS, John PERSONS, and David SPENCE. Signed: John (X) CAIN.

Page 18.   16 October 1793.   John RANDLEMAN, Stokes County, to Meredith HUTCHENS, 106 pounds, 200 acres both sides Hugh branch waters Deep Creek adjoining HUDSPETH and Geo. HOLCOMB. Witnesses: John JOHNSON, John WILLIAMS, and Job MARTIN. Signed: John RANDLEMAN.

Page 19.   11 November 1793.   John McCOLLUM and wife, Catharine, to Archelus STANDLEY, 50 pounds, 150 acres Fall branch adjoining WILLIAMS, BRAMBLETT; land granted said McCOLLUM. Witnesses: John JOHNSON, Jonathan JOHNSON, and Jemima JOHNSON. Signed: John McCOLLUM and Catharine (X) McCOLLUM.

Page 20.   2 November 1792.   William DAVIS, Rowan County, to Lindsay CARLTON, 40 pounds, 200 acres waters South fork Deep Creek; part land granted Pilgrim POPE; to said DAVIS by Elijah POPE and Nathan POPE, heirs said Pilgrim, deceased, adjoining SURGENER. Witnesses: Michael SWAIM and Jon. HAINES. Signed: William DAVIS.

Page 21.   22 April 1791.   Peter EATON, Rowan County, to Daniel COCKERHAM, 150 pounds, 300 acres little Red Creek. Witnesses: William McBRIDE and John McBRIDE. Signed: Margaret EATON and Peter EATON.

Page 21.   18 June 1793.   Robert DOAK, Guilford County, to Leonard DAVIS, 200 pounds, 300 acres South side Stewarts Creek. Witnesses: Henry HERRING, Matthew DAVIS, and John DAVIS. Signed: Robert DOAK and Hannah DOAK.

Page 22.   2 February 1793.   James LAURANCE, Union County, South Carolina, to Richard LAURANCE, 100 pounds, 150 acres both sides Tarraret River, land where William CARTER formerly lived adjoining corner, original deed granted William BURRUS. Witnesses: Joseph LAURANCE, Thomas WORD, and Richard LAURANCE, Junr. Signed: James LAURANCE.

Page 23.   1 November 1793.   Calburn LAURANCE to Thomas CHAMBERLAIN, 220 pounds, 200 acres Pauls Creek called Naked Bottom. Witnesses: Job McCRAW, Charles SMITH, and William BURRUS. Signed: Claburn (X) LAURANCE and Mary LAURANCE.

Page 24.   25 April 1792.   Edward LOVELL to Daniel BARROW, 100 pounds, 200 acres both sides Toms Creek. Witnesses: Corder STONE and Thomas STONE. Signed: Edward LOVILL.

Page 24. 22 February 1791. Ratliff BOON, Pendleton County, South Carolina, to John McKINNEY, 80 pounds, 200 acres Rutledge Creek. Witnesses: William BRUCE, Robert HARRIS, and John JACKSON. Signed: Ratliff BOON.

Page 25. 9 August 1787. North Carolina Grant Abner GREENWOOD 200 acres South side Yadkin River on Fall Creek adjoining Obediah BOHANNON, James YORK, James LINDSEY and Stephen HIDE.

Page 26. 4 May 1795. North Carolina Grant Gottlieb SHOBER, 40,000 acres Tarrarat River adjoining Thos. DUNNAGAN, Jeremiah WOOTEN, Daniel SMITH, William BRUCE, FLEMMING, Jas. HANNA, Doak HANNA, FROST & SNOW, John COX, Stewarts Creek, BLEDSOE, top Nettler Nob on little Fish River, Moses COCKERHAM, Henry NORMAN, RABON, TALIAFERRO, PORTER, ROSS, TUCKER, CLARK, Coleby CREED, Benjamin McCRAW, CLASBY, LOCKHART, MACKEY, John GITTENS, Big Fisher River, Val HOLDER-FIELD, John HORN, Isaac COPELAND, WEAVER and Littleberry BRAY.

Page 27. 4 May 1795. North Carolina Grant Gottlieb SHOBER 4,084 acres waters Mitchells River including part waters Snow Creek adjoining Rachel PETTIT, David COCKERHAM, Edward WILBURN and Andrew KING.

Page 28. 4 May 1795. North Carolina Grant Gottlieb SHOBER 4,219 acres waters Snow Creek and Mitchells River adjoining Ezekiel WILMOTH and Henry SOUTHARD.

Page 29. 4 May 1795. North Carolina Grant Gottlieb SHOBER 1,117 acres waters Snow Creek adjoining Jacob SNOW.

Page 30. 4 May 1795. North Carolina Grant Gottlieb SHOBER 5,953 acres waters Big Fisher River adjoining HOWARD.

Page 30. 4 May 1795. North Carolina Grant Gottlieb SHOBER 5,387 acres waters Fishers and Mitchells River adjoining John ROBERTS, John HUGHES, Richard MURPHEY and David RIGGS.

Page 31. 5 May 1795. North Carolina Grant Gottlieb SHOBER 4,343 acres waters Mitchells River adjoining Moses WILLIAMS and SNOW.

Page 32. 5 May 1795. North Carolina Grant Gottlieb SHOBER 5,649 acres waters Mitchells River adjoining James FINLEY, Wilkes County line, top ridge between Elkin and Mitchel Rivers being dividing line between Wilkes and Surry Counties.

Page 33. 9 July 1794. North Carolina Grant Jabez JARVIS 71 acres forks Yadkin and Fish Rivers.

Page 34. 9 July 1794. North Carolina Grant John BURCHAM
          100 acres Toms Creek adjoining his former survey
conditional line between BURCHAM and Samuel PARKER.

Page 34. 9 July 1794. North Carolina Grant Henry BURCHAM
          100 acres branch Tomas Creek adjoining BURCHAMS
former survey.

Page 35. 9 July 1794. North Carolina Grant Isaac COPELAND
          100 acres waters Fish River.

Page 36. 9 July 1794. North Carolina Grant Joseph WALKER
          200 acres Bever Creek.

Page 36. 9 July 1794. North Carolina Grant Richard LAURANCE
          250 acres waters Tarrarat River adjoining HUMPHREY.

Page 37. 9 July 1794. North Carolina Grant Richard LAURANCE
          100 acres West side Renfroes Creek on Pomysreon(?)
Branch.

Page 37. 9 July 1794. North Carolina Grant Richard LAURANCE
          100 acres Renfroes Creek in an Island adjoining his
East corner.

Page 38. 10 December 1790. North Carolina Grant John MARTIN
          300 acres Great Creek adjoining Adam TATE.

Page 39. 9 August 1787. North Carolina Grant Charles DUDLEY
          100 acres South side Yadkin River.

Page 39. 9 July 1794. North Carolina Grant Jonathan HARRIS
          100 acres Cooks Creek including Thos. ROSS improve-
ment conditional line between ROSS and Elijah GILLASPY.

Page 40. 9 October 1793. Charles HUDSPETH to Jiles
          HUDSPETH "consideration of rents" Farmlets 208
acres Yadkin River, North side Josephs Creek adjoining
H(enry) SPEER: being land Jiles HUDSPETH sold Charles
HUDSPETH 9 February 1790 but Jiles and wife, Elizabeth, to
have lifetime claim by paying a yearly rent of 10 shillings
to said Charles HUDSPETH. Witnesses: William THORNTON and
George HUDSPETH. Signed: Charles HUDSPETH.

'Page 41. 31 December 1792. Ambrose BRAMLETT "now residing
          in Surry County" to Daniel VESTAL, 267 pounds,
10 shillings for 475 acres waters North fork Deep Creek
adjoining Iron Works road, James VESTAL and Simon HADLEY.
Witnesses: Thomas HADLEY and Simon HADLEY, Junr. Signed:
Ambrose BRAMLETT.

Page 42. 19 October 1774. Jonathan OSBORNE to Jain COYLE,
          widow of Patrick COYLE, deceased, 20 pounds
Virginia money, 100 acres North side Lovens Creek, middle
fork Tarrarat River in the Hollow; part GRANVILLE granted
Patrick COYLE, deceased, 400 acres 10 May 1762; to said
OSBORNE by James COYLE, son of said Patrick 1774; being
1/3 and right of dower of said Jain COYLE. Witnesses:

84

Mart(in) ARMSTRONG and George PARIS. Signed: Jonathan
OSBORNE. . . .4 October 1793 by order Court, Martin ARMSTRONG
came before George HAUSER and Christian LASH, J.P.'S and
declares he Seen Jonathan OSBORNE signe above deed and
George PARIS was a witness with said ARMSTRONG.

Page 44. 12 December 1792. Benjamin CLANTON to James
          HUTCHENS, 100 pounds, 251 acres South side North
fork Deep Creek adjoining Grimes HOLCOMB, Robt. JOHNSON and
John RANDLEMAN; land CLANTON bought of George HOLCOMB, Senr.
Witnesses: Abner GREENWOOD, Archebald (X) JOHNSON, and Ann
(X) GREENWOOD. Signed: Benjamin (X) CLANTON.

Page 45. 25 December 1793. George ALSTON, Granville County,
          North Carolina, to William HAYNES, Franklin County,
North Carolina, 231 pounds current money of Virginia, 640
acres adjoining Christian MILLER, agreed line between John
BLALOCK and William MASTERS. Witnesses: John HALL, Drury
KIMBRELL, and John HANES. Signed: George ALSTON.

Page 45. 20 December 1791. North Carolina Grant John Thomas
          LONGINO 200 acres adjoining William BILLS near
Fall Creek.

Page 46. 20 December 1791. North Carolina Grant John Thomas
          LONGINO 300 acres Bean Shole Creek adjoining
Stephen HIDE.

Page 47. 20 December 1791. North Carolina Grant John
          Thomas LONGINO 383 acres adjoining DEVENPORT, Wm.
ROBESON, BROWN, John SPEER, SPRINKLE and RIDENS.

Page 47. 20 December 1791. North Carolina Grant John
          Thomas LONGINO 200 acres waters North fork Deed
Creek adjoining Daniel and James VESTAL, corner 50 acres
said LONGINO, including where he now lives.

Page 48. 9 July 1791. North Carolina Grant John Thomas
          LONGINO 50 acres waters North fork Deep Creek
adjoining Daniel and James VESTAL and BOHANNON.

Page 48. 20 December 1791. North Carolina Grant Henry
          SPEER 100 acres Fishing Branch adjoining Ann
WHITEHEAD.

Page 49. 11 November 1794. George LOGAN to John LOGAN,
          Yeoman, 50 pounds, lot No. 39 in Huntsville on
High Street. Witnesses: Hugh LOGAN and Samuel B. SHEPPARD.
Signed: George LOGAN.

Page 50. 30 October 1783. North Carolina Grant Thomas
          WRIGHT 400 acres waters Deep Creek a mile above
Buck Shole.

Page 50. 24 December 1792. North Carolina Grant John
          WRIGHT 300 acres waters Millers Creek adjoining
Samuel ARNOLD, WEATHERMAN and Lewis ELLIOTT.

Page 51.   9 July 1794.   North Carolina Grant Lewis FORKNER
            10 acres Big Creek Dan River.

Page 52.   9 July 1794.   North Carolina Grant Abraham REESE
            100 acres waters McFees Creek adjoining James
LINDSEY, said REESE and William SUGART.

Page 53.   3 November 1784.   North Carolina Grant Robert
            HARRIS 150 acres waters Cadles Creek.

Page 54.   3 November 1784.   North Carolina Grant Robert
            HARRIS 50 acres waters Tarrarat River.

Page 54.   8 August 1787.   North Carolina Grant Kizia DEAN
            50 acres Mitchells River.

Page 55.   3 November 1784.   North Carolina Grant Keziah DEAN
            50 acres Mitchells River mouth Reedy Fork.

Page 56.   17 February 1795.   John MARTIN to John McDANIEL,
            60 pounds, 100 acres East side Canada Creek.
Witnesses: Nimrod ELLIOTT and Nicholas MASTERS.   Signed:
John (X) MARTIN.

Page 56.   9 July 1794.   North Carolina Grant Joshua BROWN
            150 acres waters Hamons Creek adjoining William
CAIN, Leonard WISHON, UPTIGROVES old Mill.

Page 57.   2 August 1794.   Mortgage Deed from Henry SPEER to
            KENNEDY and MacPHERSON of the Shallowford; 90
pounds, 10 shillings, 9 pense North Carolina Currency, 292
acres both sides Deep Creek; land surveyed for Abraham
CRESON 13 January 1759 and adjoining Wiatt GARNER (reserving
full power, releasing said land by paying KENNEDY and Mac-
PHERSON specified amount before 20 December 1794).   Witnesses:
Dugal CAMPBELL and Kenneth CAMPBELL.   Signed: H. SPEER.

Page 58.   11 August 1792.   Mortgage Deed from George HOLCOMB
            to John KENNEDY, merchant, of Shallowford, 1 pound,
140 acres waters Deep Creek by deed Jacob PETTEJOHN to
George HOLCOMB 30 April 1792.   Witnesses: James TODD and
Dugal CAMPBELL.   Signed: George (X) HOLCOMB.

Page 59.   10 December 1790.   North Carolina Grant William
            HOUGH (also spelled HUGH in this Grant), 90 acres
waters North fork Deep Creek adjoining Simon HADLEY, JOHNSON,
John WILLIAMS, said William HUGHS corner and John MARTIN.

Page 59.   20 December 1791.   North Carolina Grant Samuel
            CALLOWAY 300 acres Pattersons Mill Creek adjoining
MILLER in Glade, Cranberry Creek.

Page 60.   10 August 1795.   North Carolina Grant Jesse LESTER
            20,000 acres South side Yadkin River, Forbis
Creek below Stephen HOBSONS Saw Mill adjoining Moses AYERS
and Wm. RICH.

Page 61.   10 December 1790.   North Carolina Grant Solomon

HUMPHREY 300 acres waters Tarrat River adjoining Richard GIDINGS and Daniel HUMPHREY and GITTINS.

Page 62.   10 December 1790. North Carolina Grant John BRYSON 50 acres Lovings Creek adjoining BRYSONS former survey.

Page 63.   20 December 1791. North Carolina Grant James BRYSON 50 acres Stewarts Creek adjoining James MATTHEW and BRYSON.

Page 63.   9 July 1794. North Carolina Grant William McBRIDE 640 acres Red Creek draft, Yadkin River adjoining Peter EATON and John MARTIN.

Page 64.   9 July 1794. North Carolina Grant William MAYES 200 acres Cooks Creek including Dudley WARES improvement, adjoining Elijah GALLASPEY and ROSS.

Page 65.   9 July 1794. North Carolina Grant John CASTEVENS 50 acres waters Deep Creek adjoining corner 200 acres of Noel WADDLE and corner 400 acres of John ELSBERRY.

Page 65.   9 July 1794. North Carolina Grant Joel MACKEY 150 acres Beach Creek, waters Tararat River including improvement where Wm. CALLAHAN lived and adjoining Robert DOAK.

Page 66.   6 March 1792. Leven SAVAGE to James MORPHEW, 40 pounds, 92 acres Cabbin Branch adjoining Levi SPEER. Witnesses: Ezekiel RUNELS and Thomas LONGINO. Signed: Levin (X) SAVAGE.

Page 67.   9 July 1794. North Carolina Grant Martin BRIDGE, farmer, 60 acres adjoining his own corner and Rowan County line, MOSBYS line, including his fishing place.

Page 68.   9 July 1794. North Carolina Grant George HOLCOMB 200 acres Fall Creek.

Page 68.   3 March 1794. Lease from Joshua CRESON to William DAVIS, now of Surry County, late from Berkley County, Virginia, considerations to be paid at different times and seasons, in each year for term eight years, land on Yadkin River above mouth Deep Creek adjoining Henry SPEER; said DAVIS be allowed to clear 20 acres river bottom and work, plant, seed, and give CRESON ½ part yearly. Witnesses: Henry SPEER and Perry (X) CHINN. Signed: Joshua CRESON.

Page 69.   13 February 1788. Philimon HOLCOMB to James WRIGHT, 100 pounds, 250 acres Fall Creek draft Yadkin River adjoining Grimes HOLCOMB. Witnesses: H(enry) SPEER, Jerry LESTER, and Justus REYNOLDS. Signed: Philimon (X) HOLCOMB.

Page 70.   8 December 1787. North Carolina Grant William Terrell LEWIS 200 acres South side Yadkin River

adjoining his own line (formerly Peter SALLES) and Richard
DENNIS.

Page 71. 8 December 1787. North Carolina Grant William
        Terrell LEWIS 200 acres Yadkin River above fish
pot adjoining his own line.

Page 72. 4 May 1795. North Carolina Grant William HOWARD
        60 acres Waters Turners Creek adjoining Henry
SPEER and Jacob SPEER.

Page 72. 9 July 1794. North Carolina Grant Rezia JARVIS
        100 acres Pheasants Branch, waters Fishers River,
North side Frosts path.

Page 73. 9 July 1794. North Carolina Grant John BURCH 100
        acres North Yadkin River adjoining WOODRUFF.

Page 73. 20 December 1791. North Carolina Grant Jesse
        REVIS 100 acres North fork Dutchmans Creek.

Page 74. 24 November 1790. North Carolina Grant Jacob
        GALLION 250 acres in Wilkes County, North Carolina
on Wooten Branch, North fork Fishes River adjoining Moses
WRIGHT.

Page 75. 18 May 1789. North Carolina Grant Joseph WILLIAMS
        1,000 acres waters Panther Creek adjoining his own
land, MOSBY, HOWARD, Shallowford Road, LANIER, Allens Branch,
and JOHNSON.

Page 75. 17 July 1795. Gottlieb SHOBER, Stokes County, to
        Timothy PICKERING, Philadelphia, Pennyslvania,
$4,800 for 4,000 acres Tarrarat River adjoining Thos.
DUNNAGAN, Jeremiah WOOTEN, Danl SMITH, Wm. BRUCE, FLEMING,
James HANNA, Doak HANNA, FROST & SNOW, Wm. GOLDEN, John COX,
Stewarts Creek, BLEDSOE, top Nettles Nob on little Fish
River, Henry NORMAN, RABON, ROSS, TUCKER, Coleby Creek,
McCRAW & CLASBY, LOCKHART, MACKEY, Val HOLDERFIELD, John
HORN, Isaac COPELAND and Littleberry BRAY. Witnesses:
Samuel LEWIS, Philip TRANSOU, and William THORNTON. Signed:
Gottlieb SHOBER.

Page 77. 17 July 1795. Gottlieb SHOBER, Stokes County, to
        Timothy PICKERING, Philadelphia, Pennyslvania,
$3,700 for 4,084 acres waters Mitchells River and Snow
Creek adjoining Rachel PETTIT, David COCKERHAM, Edward
WILBORN, Andrew KING; also 4,219 acres waters Snow Creek
and Mitchell River adjoining Ezekiel WILMOTH, Henry SOUTHARD:
also 1,117 acres adjoining Jacob SNOW waters Snow Creek;
also 5,953 acres waters Big Forbis Creek adjoining HOWARD:
also 5,387 acres waters Fishes and Mitchells Rivers adjoining John ROBERTS, John HUGHES, Richard MURPHEY, David RIGGS;
also 4,353 acres Mitchells River adjoining Moses WILLIAMS
and SNOW; also 5,649 acres waters Mitchell River adjoining
James FINDLEY, Wilkes County line, being dividing ridge
between Elkin and Mitchell Rivers and between Wilkes and
Surry Counties. Witnesses: Samuel LEWIS, Philip TRANSOU,

and William THORNTON. Signed: Gottlieb SHOBER.

Page 80. 9 July 1794. North Carolina Grant Benjamin
        HUTCHENS 160 acres adjoining his own land.

Page 81. 24 December 1792. North Carolina Grant Jarman
        BALLARD 50 acres Bear Branch waters Tarrarat River
near road.

Page 81. 8 February 1794. Henry BURCHAM and wife, Sarah, to
        Andrew KINCANNON and Martin ARMSTRONG, 50 pounds,
2 acres including Iron Ore Bank; granted Abraham COOLEY 1783,
and sold to said BURCHAM on waters Toms Creek. Witnesses:
John DUNNAGAN and Francis KINCANNON. Signed: Henry BURCHAM
and Sarah (X) BURCHAM.

Page 82. 20 March 1786. Abraham COOLEY and wife, Sarah, to
        Henry BURCHAM, 100 pounds, 400 acres waters Toms
Creek; State granted COOLEY 13 October 1783. Witnesses:
Samuel PARKER and James MACKENNY. Signed: Abraham (X)
COOLEY and Sarah (X) COOLEY.

Page 83. 25 February 1793. John WILLIAMS and wife, Jane, to
        William HOUGH, 80 pounds, (no acreage), waters
North fork Deep Creek, part State granted WILLIAMS adjoining
PETTIJOHN. Witnesses: John Thomas LONGINO and H(enry)
SPEER. Signed: John WILLIAMS and Jane (X) WILLIAMS.

Page 84. 9 August 1791. Humphrey COCKERHAM to John McBRIDE,
        50 pounds hard money, 52 acres between Yadkin
River and Pipes Creek adjoining John PIPES. Witnesses:
William McBRIDE and Gideon WOODRUFF. Signed: Humphrey (X)
COCKERHAM and Jemima (X) COCKERHAM.

Page 85. 12 February 1794. Justice REYNOLDS to Jonathan
        HAINES, 80 pounds, 150 acres North fork Forbis
Creek. Witnesses: Thomas HADLEY and Abraham VANWINCLE.
Signed: Justice REYNOLDS.

Page 86. 9 August 1791. Humphrey COCKERHAM to John McBRIDE,
        50 pounds, 100 acres Pipes Creek South side Yadkin
River adjoining PIPES. Witnesses: William McBRIDE and
Gideon WOODRUFF. Signed: Humphrey (X) COCKERHAM and Jemima
(X) COCKERHAM.

Page 87. 22 May 1793. John CARLTON, Spartanburg County,
        South Carolina, to Edward BASS, 10 pounds, 100
acres waters Forbis Creek crossing Colemans Branch.
Witnesses: John SHUGART and David MOORE. Signed: John (X)
CARLTON.

Page 88. 22 May 1793. John CARLTON, Spartanburg County,
        South Carolina, to John DAVIS, 10 pounds, 100
acres waters Forbis Creek adjoining Edward BASS. Witnesses:
John SHUGART and David MOOR. Signed: John (X) CARLTON.

Page 89. 16 March 1793. Charles HUNT, Salisbury, Rowan
        County, to Abraham EATON, 9 pounds, 1 shilling,

Lot NO. 7 in Huntsville on High Street. Witnesses: William THORNTON and Isham FROHOCK. Signed: Chas. HUNT.

Page 89. 2 September 1793. John Thomas LONGINO to Garsham BILLS, 50 pounds (no acreage), waters Yadkin River, Falls Creek adjoining James YORK, James LINDSEY and Stephen HIDE. Witness: Stephen WOOD. Signed: John Thomas LONGINO.

Page 90. 9 December 1793. William BURRUS to Richard LAURANCE, Jr., 150 pounds, 150 acres Pauls Creek, waters Tarrarat River. Witnesses: David HUMPHREY, Richard LAURANCE, and Samuel LAURANCE. Signed: William (X) BURRUS.

Page 91. 28 December 1793. William BURRUS to Francis McCRAW 100 pounds Specie, 200 acres Pauls Creek known by Lem JONES old place adjoining county line. Witnesses: Jacob McCRAW and Charles SMITH. Signed: William (X) BURRUS.

Page 92. 6 February 1793. Thomas WOOTEN, Sr. to Samuel DENNY, 100 pounds, (no acreage), Tarrarat River including plantation where Thos. WOOTEN once lived; granted him 1784. Witnesses: James (X) GUNSTON and George (X) WOOTEN. Signed: Thomas (X) WOOTEN.

Page 93. 13 January 1794. John and Ellinor ALLEN to David THOMASON, 100 pounds, 100 acres Fishers River adjoining Yadkin River and Peter HAMLIN. Witnesses: Thomas HAMLIN and Sherwod (X) BROCK. Signed: John (X) ALLEN and Ellenor (X) ALLEN.

Page 94. 21 April 1788. Samuel KANIDAY to Moses WILLIAMS, 20 pounds, 30 acres Wilkes County in County line, little Reedy fork; part land where Samuel now lives conveyed to him by Jesse FRANKLIN. Witnesses: Mark KANIDAY, Thomas ROSS, and John WILLIAMS. Signed: Samuel KANIDAY.

Page 95. 29 January 1792. Gibson MAYNARD, Wilkes County, North Carolina, to William BEAN, 30 pounds proclamation money, 100 acres in Wilkes County, North fork Christians Creek. Witnesses: Jesse FRANKLIN and Matthew DUGLASS. Signed: Gibson (X) MANARD.

Page 95. 2 January 1794. Archelus STANDLEY and wife, Elizabeth, to Peter FITZGERRAL, 64 pounds Specie, 150 acres Fall Branch which Archelus bought of John McCOLLUM adjoining WILLIAMS and BRAMLETT. Witnesses: Nicholas HUTCHENS, Sarah HUTCHENS, and Jesse (X) STANDLEY. Signed: Archeleus (X) STANDLEY and Elizabeth (X) STANDLEY.

Page 96. 15 April 1793. John HANNA to John Doak HANNA, 100 pounds North Carolina money, 200 acres Moores fork, waters Tarrarat River adjoining John HANNA. Witnesses: Robert HAMMOCK, Christr. ROWLES, and Nathaniel DOAD. Signed: John HANNA.

Page 97. 15 April 1793. John HANNA to John Doak HANNA, 500 pounds, 136 acres Stewarts Creek, West fork Arrarat River adjoining Thomas BURRUS. Witnesses: Robert

HAMMOCK, Chrisr. ROWLES, and Nathaniel DOAK. Signed: John HANNA and Martha (X) HANNA.

Page 97. 15 April 1793. John HANNA to John Doak HANNA, 100 pounds North Carolina money, 200 acres Stewarts Creek, waters Tarrarat River adjoining BAILEY. Witnesses: Robert HAMMOCK, Chrisr. ROWLES, and Nathaniel DOAK. Signed: John HANNA and Martha (X) HANNA.

Page 98. 10 August 1792. Nicholas GENTRY to Artha GENTRY, 100 pounds, 100 acres South side Yadkin River adjoining GARROTT. Witnesses: James BADGETT and Blunt GARROT. Signed: Nicholas GENTRY.

Page 99. 1787. Nicholas GENTRY to Blunt GARROT, 65 pounds, 100 acres Yadkin River including GARROTS plantation. Witnesses: James BADGETT and Artha (X) GENTRY. Signed: Nicholas GENTRY.

Page 100. 7 February 1794. Henry SPEER to John GROCE, 60 pounds, 123 acres waters Deep Creek; granted Joseph WINSTON and conveyed to SPEER adjoining WELLS and GROCE. Witnesses: John CARTER, James TODD, and Jacob (X) EDDLEMAN. Signed: H. SPEER.

Page 101. 10 February 1794. Obediah Martin BENGE to John FLETCHER, Patrick County, Virginia, 150 pounds, 155 acres Yadkin River top ridge opposite Tumbling Falls Creek. Witnesses: William FLETCHER, Richard WILBURN, and J.M. LEWIS. Signed: Oba. M. BENGE.

Page 101. 12 July 1793. Richard LAURANCE to Bowater SUMNER, 40 pounds, 200 acres both sides Seed Cane; granted LAURANCE 20 December 1791. Witnesses: William FORKNER, George REED, and William (X) BURCH. Signed: Richard LAURANCE.

Page 102. 9 March 1793. Joseph ASHLEY to Tyre HARRIS, 66 pounds, 100 acres Flat Shoal Creek and Tarrarat River. Witnesses: Edward LOVELL, George HEARD, and John HEARD. Signed: Joseph ASHLEY.

Page 103. 13 June 1793. John STANDLEY to William HARDING, 26 pounds, 13 shillings, 4 pence for 100 acres waters Forbis Creek adjoining COGBURN; tract granted William RAMEY 9 August 1787. Witnesses: John JOHNSON and Jonathan JOHNSON. Signed: John STANDLEY.

Page 104. 5 February 1794. Charles SMITH to Stephen K. SMITH, 100 pounds, 216 acres West side Renfroes Creek, North fork Arrarat River. Witnesses: William HUGHLETT and Fra. POINDEXTER. Signed: Chas. SMITH.

Page 104. 28 August 1793. Abijah ELMORE to Perrin CHIN, 10 pounds (no acreage), waters Forbis Creek adjoining corner 200 acres granted Abijah 20 December 1791. Witnesses: H(enry) SPEER and John WILLIAMS. Signed: Abijah ELMORE.

Page 105. 11 March 1793. William COCKERHAM to Joshua PRESTON
55 pounds, 160 acres near head Cogdels Branch,
agreed line between COCKERHAM and Abraham DOWNEY. Witnesses:
William McBRIDE and Martha (X) McBRIDE. Signed: William (X)
COCKERHAM.

Page 106. 17 October 1793. Jacob RUDOLPH, Tennery County,
State of Mero by his Atty. Henry SPEER to Charles
FRADA, 90 pounds, 87 acres waters Deep and Turners Creek
adjoining Patrick BURNS, road leading from Shallowford on
Yadkin to an Island on Cataba; line 100 acres surveyed for
Matthias STEELMAN adjoining James HOWELL; part 225 acres
granted William STEELMAN, then to Joseph WALKER. Witnesses:
Joshua (X) BROWN and Thomas (X) BROWN. Signed: H. SPEER,
Atty. for Jacob RUDOLPH.

Page 107. 28 April 1793. Jacob WEAVER to John McMICKLE, Jr.,
115 pounds, 300 acres Branch McFees Creek adjoining Wm. MOORE, Simeon CARTER, Richmond Road, agreed line
with James JONES. Witnesses: John (X) McMICKLE, Senr. and
Dougal McMICKLE. Signed: Jacob (X) WEAVER.

Page 108. 1 June 1787. James FIELDER to Henry SOUTHARD, 20
pounds, 200 acres South fork Mitchells River.
Witnesses: Isaac SOUTHARD, John PIPES, and Richard MURPHEY.
Signed: James (X) FIELDER and Sarah FIELDER.

Page 108. 12 May 1794. Leonard DAVIS and Garner TUCKER to
Matthew DAVIS, 300 pounds, 230 acres both sides
little Fishers River adjoining MOORE. Witnesses: John
ROBERTS, John ROBERTS, Junr., and John DAVIS. Signed:
Leonard DAVIS and Garner (X) TUCKER.

Page 109. 4 January 1796. North Carolina Grant Peter TERRY
30,000 acres waters Mitchell and Fishers Rivers
including 46 Entrys of 640 acres each and one 560 acres, all
adjoining each other entered 3 January 1795 adjoining BRAHAM,
Fishers Peak in Virginia line, Mountains in Wilkes County
line, John WILLIAMS, Marshalls nob and Richard MURPHEY.

Page 110. 2 November 1793. Samuel DAVIS to William DAVIS,
500 pounds, 100 acres Fishers River. Witnesses:
Ephraim WITCHER, Stephen POTTER, and Larkin (X) STRAWN.
Signed: Samuel DAVIS.

Page 111. 11 February 1792. Aaron SPEER, Senr. to Jacob
WEAVER, 100 pounds, 300 acres head Branch McFees
Creek adjoining Wm. MOORE, Simeon CARTER, Richmond road and
James JONES. Witnesses: William COOK, Thomas HOLCOMB, and
William JACKSON. Signed: Aaron SPEER.

Page 111. 21 October 1793. Henry SPEER to James ROTEN, 10
pounds, 100 long Branch Hunting Creek, East end
600 acres granted H. SPEER 20 November 1791, dividing line
between Joshua TULBERT and Josiah ROTEN. Witnesses: Josiah
ROUGHTON and Christian BROWN. Signed: H. SPEER.

Page 112. 30 August 1793. Laughlin McALYEA to David Taylor,

100 pounds, (no acreage), waters Deep Creek adjoining Nathan HAINES formerly David MARTINS. Witnesses: David SPENCE and Hugh McALYEA. Signed: Laughlin (X) McALYEA.

Page 113. 21 October 1793. John ALLEN to Joshua TULBERT, 75 pounds, 68 acres North fork Hunting Creek adjoining Haystack Meadow, Josiah ROTEN, Edward RILEY; part 200 acres granted ALLEN 9 August 1787. Witnesses: Josiah ROUGHTON and William MacPHERSON. Signed: John ALLEN.

Page 114. 30 October 1793. Josiah KERBY to Philip KERBY, 500 pounds North Carolina currency, 100 acres both sides big Fisher River. Witnesses: Ephraim WITCHER, Stephen POTTER, William REGNY(?), and Larkin (X) STRAWN. Signed: Josiah (X) KERBY.

Page 114. 23 October 1793. David ROTEN to Josiah ROTEN, 5 pounds, 61 acres South side, North fork Hunting Creek; part 240 acres granted John ALLEN 3 November 1784. Witnesses: Joseph SALMON and James ROUGHTON. Signed: David (X) ROTEN.

Page 115. 21 October 1793. David ROTEN to Jacob ROTEN, 5 pounds, 179 acres North side Hunting Creek; part 240 acres granted John ALLEN 3 November 1784 adjoining John BROWN. Witnesses: H(enry) SPEER and Josiah ROUGHTON. Signed: David (X) ROTEN.

Page 116. 16 March 1793. John TILLEY to Jonathan HANES, 45 pounds, 175 acres waters Tarrarat River, conditional line Nathaniel WILLIAMS made to Henry TILLEY 14 November 1787; part 400 acres granted Charles DUDLEY. Witnesses: Jeremiah EARLY, William FINLEY, and John LANGLEY. Signed: John (X) TILLEY.

Page 117. 26 September 1789. Gilbert KEEN to Abraham DOWNEY, 200 pounds, 200 acres Beaver Dam Creek adjoining Josiah KEEN and Zeno BALDWIN. Witnesses: Samuel CRAWLEY and Nathaniel MORRIS, Junr. Signed: Gilbert (X) KEEN.

Page 117. 19 December 1782. Jacob FEREE, State of Pennsylvania, to Henry SPEER, 100 pounds, 500 acres North fork Deep Creek adjoining Samuel SHIN, Peter MYERS, Simon HADLEY, Francis BAKER, Ambrose BRAMLETT, George HOPPES and crossing Hoppes Creek. Witnesses: Lemuel JONES and Henry HATH. Signed: Jacob FEREE. . . .Acknowledged by James JONES to be act of Jacob FEREE 17 February 1794, witness by Daniel BILLS and John THAGAN and signed by said JONES.

Page 118. 3 April 1794. George LOGAN to Hugh LOGAN, 380 pounds, 300 acres North fork Josephs Creek adjoining John LOGAN. Witnesses: George HEAD and James LOGAN. Signed: George LOGAN and Sarah (X) LOGAN.

Page 119. 11 September 1793. William WATTS, planter, to Charity WATTS, one peppercorn, 100 acres Brushy fork Mitchells River. Witnesses: John UNDERWOOD, Joel UNDERWOOD and William UNDERWOOD. Signed: William WATTS.

Page 120.   18 November 1793.   Charles HUDSPETH to Isaiah COE,
         410 pounds, 280 acres West side Yadkin River, North
side Josephs Creek where Charles "do now live", part 558
acres GRANVILLE granted Robert FORBIS adjoining John JOYNER
and Edmond WOOD. Witnesses: George HEAD and Pat HUDSPETH.
Signed: Charles HUDSPETH.

Page 121.   16 March 1793.   Charles HUNT, Salisbury, Rowan
         County, to Jacob SPEER, Junr., 16 pounds, 1 penny,
Lot No. 39, town Huntsville, High and 3rd Streets. Witnesses:
William THORNTON and Jo HUNT. Signed: Chas. HUNT.

Page 121.   21 October 1793.   Henry SPEER to Andrew HERREN,
         10 pounds, 200 acres West end 600 acres granted
SPEER on Long Branch 20 November 1791. Witnesses: James
ROUGHTON and Ann Apple (X) ROTEN. Signed: H. SPEER.

Page 122.   October 1793.   John ALLEN to Josiah ROWTEN, 25
         pounds, 100 acres South side North fork Hunting
Creek adjoining 200 acres granted said ALLEN 9 August 1787
including Haystack Meadow. Witnesses: Joshua (X) TULBERT
and (blur) MacPHERSON. Signed: John ALLEN.

Page 123.   10 May 1794.   Samuel HUMPHREYS to Thomas BALL, 65
         pounds, 100 acres part HUMPHREYS original granted
3 May 1789, big Flat Shole Creek. Witness: D. HUMPHREY, Junr.
Signed: Samuel HUMPHREYS.

Page 123.   4 November 1793.   Henry SPEER to Jacob SALMON, 20
         pounds, 300 acres Long Branch Hunting Creek; part
600 acres granted SPEER 2 December 1791 adjoining Andrew
HERRIN. Witnesses: John CARTER, Josiah ROUGHTON, and John
SKIDMORE. Signed: H. SPEER.

Page 124.   22 November 1793.   David HUDSPETH to George
         HUDSPETH, Sr., 150 pounds, 250 acres East side
Yadkin River; part land formerly granted by GRANVILLE to
John HOWARD; from HOWARD to Elijah SKIDMORE; by SKIDMORE to
John HUDSPETH; from John to Ralph HUDSPETH, Sr. and Willed
by Ralph Sr. to David HUDSPETH. Witnesses: Airs HUDSPETH
and Joel HUDSPETH. Signed: David HUDSPETH.

Page 125.   8 November 1793.   Thomas Adams WORD to Alexander
         BRYSON, 80 pounds Proclamation money, 90 acres
middle fork Tarrarat River, Bleckers Creek adjoining Andw.
BAILEY. Acknowledged. Signed: T.A. WORD.

Page 126.   12 March 1794.   John HEIXT, Stokes County, to
         George FITZGARREL, 60 pounds, 70 acres, Stokes
County, Branch Double Creek adjoining BAGGE, HARVY (formerly
PHILLIPS). Witnesses: William THORNTON and William VEST.
Signed: John HEYXT.

Page 127.   5 June 1794.   Zachariah SHUGART to Nathan FARMER,
         24 pounds, 100 acres waters North fork Deep
Creek; part SHUGARTS original grant. Witnesses: John SHUGART
and Leonard SHUGART. Signed: Zachariah SHUGART.

Page 127.   25 January 1792.   James SANDERS, Junr., Wilkes
            County, Georgia, to James Taylor RILEY, 110 pounds
Specie, 250 acres waters North Hunting Creek adjoining John
ANDERSON and George WOOTEN. Witnesses: Ninean RILEY, Junr.,
and Briattin SANDERS. Signed: James SANDERS.

Page 128.   8 August 1794.   Benjamin SCOTT and wife, Ellener
            to Ephraim Witcher, 50 pounds, 50 acres Mitchells
River. Witnesses: Richard MURPHEY and Martha (X) ROBINSON.
Signed: Benjamin SCOTT and Ellener SCOTT.

Page 129.   13 August 1794.   Hugh ARMSTRONG, late Sheriff, to
            Abraham STOW, planter, (land lost by Thos. FLOYD
and wife, Mary, by indictment by Grand Jury for sundry
misdemeners), 300 acres South side Yadkin River, Baleys
Creek (surveyed 23 July 1788; granted 14 December 1792.)
Acknowledged. Signed: Hugh ARMSTRONG, Sheriff.

Page 130.   20 July 1793.   Joshua CRESON to William HAGENS,
            90 pounds, 10 shillings, 145 acres below Shallow-
ford of Yadkin River on waters Turners Creek; part 250 acres
granted Abraham CRESON 3 November 1784 adjoining SCOTT near
Salisbury road. Witnesses: William MacPHERSON and H(enry)
SPEER. Signed: Joshua CRESON.

Page 130.   5 February 1794.   Ninian RILEY, Senr., to Isaac
            WINDSOR, 50 pounds, 400 acres Buck Shole Branch,
waters Hunting Creek adjoining MIERS, Hamblins road.
Witnesses: Stephen WOOD and Bennat WOOD. Signed: Ninian
RILEY.

Page 131.   3 August 1793.   John WILLIAMS, planter, to Jacob
            GALLION, Junr., planter, 37 pounds, 100 acres
waters Deep Creek, North fork Shole Branch; part 400 acres
granted WILLIAMS. Witnesses: John Thomas LONGINO and Edward
LOVELL. Signed: John WILLIAMS.

Page 132.   26 December 1793.   Ezekiel REYNOLDS to Robin HEAD,
            65 pounds, 200 acres Beaver Can Creek, waters
Yadkin River; part State granted John BRASWELL. Witnesses:
George HEAD and Willis (X) JOYNER. Signed: Ezekiel (X)
REYNOLDS.

Page 133.   15 August 1794.   Thomas Adams WORD to William
            WORD, brother of said Thos. for love, 85 acres
Bledsoe Creek waters, Tarrarat River adjoining land Thomas
Adams WORD sold Alexander BRYSON. Acknowledged. Signed:
T.A. WORD.

Page 133.   13 December 1793.   George RIDENS to Peter ELDER,
            100 pounds, 500 acres draft Yadkin River adjoining
John Thomas LONGINO and Michael SPRINKLE. Witnesses: George
HEAD and Robin HEAD. Signed: George (X) RIDENS.

Page 134.   16 February 1792.   Jesse LESTER to Thomas AYERS,
            Patrick County, Virginia, 5 shillings, 1½ acres
waters Yadkin River adjoining Moses AYERS, Nathanil AYERS

Cabbin. Witnesses: Aires HUDSPETH and Gentry (X) AYERS. Signed: Jesse LESTER.

Page 135. 13 May 1793. Solomon HUMPHREY to Drury McGEE, 30 pounds Virginia money, 300 acres Seed Cain adjoining land now occupied by Rich GITENS and adjoining Dan'l. HUMPHRIES. Witnesses: David HUMPHRIES, Elijah SMALLWOOD, and Bowater SUMNER. Signed: Solomon HUMPHREY.

Page 136. 10 November 1794. Samuel RIGGS to Ephraim WITCHER, 400 pounds, 22 acres Mitchells River adjoining Joseph LACEWELL. Witnesses: Joseph MURPHEY, Abednego FRANKLIN, and Silas RIGGS. Signed: Samuel RIGGS.

Page 136. 8 August 1794. Benjamin SCOTT to Ephraim WITCHER, 50 pounds, 92 acres Mitchell River. Witnesses: John SCOTT, Joseph MURPHEY, and Zadock RIGGS, Junr. Signed: Benjamin SCOTT and Ellener SCOTT.

Page 137. 20 September 1794. Benjamin SCOTT to John SCOTT, 100 pounds, 45 acres Mitchell River adjoining county line. Witnesses: Joseph MURPHEY, Ephraim WITCHER, and Zadock RIGGS, Junr. Signed: Benjamin SCOTT and Ellenner SCOTT.

Page 138. 11 October 1794. Samuel RIGGS to John SCOTT, Wilkes County, North Carolina, 50 pounds, 48 acres South side Mitchells River; part 400 acres RIGGS now lives on adjoining Wilkes County. Witnesses: Joseph MURPHEY and Richard MURPHEY. Signed: Samuel RIGGS.

Page 139. 11 October 1791. Icabud BLACKLEDGE gives Power of Attorney to Joel LEWIS to execute deed to Obediah Martin BENGE for 140 acres that Icabud sold said BENGE lying on main road leads from Iron Works to Fishers Gap and plantation where BLACKLEDGE now lives. Witnesses: William LEWIS and Obediah MARTIN. Signed: Ichabud BLACKLEDGE.

Page 139. 5 October 1792. Icabod BLACKLEDGE to Obediah Martin BENGE by Atty. Joel LEWIS, 50 pounds, 140 acres waters Yadkin River adjoining Nathan CARTER and HAINES. Witnesses: William T. LEWIS and John McCONNELL. Signed: Ichabod BLACKLEDGE by Atty. Joel LEWIS.

Page 140. 16 September 1793. Henry SPEER to John DINKINS, 10 pounds, 100 acres waters North fork Deep Creek adjoining Christian WEATHERMAN. Witnesses: James PILCHER, Daniel (X) PILCHER, and William (X) CHEOWOON. Signed: H. SPEER.

Page 140. 8 November 1794. Henry SPEER to Thomas ROACH, 50 pounds, 300 acres waters Adar Creek adjoining Rowan County line, Thomas HORN; part 400 acres to SPEER 28 November 1792. Witnesses: William SPEER and Samuel SPEER. Signed: H. SPEER.

Page 141. 8 August 1793. Abijah ELMORE to Daniel PILCHER, 5 pounds, 53 acres waters Deep Creek; part 200 acres granted said ELMORE 20 December 1791, adjoining PILCHER and CHINN. Witnesses: H(enry) SPEER and John WILLIAMS. Signed: Abijah ELMORE.

Page 142. 4 August 1794. William SILVY to Obediah MARTIN, 57 pounds, 10 shillings, 100 acres waters Double Creek, waters Yadkin River adjoining HORN. Witnesses: Jonathan HAINES, John EMARS(?), and Corn. PHILLIPS. Signed: William (X) SILVY.

Page 142. 5 November 1794. John PETTIJOHN and wife, Sarah, to Martha JOHNSON, 80 pounds, 157 acres waters North fork Deep Creek adjoining John WILLIAMS, PETTIJOHN, Peter MIERS, and Samuel BROWN. Witnesses: John SCOTT and William JOHNSON. Signed: John PETTEJOHN and Sarah (X) PETTEJOHN.

Page 143. 7 November 1794. Abraham VANWINKLE to John SPENCER 120 pounds, 150 acres Grassy Creek adjoining MARTIN. Witnesses: D.W. ??? and Peter SALLE. Signed: Abraham VANWINKLE.

Page 144. 23 October 1793. John ELSBERRY, Wilkes County, North Carolina, to Samuel MARSH, 60 pounds Specie, 299 acres North Hunting Creek adjoining PENNELL. Witnesses: Stephen WOOD and Sidness MAXWELL. Signed: John ELSBERRY.

Page 145. 4 November 1794. Ninian RILEY, Senr. to "my 3 eldest sons" viz Ninian, James and Gerrard RILEY for love have deeded them their proportional part my lands and my youngest son, John RILEY has just arrived at age 21 years, I now for love deed remainder my lands to him, said John; also furniture and c. Witnesses: Stephen WOOD and James DEBORD. Signed: Ninian RILEY.

Page 145. 9 February 1791. John ALLEN, George KIMBROUGH, Gol(d)man KIMBROUGH and Marmaduke KIMBROUGH, Quit Claim ½ tract land on which Wyatt GARNER now lives adjoining LANIER, Henry SPEER and including eastern half, being part tract assigned to said GARNER by committee (and by consent Legatees) appointed by Court to divide estate Marmaduke KIMBROUGH, deceased. Witnesses: William THORNTON and H(enry) SPEER. Signed: John ALLEN, George KIMBROUGH, and Goldman KIMBROUGH, (No signature for Mduke (Jr.)).

Page 146. 12 October 1794. Anne WRIGHT, Executrix, estate of John WRIGHT, deceased, to Samuel ROBERTS, 20 pounds Specie, 120 acres Pole Branch waters Hunting Creek. Witnesses: Stephen WOOD and John STEPHENS. Signed: Anne WRIGHT.

Page 147. 1 August 1793. William SPARKS, Junr. to Hugh McALYEA, 70 pounds, 100 acres Rich Nob, one of the Brushy Mountains; granted SPARKS 9 August 1787 adjoining his survey. Witnesses: David SPENCE and Jeremiah (X) SPARKS. Signed: William SPARKS, Junr.

Page 147. 30 December 1793. John SHUGART to William SHUGART,

50 pounds, 100 acres South fork McFees Creek.
Witnesses: Zachariah SHUGART and Nathan FARMER. Signed: John
SHUGART.

Page 148. 13 December 1793. Joseph WILLIAMS to Phillip
           HOWARD, 10 pounds, 2 acres Williams Spring Branch.
Witnesses: John Thomas LONGINO, Jo WILLIAMS, Junr., and John
WILLIAMS. Signed: Jo WILLIAMS.

Page 149. 13 December 1793. Philip HOWARD to Joseph WILLIAMS
           10 pounds, 2 acres Williams Spring Branch near
said Williams Spring. Witnesses: John Thomas LONGINO and
Jo WILLIAMS. Signed: Philip HOWARD.

Page 149. 23 October 1794. James MATTHEWS, Mecklenburg
           County, North Carolina, to Joseph WILLIAMS, 200
pounds, 100 acres middle fork Tarrarat River adjoining James
ROBERT and place where Jonathan OSBURN lives; State granted
MATTHEWS by Gov. A. MARTIN 1784. Witnesses: Robert WILLIAMS,
Junr. and William THORNTON. Signed: James MATTHEWS.

Page 150. 23 October 1794. James MATTHEWS, Mecklenburg
           County, North Carolina, to Joseph WILLIAMS, 300
pounds, 200 acres waters Toms Creek adjoining Abraham
COOLEY; State granted MATTHEWS 3 November 1784. Witnesses:
Robert WILLIAMS and William THORNTON. Signed: James MATTHEWS.

Page 151. 20 September 1794. Wyott GARNER to Joseph
           WILLIAMS, 200 pounds, 191½ acres adjoining CRESON,
SPEER and being part land conveyed by Thos. TURNER to
Marmaduke KIMBROUGH 4 March 1768 and assigned to Wyott GARNER
as Legatee to said Marmaduke KIMBROUGH, deceased. Witnesses:
Jo WILLIAMS, Junr. and John WILLIAMS. Signed: Wiott GARNER.

Page 151. 22 December 1794. Edward WILLIAMS, Yeoman, and
           wife, Nancy, to Robert WALKER, Union County,
South Carolina, 500 pounds, 652 acres South side North fork
Hunting Creek, formerly property of a certain SANDERS: by
SANDERS to WILLIAMS adjoining old Still House, Johnson
County line and waggon road. Witnesses: Daniel (X) JONES,
Laurance OWEN, and (blur) (X) PARKER. Signed: Edward (X)
WILLIAMS and Nancy WILLIAMS.

Page 153. 8 January 1794. George WATKINS to Littleberry
           BRAY, 300 pounds, 300 acres Bullrun. Witnesses:
Jeremiah EARLY, Nehemiah BLOOMER, and Samuel HUMPHREYS.
Signed: George (X) WATKINS.

Page 153. 12 December 1794. William and Jacob McCRAW to
           Hugh ARMSTRONG, 400 pounds, 403 acres, part
larger tract purchased of James BROWN in the Hollows adjoining Majr BAYLIES and David BROWN, both sides Stewarts little
Creek. Witnesses: William (X) BURRUS, Samuel McCRAW, and
Joseph HARVEY. Signed: William McCRAW and Jacob McCRAW.

Page 154. 12 May 1792. Jacob FREEMAN to Richard WILBORN,
           400 pounds, 100 acres Hogans Creek concluding
plantation known as old Mill place. Witnesses: Jeremiah

EARLEY, Samuel FREEMAN, and Littleberry BRAY. Signed:
Jacob FREEMAN.

Page 155. 12 May 1792. William FREEMAN to Richard WILBORN,
100 pounds, 105 acres both sides Hogans Creek
adjoining Captain FREEMANS. Witnesses: Jeremiah EARLEY,
Samuel FREEMAN, and Littleberry BRAY. Signed: William FREEMAN.

Page 156. 8 December 1794. Charles VANDEVER to George
VANDEVEER, 15 pounds, 121 acres waters Forbis
Creek. Witnesses: James MORPHEW and Joseph HEEGAMAN. Signed:
Charles VANDEVEER.

Page 156. 5 December 1794. William DOWLING to John DOWLING,
100 pounds, 300 acres waters Frobis Creek adjoining William DEVONPORT; granted said William 24 December 1792.
Witnesses: H(enry) SPEER, Thomas SPEER, and Moses BAKER.
Signed: William DOWLING.

Page 157. 21 May 1794. Henry SPEER to Thomas SPEER, 5
shillings, 240 acres waters Forbis Creek adjoining Stephen DINKINS, Joseph MURPHEY, John WYATT, Francis
LACKEY, and ELLIOT; part 400 acres granted SPEER 24 December
1792. Witnesses: William DOWLING, Francis (X) LACKEY, and
Maner (X) LACKEY. Signed: H. SPEER.

Page 158. 7 February 1795. Isaac EMANUEL to Samuel COOK,
20 pounds (no acreage), branch Double Creek.
Witnesses: William COOK and Mary SHORES. Signed: Isaac (X)
EMANUEL.

Page 158. 10 February 1794. William COOK, Sheriff, to
Charles HUNT (execution against Executors of
Isaac SESSION, deceased, obtained by WHEATON & TISDALE), 100
acres adjoining Abraham CRESONS 300 acre tract, Gold.
KIMBROUGH and Leonard RICHARD. Acknowledged. Signed:
William COOK, Sheriff.

Page 159. 16 December 1791. Aaron LISBY and wife, Milly,
to David DAVIS, 200 pounds, 200 acres waters
Meeks Creek. Witnesses: John (X) STUDIVANT, William BATES,
and David (X) CLARK. Signed: Aaron LISBY and Milly (X)
LISBY.

Page 160. 13 January 1795. Elias TURNER to Benjamin SPEER,
102 pounds, 102 acres Turners Creek, Irish ford
road leading from Shallowford to Salisbury adjoining Andrew
SPEER, Charles VANDEVER, Joseph WILLIAMS; part 204 acres
John Earl GRANVILLE granted to Roger TURNER 8 February 1755.
Witnesses: H(enry) SPEER and James (X) STEELMAN. Signed:
Elias TURNER.

Page 160. 29 December 1794. Jabez JARVIS, Senr. to Jabez
JARVIS, Junr., 200 pounds, 191 acres fork Fishers
and Yadkin Rivers. Witnesses: William MEREDITH, Robert
ANDERSON, and Joseph NOBLIT. Signed: Jabez JARVIS, Senr.

Page 161. 28 August 1793. Abijah ELMORE to John WILLIAMS,

Esq., 5 pounds, 62 acres waters Forbis Creek
adjoining 200 acres tract granted ELMORE 20 December 1791,
Brooks old road. Witnesses: H(enry) SPEER and John (X)
DINKINS. Signed: Abijah ELMORE.

Page 162. 12 February 1795. Jacob SHEPPERD to Joseph KERBY,
200 pounds, 222 acres Grassy Creek; by State
granted 1787. Acknowledged. Signed: J. SHEPPERD.

Page 163. 14 October 1794. Anne BAKER, James BAKER, David
BAKER, Samuel JONES, Evan JONES, John BAKER, Peleg
BAKER, Joseph BAKER, Jonathan BAKER, and Joshua BAKER (all
of State of Kentucky and heirs and legatees Michael BAKER,
deceased, of North Carolina), appointed our Brother Moses
BAKER of North Carolina, our lawful Attorney to sell, etc.,
tract land Surry County, North Carolina, whereon Michael
BAKER died. Signed: Anne BAKER, David BAKER, Evan JONES,
Peleg BAKER, James BAKER, Samuel JONES, John BAKER, and
Joseph BAKER. . . .Town Lexington, Fayette County, Kentucky,
above letter Attorney produced in Court and ordered recorded
17 October 1794 and 3rd year Commonwealth. Signed: Levi
TODD, C.C., Surry County, North Carolina, February Term 1795,
above letter Attorney produced in Court and ordered recorded.
Signed: Jo WILLIAMS, C.C.

Page 163. 5 December 1794. Moses BAKER, Attorney for heirs
of Michael BAKER, deceased, to Wm. SPILMAN, 25
pounds, 32 acres waters Forbis Creek adjoining John BOREN,
Bakers Creek; part 500 acres sold by George FORBIS to
Michael BAKER 21 May 1765. Witnesses; H(enry) SPEER and
Thomas SPEER. Signed: Moses BAKER, Heir at Law and Attorney.

Page 164. 5 December 1794. Moses BAKER, Attorney for heirs
of Michael BAKER, deceased, to William DOWLING,
150 pounds, 312 acres waters Forbis Creek adjoining John
DOWLING, Bakers old line, Wm. DOWLING; part 400 acres sold
by Geo. FORBIS to Michael BAKER 21 May 1765. Witnesses:
H(enry) SPEER and Thomas SPEER. Signed: Moses BAKER, Heir
at Law and Attorney.

Page 165. 24 December 1792. North Carolina Grant Airs
HUDSPETH 300 acres Deep Creek adjoining WAGGONER.

Page 165. 15 December 1794. Millington BLALOCK to Thomas
ANTHONY, 133 pounds, 440 acres adjoining 640
acres Granted to said BLALOCK 24 December 1792. Witnesses:
H(enry) SPEER and Henry HAMRICK. Signed: Millington BLALOCK.

Page 166. 15 October 1794. Henry SPEER to Samuel AYERS,
70 pounds, 100 acres waters Forbis Creek adjoining Cooleys path, Jos. MURPHEY; part 400 acres granted
SPEER 24 December 1792. Witnesses: John WYATT and Samuel
SPEER. Signed: H. SPEER.

Page 167. 15 October 1794. Henry SPEER to Jesse STANDLEY,
5 shillings, 100 acres waters Forbis Creek adjoining Joseph MURPHEY, John DOWLING; part 500 acres granted
SPEER. Witnesses: Samuel AYERS and John Wyatt. Signed: H.
SPEER.

Page 167.   17 February 1795.   Thomas ROSS to John ROSS, 70
            pounds, 80 acres Mitchells River adjoining John
DUN; Granted 1790. Witnesses: Thomas A. WORD and Rezia JARVIS.
Signed: Thomas ROSS.

Page 168.   22 January 1793.   William WATTS, Wilkes County,
            North Carolina, to Caleb WINFREE, Wilkes County,
North Carolina, 200 pounds, 199 acres South fork Mitchells
River adjoining Thomas PAYN. Witnesses: William BURCH and
Obediah WINFREE. Signed: William (X) WATTS.

Page 169.   4 February 1795.   John HOLDER to Cornelius KEITH,
            Junr., 100 pounds, 100 acres Stewarts Creek adjoin-
ing Virginia line. Witnesses: Hugh ARMSTRONG, Edward STEWART,
and Martha ARMSTRONG.   Signed: John (X) HOLDER and Agnes (X)
HOLDER.

Page 169.   27 August 1790.   Thomas MASON to Henry SPEER, 150
            pounds, 800 acres Beach fork in Jefferson County,
Virginia adjoining Michael TORELMANS 500 acres granted;
granted MASON 1786. Witnesses: John (X) GROCE, Samuel
CROCKET, Abraham (X) SKIDMORE, and Thomas MOSBY. Signed:
Thomas MASON.

Page 170.   11 February 1795.   Hugh ARMSTRONG to Jacob McCRAW,
            400 pounds North Carolina Curency, 403 acres;
part larger tract bought of James BROWN in the Hollows
adjoining Majr BAYLISS and David BROWN on Stewarts little
Creek. Acknowledged. Signed: Hugh ARMSTRONG.

Page 171.   20 December 1794.   William COOK, Sheriff, to John
            MARTIN, tanner, (land lost by George HOLCOMB and
wife, Elizabeth, labourer, action brought by Jesse LESTER,
John HORN, J.P.), no acreage, South fork Deep Creek adjoining
Daniel LIVERTON, Peter SHERMER and Peter SPRINKELS old line.
Acknowledged. Signed: William COOK, Sheriff.

Page 172.   3 February 1795.   Henry SPEER to John BINKLEY, 50
            pounds, 150 acres waters Forbis Creek. Witnesses:
Daniel LIVERTON and Frederick (X) SHORE. Signed: H. SPEER.

Page 173.   13 March 1794.   William DAVIS, Rowan County, to
            May HOLCOMB, 44 pounds, 440 acres mouth South
fork Deep Creek, North part land said DAVIS bought of Heirs
of Pilgrim POPE adjoining widow WHITEHEAD and Lindsey KARLTON.
Witnesses: Solomon DAVIS and Henry DAVIS.   Signed: William
DAVIS.

Page 173.   27 December 1794.   Thomas Adams WORD to Lewis
            FORKNER, Edmund HODGES and Obediah BAKER, Elders
of Baptist Church in Hollow Settlement for "desire said WORD
has to promote worship of the only true God and encouragement
of Schools of Knowledge", 10 acres waters Lovins Creek,
middle fork Tarrarat River, Donaldsons School House Branch;
part State granted Charles WORD (specifies Elders give free
privelege for worship of God of other established churches
except when in use by Baptist, to keep up Schools and by no
means erect Dwelling houses, houses of Public Drinking places

or any other practice of immorality). Witnesses: Richard
LAURANCE, Matthew DAVIS, and John McKINNEY, Senr. Signed:
T.A. WORD.

Page 174. 17 June 1791. Elijah and Nathan POPE, both formerly
          of Rowan County, Heirs at Law of their Honored
Father, Pilgrim POPE, deceased, to William DAVIS, Rowan County,
60 pounds, 640 acres South fork Deep Creek; State granted
Pilgrim POPE, adjoining SURGENOR and widow WHITEHEAD. Witness-
es: Solomon DAVIS and Henry DAVIS. Signed: Elijah POPE and
Nathan POPE.

Page 175. 16 July 1794. Daniel LIVERTON to Thomas HUTCHENS,
          60 pounds, 300 acres South fork Forbis Creek
adjoining Benjamin HUTCHENS. Witnesses: John JOHNSON and
Benjamin JOHNSON. Signed: Daniel LIVERTON.

Page 176. 9 June 1792. Moses BAKER to Thomas ROSS, 60 pounds,
          100 acres Mitchells River. Witnesses: Moses
WILLIAMS and John ROSS. Signed: Moses BAKER.

Page 176. 3 January 1795. Thomas THORNTON to Simon HADLEY,
          Senr., 50 pounds, 200 acres McFees Creek adjoining
Aaron SPEER, MOORE; land entered by James JONES; by JONES to
THORNTON. Witnesses: Adam COFFIN, Francis BARNARD, and
Simon HADLEY, Junr. Signed: Thomas THORNTON.

Page 177. 16 March 1793. Charles HUNT, Salisbury, Rowan
          County, to George LOGAN, 8 pounds, 1 shilling,
lot No. 39, Huntsville on High Street. Witnesses: William
THORNTON and John HUNT. Signed: Chas. HUNT.

Page 178. 9 December 1794. William ALNUTT and wife, Mary,
          to John JOHNSON, 55 pounds, 500 acres Buck Shole
Branch, waters Hunting Creek adjoining WINSOR. Witnesses:
Elisha JOHNSON and Benjamin JOHNSON. Signed: William
ALLNUTT and Mary ALLNUTT.

Page 179. 3 January 1795. Edmund WOOD, Green County, and
          Ceded Territory, Southwest of river Ohio, to
William HODGES, 50 pounds, 10 shillings, 125 acres little
Beaver Dam Creek adjoining WOODS former line. Witnesses:
Jo MURPHEY, James JENNINGS, and John HODGES. Signed: Edmund
(X) WOOD.

Page 179. 13 September 1793. Charles HUNT and wife,
          Elizabeth, Huntsville, to Peter EATON, Rowan
County, 25 pounds, 15 shillings, Lot No. 9, Huntsville,
High and Pine Streets. Witnesses: John HUNT and Robert
BRIGGS. Signed: Chas. HUNT and Elizabeth HUNT.

Page 180. 19 February 1793. Valentine MOLER to Samuel
          ERWIN, Iredell County, 400 pounds Specie, 248
acres North Hunting Creek adjoining SANDERS and Johnsons
Branch. Witnesses: Stephen WOOD and William BALL, Senr.
Signed: Valentine MOLER and Christinah (X) MOLER.

Page 181. 9 January 1793. John ELSBERRY to John STEPHENS,
                25 pounds Specie, 300 acres North fork Hunting
Creek adjoining Isaac ELSBERRY. Witnesses: Stephen WOOD
and Robert FRAZIER. Signed: John ELSBERRY.

Page 181. 29 April 1795. George LONG to George DEBOARD, 2
                pounds Specie, 100 acres waters Fishers Creek
adjoining John PENDRY and MOSELY. Witnesses: Thomas WRIGHT
and Joseph WARBINTON. Signed: George LONG.

Page 182. 16 March 1793. Charles HUNT, Salisbury, Rowan
                County, to James LOGAN, 8 pounds, 10 shillings,
Lot No. 67, Huntsville, High and Third Streets. Witnesses:
William THORNTON and John HUNT. Signed: Chas. HUNT.

Page 182. 13 May 1795. William COOK, Sheriff, to John
                MARTIN, farmer, (land lost by George HOLCOMB,
labourer, by James LESTER before John HORN, J.P.; judgement
received against George and Drury HOLCOMB), 5 acres South
fork Deep Creek. Acknowledged. Signed: William COOK, Sheriff.

Page 183. 17 February 1795. May HOLCOMB to George HOPPES,
                35 pounds, 240 acres waters Deep Creek adjoining
Linsey CARLTON. Witnesses: John Thomas LONGINO and Thomas
WRIGHT. Signed: May HOLCOMB.

Page 184. 17 February 1795. May HOLCOMB to Lindsey CARLTON,
                25 pounds, 100 acres waters Deep Creek adjoining
said CARLTON. Witnesses: John Thomas LONGINO and Thomas
WRIGHT. Signed: May HOLCOMB (male).

Page 185. 16 August 1792. William T. LEWIS to David BARY,
                Junr., 75 pounds, 200 acres Codys Creek, land
sold sometime ago to said LEWIS by David BRAY, Senr.
Witnesses: Nathan (X) BRAY and Zenas BALDWIN. Signed: Wm.
T. LEWIS.

Page 185. 17 March 1794. James FAREZ to William Lucket
                DAVIS, 100 pounds Specie, 200 acres North
Hunting Creek adjoining MOLER and MOSBY. Witnesses: Stephen
WOOD and Zenas BALDWIN. Signed: James (X) FAREZ.

Page 186. 20 April 1789. Joshua FREEMAN to Samuel FREEMAN,
                600 pounds, 267 acres Yadkin River, mouth Hogans
Creek adjoining Morgan BRYANT, Arrarat River, GRANVILLE
granted Morgan BRYAN, Senr. 28 October 1752. Witnesses:
William FREEMAN, Edward SMITH, and Ephraim (X) PHILIPS.
Signed: Joshua FREEMAN.

Page 187. 11 May 1795. Daniel VESTAL to Thomas HADLEY,
                300 pounds, 475 acres waters North fork Deep
Creek in Iron Works road adjoining James VESTAL and Simon
HADLEY, conveyed by Ambrose BRAMLET to Daniel VESTAL.
Witnesses: Simon HADLEY, Senr. and Simon LACKEY. Signed:
Daniel VESTAL.

Page 187. 2 February 1795. Henry SPEER to Daniel LIVERTON,
                95 pounds, 200 acres North fork Deep Creek

adjoining DEFREE, old corner Morgan BRYAN known as Kimbrough
Bottom, Iron Work road, Jacob DOUTHIT, John MASH, THOMPSON
and GIBBEN. Witnesses: James TODD and John (X) MASON.
Signed: H. SPEER.

Page 188. 13 January 1795. Henry SPEER to James PERRY, 20
          pounds, 240 acres waters Hunting Creek adjoining
Matt SPARKS, WOOLDRIDGE; part land granted SPEER 20 December
1791 Witnesses: Labon HICKS and John KELLY. Signed: H.
SPEER.

Page 189. 20 January 1795. Henry SPEER to James PERRY, 20
          pounds, 200 acres waters North Hunting Creek
adjoining Richard GOOD in Bryshy Mountain, Ambrose Chappel,
Wilkes County line. Witnesses: Labon HICKS and John KELLY.

Page 190. 10 May 1795. Charles DUDLEY to Blunt GARRETT,
          100 pounds, 100 acres South side Yadkin River.
Witnesses: William THORNTON and Meals GARRETT. Signed:
Chas. DUDLEY.

Page 190. 10 March 1795. Samuel RICE, Madison County,
          Kentucky, to Heirs of Michael RICE, deceased,
late King William County, Virginia, 200 pounds Virginia
money, 56 acres North side Yadkin River. Witnesses: Alex
CARNES, William CUNNINGHAM, and John DAVIS. Signed: Samuel
RICE.

Page 191. 9 February 1795. Samuel RICE, Madison County,
          Kentucky, to Heirs of Michael RICE, deceased,
late of King William County, Virginia, 200 pounds, 270 acres,
North side Yadkin River adjoining John HARVEY, Adam BLACK,
and John Butterworth COLVARD. Witnesses: Alexander CARNES,
William CUNNINGHAM, and John DAVIS. Signed: Samuel RICE.

Page 192. 14 May 1795. William COOK, Esq., Sheriff, to
          Henry SPEER (land lost by Stephen DAVIS; action
by Geo. STEELMAN), 443 acres Hannas Creek adjoining Chas.
VANDEVEER, Rowan County line, Jacob SPEER and John DANNELS.
Witnesses: Moses BAKER and Andrew SPEER. Signed: William
COOK, Sheriff.

Page 193. 22 January 1793. William WATTS to Caleb WINFREE,
          100 pounds, 60 acres South fork Mitchells River
adjoining PEARSON. Witnesses: William BURCH and Obediah
WINFREE. Signed: William (X) WATTS.

Page 193. 10 January 1795. Henry SPEER to Peter SPRINKLE,
          5 pounds, 30 acres waters Deep Creek adjoining
REESE, JOHNSON; part 300 acres granted SPEER. Witnesses:
John BINKLEY, Jonathan SPRINKLE, and Thomas (X) CLANTON.
Signed: H. SPEER.

Page 194. 24 February 1795. Henry PATTILLO, Junr. to
          Jonathan HAINES, 100 pounds, 80 acres North side
North fork Deep Creek adjoining DINKINS: granted PATTILLO
20 December 1791. Witnesses: H(enry) SPEER and Rd. RAIFORD.
Signed: Henry PATTILLO, Junr.

Page 195. 8 February 1795. Thomas PUCKET to John STUTHARD, 35 pounds, (no acreage), head Flat Shole Creek; part 220 acre tract. Witnesses: Richard PUCKETT and Samuel PARKER. Signed: Thomas PUCKET.

Page 195. 4 August 1792. Jesse COUNCIL, Wilkes County, North Carolina, to Peter COOK, 100 pounds, 400 acres middle fork Forbis Creek adjoining John ENGLAND and William MOORE. Witness: John WILLIAMS. Signed: Jesse COUNCILL.

Page 196. 14 November 1793. William THORNTON, Stephen WOOD, John Thomas LONGINO, Jacob SHEPPERD and David HUMPHREYS, Commissioners, Town of Rockford, to Reuben GRANT, 10 pounds, 5 shillings, Lot No. 11, High Street. Acknowledged. Signed: All Commissioners signed.

Page 197. 3 January 1793. Chas. HUNT, Huntsville, to George EARNEST, Huntsville, 10 pounds, Lot No. 8, town of Huntsville. Witnesses: Nathan CHAFFIN and John TURNER. Signed: Chas. HUNT.

Page 198. 13 May 1795. Daniel BILLS, Esq. to Airs HUDSPETH, Junr., 250 pounds, 250 acres waters Forbush Creek adjoining Jonas REYNOLDS, Benj HUTCHENS, BASS, GUINN, and John MARTIN. Acknowledged. Signed: Daniel BILLS.

Page 198. 16 December 1794. Thomas CLARKE, Spartanburg County, South Carolina, to James REAVIS, Senr., 110 pounds, 112 acres South side Deep Creek adjoining RUTLEDGE and Hoppes Creek. Witnesses: James REAVIS, James DOYLE, and Mary DOYLE. Signed: Thomas CLARKE.

Page 199. 14 August 1794. Richard and Andrew SPEER to Frederick LONG, 20 pounds, 108 acres waters South fork Deep Creek adjoining SPEERS 400 acres granted, LONG and HUDSPETH. Witnesses: H(enry) SPEER, Robert CLARK, and Samuel CORCKET. Signed: Andrew SPEER and Richard SPEER.

Page 200. 20 November 1795. North Carolina Grant Martin ARMSTRONG 200 acres waters Grassy Creek.

Page 200. 20 November 1795. North Carolina Grant Martin ARMSTRONG 300 acres waters Toms Creek.

Page 201. 20 November 1795. North Carolina Grant Martin ARMSTRONG 250 acres waters Toms Creek.

Page 201. 16 March 1795. Miner MARSH and wife, Ann, to John MARSH, Junr., 50 pounds, 75 acres West side Fishers River. Witnesses: Jesse LESTER, Larkin BLEDSOE, and Thomas MARSH. Signed: Miner (X) MARSH and Ann (X) MARSH.

Page 202. 20 November 1795. North Carolina Grant Martin ARMSTRONG 300 acres waters Toms Creek.

Page 202. 20 February 1795. John McMICKLE, Junr. to Aaron SPEER, 127 pounds, 300 acres head McFees River

adjoining Wm. MOORE, Simion CARTER, Richmond road and James
JONES. Witnesses: Dougal McMICKLE and John (X) McMICKLE.
Signed: John McMICKLE, Junr.

Page 203.   20 November 1795.   North Carolina Grant Martin
            ARMSTRONG 200 acres waters Grassy Creek.

Page 204.   20 November 1795.   North Carolina Grant Martin
            ARMSTRONG 400 acres waters Tarrarat River.

Page 204.   20 November 1795.   North Carolina Grant Martin
            ARMSTRONG 350 acres waters Tarrarat River.

Page 205.   20 November 1795.   North Carolina Grant Martin
            ARMSTRONG 1,000 acres waters both Grassy Creeks.

Page 205.   24 December 1795.   North Carolina Grant Thomas
            WEAVER 300 acres adjoining KELL.

Page 206.   20 November 1795.   North Carolina Grant Martin
            ARMSTRONG 500 acres Powels Creek.

Page 206.   20 November 1795.   North Carolina Grant Martin
            ARMSTRONG 300 acres waters Powels Creek.

Page 207.   20 November 1795.   North Carolina Grant Martin
            ARMSTRONG 200 acres Yadkin River.

Page 207.   16 July 1795.   North Carolina Grant Job MARTIN
            300 acres South side Yadkin River adjoining John
MARTIN, North side Baileys Creek and Alexander CAR(R).

Page 208.   20 November 1795.   North Carolina Grant Martin
            ARMSTRONG 300 acres little Grassy Creek.

Page 208.   20 November 1795.   North Carolina Grant Martin
            ARMSTRONG 640 acres waters Pilot Creek.

Page 209.   20 November 1795.   North Carolina Grant Martin
            ARMSTRONG 200 acres waters Tarrarat River.

Page 209.   9 July 1794.   North Carolina Grant Jebez JARVASS
            400 acres waters Codys Creek between Henry SNOW
and West MOSELEYS.

Page 210.   20 November 1795.   North Carolina Grant Martin
            ARMSTRONG 400 acres both sides little Grassy Creek.

Page 210.   20 November 1795.   North Carolina Grant Martin
            ARMSTRONG 250 acres waters Tarrarat River.

Page 211.   20 November 1795.   North Carolina Grant Martin
            ARMSTRONG 300 acres waters Toms Creek.

Page 212.   20 November 1795.   North Carolina Grant Martin
            ARMSTRONG 300 acres North side Pilot Creek adjoin-
ing Jonathan HAINES.

Page 212.   20 November 1795.   North Carolina Grant Martin
             ARMSTRONG 200 acres waters Grassy Creek.

Page 213.   20 November 1795.   North Carolina Grant Martin
             ARMSTRONG 500 acres waters little Grassy Creek
adjoining General SUMNER.

Page 213.   24 July 1792.   Thomas PINNION to Frederick DESARN,
             200 pounds, 100 acres East side Tarrarat River.
Witnesses: Samuel FREEMAN, Edward SMITH, and Valentine
HOLIFIELD.   Signed: Thomas (X) PINNION.

Page 214.   20 November 1795.   North Carolina Grant Martin
             ARMSTRONG 400 acres waters Powels Creek.

Page 214.   9 July 1794.   North Carolina Grant Nathan FARMER
             121 acres waters North fork Deep Creek adjoining
Abraham REESE and Zachariah SUGART.

Page 215.   20 November 1795.   North Carolina Grant Martin
             ARMSTRONG 200 acres waters Tarrarat River.

Page 215.   20 November 1795.   North Carolina Grant Martin
             ARMSTRONG 640 acres Standleys Creek.

Page 216.   20 November 1795.   North Carolina Grant Martin
             ARMSTRONG 150 acres waters Grassy Creek.

Page 217.   20 November 1795.   North Carolina Grant Martin
             ARMSTRONG 300 acres waters Tarrarat River.

Page 217.   9 July 1794.   North Carolina Grant John BURCHAM
             50 acres Buck Horn Branch adjoining JESSOP.

Page 218.   20 November 1795.   North Carolina Grant Martin
             ARMSTRONG 300 acres waters Toms Creek.

Page 218.   9 July 1794.   North Carolina Grant Joseph HIETT
             80 acres Chiquemine Creek adjoining Benjamin
HIETT.

Page 219.   20 November 1795.   North Carolina Grant Martin
             ARMSTRONG 100 acres waters Pilot Creek.

Page 219.   20 November 1795.   North Carolina Grant Martin
             ARMSTRONG 200 acres waters Grassy Creek.

Page 220.   20 November 1795.   North Carolina Grant Martin
             ARMSTRONG 640 acres waters Yadkin River.

Page 220.   20 November 1795.   North Carolina Grant Martin
             ARMSTRONG 640 acres South side Pilot Creek.

Page 221.   20 November 1795.   North Carolina Grant Martin
             ARMSTRONG 400 acres waters Yadkin River.

Page 221.   20 November 1795.   North Carolina Grant Martin
             ARMSTRONG 150 acres Tarrarat River.

Page 222.   20 November 1795. North Carolina Grant Martin
            ARMSTRONG 400 acres waters Toms Creek.

Page 222.   9 July 1794. North Carolina Grant Joseph HIETT
            50 acres waters Toms Creek adjoining Benjamin
HEITT and Aaron HEITT.

Page 223.   20 November 1795. North Carolina Grant Martin
            ARMSTRONG 200 acres waters Tarrarat River.

Page 223.   9 July 1794. North Carolina Grant William SUGART
            90 acres waters McFees Creek adjoining John SHUGART,
Zachariah SHUGART and LINDSEY.

Page 224.   20 November 1795. North Carolina Grant Martin
            ARMSTRONG 200 acres waters Tarrarat River.

Page 224.   20 November 1795. North Carolina Grant William
            ARMSTRONG 500 acres both sides middle fork Tarrarat
River crossing Birdges Creek.

Page 225.   9 February 1795. Thompson GLEN, Stokes County,
            to Levin GROCE, 86 pounds, 500 acres middle
District waters Richland Creek of Elk River (part ½ entry
made by William SHEPPERD and Joseph PHILIPS of 5,000 in John
ARMSTRONGS office and sold to Matthew BROOKS; from BROOKS
to Jos. PHILIPS; from PHILIPS to Thompson GLEN), adjoining
Andrew PHILIPS. Witnesses: John BARNS and Jarny GROCE.
Signed: Thompson GLEN.

Page 226.   9 July 1794. North Carolina Grant Darby RYAN
            200 acres Davis Branch, waters Fishers River
adjoining LANTRIP and HUDSON.

Page 226.   9 February 1795. Thompson GLEN, Stokes County,
            to Levin GROCE, 100 pounds, 230 acres waters
Yadkin River, Josephs Creek adjoining LOGAN, FORBIS, Moses
BAKERS old line; part 351 acres State granted Timothy COE
3 April 1789; by Sheriff to John LYNCH 13 February 1789; by
LYNCH to GLEN 21 May 1792. Witnesses: John BARNS and James
(X) GROCE. Signed: Thompson GLEN.

Page 227.   18 May 1789. North Carolina Grant Isaax MIZE
            400 acres North side Hunting Creek.

Page 228.   15 April 1795. North Carolina Grant Henry SPEER
            397 acres adjoining Benjamin SPEER, South side
Yadkin, Elias TURNER, Jonathan BRYAN, RUTLEDGE, Andw. SPEER,
Wm. HOWARD, Charles VANDEVEER, James STEELMAN, John HUNT,
Leonard RICHARDS, Wyatt GARNER, North side Mulberry Field
road, Isham YOUNG, John TURNER, William HAGGES and Edward
SCOTT.

Page 229.   18 May 1795. Henry SPEER to John RUTLEDGE, 20
            pounds, 200 acres waters Hanns Creek and Elrods
Creek adjoining Andrew SPEER, Junr., Hanns old survey; part
443 acres sold Henry SPEER by Wm. COOK, Sheriff, 14 May 1795.
Witnesses: Edward SCOTT and Joseph RUTLEDGE. Signed: H. SPEER.

Page 230.　16 July 1795.　North Carolina Grant George LASH
　　　　　　200 acres Yadkin River.

Page 230.　16 July 1795.　North Carolina Grant John JOYNER
　　　　　　716 acres Yadkin River.

Page 231.　18 June 1795.　James CARSON to Isaac WILBURN, 30
　　　　　　pounds, 2 acres Forbis Creek, being part land
said CARSON now lives on.　Witnesses: Edward LOVELL and Isaac
WILBURN.　Signed: James CARSON.

Page 232.　25 February 1796.　John HUNT, Rowan County, to
　　　　　　Charles HUNT, 131 pounds, 5 shillings, 100 acres
waters Turners and Lick Run Creeks of Yadkin River adjoining
George KIMBROUGHS 100 acres he bought of James CAMPBELL;
Matthias STEELMAN and Leo RICHARDS.　Witnesses: Leonard
RICHARDS, William HUNT, and Jeffrey JOHNSON.　Signed: J. HUNT.

Page 233.　16 July 1795.　North Carolina Grant Charles HUNT
　　　　　　640 acres waters Turners Creek adjoining James
STEELMAN, Jonathan THOMPSON, Jacob SPEER, William SPEER,
Benj. SPEER, Henry RENEGOR and EDDLEMAN.

Page 235.　11 May 1795.　Thomas HADLEY to Sampson BASS, 30
　　　　　　pounds, 43 acres waters Deep Creek adjoining 200
acre tract John PETTYJOHN.　Witnesses: Simon HADLEY, Junr.
and Simon HADLEY, Senr.　Signed: Thomas HADLEY.

Page 235.　7 March 1795.　Arthur SCOTT, Stokes County, to
　　　　　　Edward LOVELL, James THOMPSON, and Isaac WELBURN,
1,000 pounds, 640 acres in Surry and Stokes Counties below
mouth little Yadkin River on Big Yadkin.　Witnesses: William
FINLEY, Samuel B. SHEPARD, Jesse KEARBY, and John THOMPSON.
Signed: Arthur SCOTT.

Page 236.　18 May 1789.　North Carolina Grant WM. T. LEWIS
　　　　　　150 acres Fox Nobb adjoining WOODRUFF.

Page 237.　9 July 1794.　North Carolina Grant Richard
　　　　　　PUCKETT 50 acres waters Flat Shole Creek adjoining
his former survey.

Page 238.　18 May 1789.　North Carolina Grant Christopher
　　　　　　ELLES, Senr. 194 acres Bullrun West Piolot Mountain.

Page 238.　16 July 1795.　North Carolina Grant Rial SIMMONS
　　　　　　60 acres Grindstone Branch, waters Toms Creek
adjoining Joseph JESSOP.

Page 239.　22 December 1795.　Letter of Attorney from Martin
　　　　　　ARMSTRONG to Thos. Adams WORD to sell following
land: 1,000 acres, 350 acres, 100 acres, 500 acres, 7,300
acre tracts, 7,400 acre tracts, 8,200 acre tracts, 2,250
acre tracts, 4,640 acre tracts, 2,150 acre tracts.　Witness:
John DAMAS.　Signed: Martin ARMSTRONG. . . .Queen Anne
County, Maryland, Martin ARMSTRONG of Surry County, North
Carolina came before John DAMAS, J.P. and acknowledged above
letter of Attorney 22 December 1795.　Surry County, North

Carolina Registered 20 August 1796. Signed: Wm. THORNTON, Register.

Page 241. 10 August 1795. John Thomas LONGINO, Deputy Sheriff and Constable to Wm. TRUITT, farmer, 80 pounds, 330 acres North fork Yadkin River; part surveys for LONGINO 28 October 1778, 17 February 1779 and 25 August 1790 adjoining Thos. ADDEMAN. Witness: Thomas VEACH, Junr. Signed: John Thomas LONGINO.

Page 242. 29 December 1794. John WARD, Wilkes County, North Carolina to Michael ROMINGER, Stokes County, 35 pounds Specie, 300 acres waters South fork Deep Creek adjoining ELLIOTT and Airs HUDSPETH. Witnesses: Stephen WOOD and John HANKS. Signed: John WARD.

Page 243. 5 November 1795. Jesse LESTER to John Brown CUTTING, Pennsylvania, $2,400 Pennsylvania Currency, 20,000 acres (State granted LESTER 28 July 1795), South side Yadkin River, East side Forbis Creek below Stephen HOBSONS Saw Mill, Fall Creek adjoining Moses AYERS and William RICH. Witnesses: James MARTIN, J.E. STOCK, and Stephen (X) HORN. Signed: Jesse LESTER.

Page 245. 7 November 1795. Before me, Thomas McKEAN, Esq., Doctor of Law, Chief Justice, State Pennsylvania, came this day Jesse LESTER, Esq. and acknowledged the above deed to be his act and deed. . . .Surry County, North Carolina, August Term 1796. The above deed acknowledged; then came Mary LESTER, wife said Jesse and relinquished her dower right. Signed: Jos. WILLIAMS, C.C.

Page 245. 20 December 1791. North Carolina Grant Zadock RIGGS 35 acres waters Mitchells River adjoining Murphey and Samuel RIGGS.

Page 246. 28 August 1795. North Carolina Grant James MURPHEY 300 acres waters Hunting Creek adjoining PARKER, MASTERS, head Cane Brake Branch of Hunting Creek.

Page 247. 9 September 1796. North Carolina Grant Gottlieb SHOBER 4,360 acres waters Fisher River and Double Creek near Isaac COPELAND, HAMBLIN, JARVIS and MELTON.

Page 248. 9 September 1796. North Carolina Grant Gottlieb SHOBER 640 acres waters Fishers River adjoining Timothy PICKERING, Horns Mill Creek and Isaac COPELAND.

Page 248. 12 March 1792. George WOOTEN to William POE, 150 pounds, 270 acres adjoining William PETTY. Witnesses: Ephraim (X) McLIMORE and Henry (X) POE. Signed: George (X) WOOTEN.

Page 249. 30 December 1793. John SHUGART to Isaac SHUGAT, Orange County, North Carolina, 50 pounds, 100 acres South fork McFees Creek. Witnesses: Zachariah SHUGART and Nathan FARMER. Signed: John SHUGART.

Page 250.   9 July 1794.   North Carolina Grant Airs HUDSPETH,
             Junr. 25 acres waters North fork Deep Creek adjoin-
ing Jonas RENDELS and PETTYJOHN.

Page 250   16 July 1795.   North Carolina Grant Peter SPRINKLE
             50 acres waters Deep Creek adjoining Benjamin
CLANTON.

Page 251.   24 January 1795.   Ann WRIGHT to James ROTEN, 22
             pounds Specie, 129 acres waters Hunting Creek.
Witnesses: Thomas WRIGHT and James WRIGHT.   Signed: Ann
WRIGHT.

Page 252.   8 December 1794.   James BURNSIDE, Yeoman, to
             Thomas VEACH, farmer, 34 pounds, 170 acres South
side North Hunting Creek adjoining David GANTT: State granted
said BURNSIDE.   Witnesses: William ALNUTT and William TRUITT.
Signed: James BURNSIDE.

Page 253.   1 August 1795.   Henry SPEER, Esq. to Josiah ROWTEN,
             10 pounds, 100 acres waters Hunting Creek near
bald Knob adjoining HICKS and COOHOON.   Witnesses: Stephen
WOOD and Jacob (X) ROWTEN.   Signed: H. SPEER.

Page 254.   20 May 1795.   Robert JOHNSTON, Stokes County, to
             Elisha JOHNSTON, 150 pounds, 217 acres North fork
Deep Creek; State granted Jacob FERREE and by Sheriff and
FEREE to Henry SPEER; by SPEER to Robert JOHNSTON on Muster
Ground Branch crossing Hoppis Creek.   Witnesses: H(enry)
SPEER and Jonathan JOHNSTON.   Signed: Robert (X) JOHNSTON.

Page 255.   9 February 1796.   John WILLIAMS to George Durram
             HOLCOMB, 20 pounds, 30 acres waters Deep Creek
adjoining WILLIAMS, Jonas REYNOLDS; granted said WILLIAMS
1 January 1794.   Witnesses: H(enry) SPEER, William HOUGH,
and William JOHNSON.   Signed: John WILLIAMS.

Page 256.   16 July 1795.   North Carolina Grant Airs HUDSPETH
             40 acres North fork Deep Creek adjoining Joshua
BROWN, BRUCE and HUTCHENS.

Page 256.   12 August 1795.   John ALLEN to Peter HAMBLIN, 50
             pounds, 100 acres North side Yadkin River, bank
Fishers River at old road, HOWARDS old ford and main waggon
road.   Witnesses: William COOK and William THORNTON.   Signed:
John (X) ALLEN.

Page 257.   18 May 1795.   Henry SPEER to Andrew SPEER, Junr.,
             100 pounds, (no acreage), adjoining Charles
VANDEVEER, crossing Hanns Creek; part 440 acres by Sheriff
to H. SPEER 14 May 1795.   Witnesses: Michael TURNIDGE and
Joseph RUTLEDGE.   Signed: H. SPEER.

Page 258.   11 August 1795.   John HINSHAW to Simon HADLEY, 75
             pounds, 100 acres North fork Deep Creek adjoining
JOHNSON and Simon HADLEY.   Witnesses: Jesse VESTAL and Jacob
DOBBINS.   Signed: John HINSHAW.

Page 258. 3 December 1793. Sarah JOHNSON, Executrix and
Joseph JOHNSON, Executor of last Will of John
JOHNSON, deceased, Wilkes County, Georgia, to Isaac JOHNSON,
50 pounds, 160 acres South side North Hunting Creek adjoining
William ALNUTT to ford in Hunting Creek. Witnesses: Solomon
DICKERSON and William ALNUTT. Signed: Sarah JOHNSON and
Joseph JOHNSON.

Page 259. 10 August 1795. William COOK, Sheriff, to John
Thomas LONGINO, Yeoman, (land lost by James
WRIGHT, labourer, to satisfy John WILLIAMS, J.P.), 250 acres
Fall Creek branch Yadkin River adjoining Grimes HOLCOMB and
Philamon HOLCOMB. Acknowledged. Signed: William COOK,
Sheriff.

Page 260. 7 June 1795. Henry SPEER, gentleman, to John
Thomas LONGINO, Yeoman, 3 pounds, 100 acres Fishing Branch adjoining Ann WHITEHEAD. Witnesses: John KELLY
and Abner GREENWOOD. Signed: H. SPEER.

Page 261. 10 August 1795. John Thomas LONGINO, Yeoman, to
Allen GENTRY, planter, 50 pounds, 312 acres waters
South Deep Creek adjoining Nicholas GENTRY, WADDLE and said
ALLEN. Acknowledged. Signed: John Thomas LONGINO.

Page 262. 15 November 1795. Amariah FELTON to John Thomas
LONGINO, 39 pounds, 312 acres waters South fork
Deep Creek adjoining NICHOLAS and Allen GENTRY. Witnesses:
John WILLIAMS and Richard (X) GENTRY. Signed: Ameriah FELTON.

Page 262. 27 July 1792. Benjamin CADLE to Daniel SMITH,
100 pounds, 55 acres South side Tarrarat River.
Witnesses: Thomas BRYSON, Joseph SMITH, and Christopher
AMBER. Signed: Benjamin (X) CADLE.

Page 263. 4 October 1796. Gottlieb SHOBER, Stokes County,
to Timothy PICKERING, Philadelphia, Pennsylvania,
10 shillings, 640 acres waters Fishers River and 4,360 acres
Fishers and Double Creek adjoining PICKERING, Horns Mill
Creek, Isaac COPELAND, JARVIS and MELTON. Witnesses: George
HANSON and John Henry HAUSER. Signed: Gottlieb SHOBER.

Page 264. 16 April 1789. Thomas and Pheby ISBELL to
Lazarus TILLEY, 64 pounds, 10 shillings Virginia
Currency, 400 acres surveyed by Geo. DEATHERAGE, Big Creek
of Dan River including his plantation. Witnesses: John
HUGHES and Ephraim HOBBS. Signed: Thomas ISBELL.

Page 265. 20 July 1793. Joshua CRESON to Edward SCOTT, 90
pounds, 10 shillings, 105 acres waters Yadkin
River below Shallowford; part 200 acres granted Abraham
CRESON 3 November 1784 adjoining TURNER, road leading from
Salisbury to Shallowford. Witnesses: William MacPHERSON
and H(enry) SPEER. Signed: Joshua CRESON.

Page 266. 23 February 1795. Alexander BRYSON and wife,
Mary, to Edwin HICKMAN, 100 pounds Virginia
Currency, 98½ acres middle fork Tarrarat River adjoining

corner GRANVILLE granted to Andrew BAILEY. Witnesses:
Thomas A. WORD, John CREED, and John BRYSON, Junr. Signed:
Alexander BRYSON and Mary (X) BRYSON.

Page 267. 4 August 1795. Henry SPEER to William ZACHORY,
        10 pounds, 76 acres waters Deep Creek adjoining
WILES, JOHNSON and SPRINKLE. Witnesses: George HOLCOMB and
D. HOLCOMB. Signed: H. SPEER.

Page 267. 9 July 1790. North Carolina Grant Chas. WORD
        250 acres between Blutchers and Tarrarat River
adjoining BAILEY and LAURANCE.

Page 268. 24 December 1792. North Carolina Grant Leonard
        WISHON 185 acres Harmons Creek adjoining Thomas
CAIN and WINSTON.

Page 269. 28 August 1795. North Carolina Grant Edmond WOOD
        200 acres both sides Beaver Dam, waters of
Fishers River.

Page 270. 9 August. North Carolina Grant Anthony BETTS
        200 acres waters Harmons Creek.

Page 270. 6 August 1793. Dabney HARRIS to John PERSONATE,
        75 pounds, 95 acres adjoining Jesse FRANKLIN and
Mark KENNEDAY. Witnesses: James (X) FRANKLING and Thomas
ROSS, and William SNOW. Signed: Dabney HARRIS.

Page 271. 21 February 1795. George FRANKLIN to Richard
        BEAN, Stokes County, 40 pounds, two surveys, 50
acres each on Christians Creek, Branch Mitchells River
adjoining KENNEDAY. Witnesses: Jesse FRANKLIN and Meshack
FRANKLIN. Signed: George FRANKLIN.

Page 272. 24 December 1795. North Carolina Grant Hezekiah
        FORRISTER 75 acres Tarrarat River, Bullrun.

Page 273. 20 September 1779. North Carolina Grant Thomas
        ALLEN 340 acres both sides Hunting Creek near
head adjoining OWENS and his own lines.

Page 273. 10 November 1792. Thomas HILL, Wilkes County,
        Georgia, to Jacob HILL, 50 pounds, 140 acres both
sides Fishers River adjoining John HILL, above, and James
HILL, below, agreeable to the conditional line made between
them and their Father, William HILL, in his lifetime and
including the place where he deceased. Witnesses: J. MACKAY,
John (X) WATSON, and Matthew (X) SIMS. Signed: Thomas HILL.

Page 274. 10 November 1792. Thomas HILL, Wilkes County,
        Georgia, to James HILL, 90 pounds, 140 acres
both sides Fishers River, lower end survey made by William
RANSEY, 380 acres adjoining conditional line made between
James and his Father, William HILL. Witnesses: J. MACKAY,
John (X) WATSON, and Matthew (X) SIMS. Signed: Thomas HILL.

Page 274. 10 November 1792. Thomas HILL, Wilkes County,

Georgia, to John HILL, 100 pounds, 100 acres both sides Fishers River adjoining conditional line between John HILL and his Father, William HILL, deceased, and 380 acres, survey, Wm. RANSEY. Witnesses: J. MACKAY, John (X) WATSON, and Matthew (X) SIMS. Signed: Thomas HILL.

Page 275. 2 September 1786. William AUSTIN, Montgomery County, Virginia, to George FRANKLIN, Wilkes County, North Carolina, 15 pounds, 50 acres in Wilkes County, both sides Christians Creek, branch Mitchells River adjoining SMITH. Witnesses: Jesse FRANKLIN and Barnard FRANKLIN. Signed: William AUSTIN.

Page 276. 2 September 1786. William AUSTIN, Montgomery County, Virginia, to George FRANKLIN, Wilkes County, North Carolina, 15 pounds, 50 acres in Wilkes County, both sides Christian Creek, waters Mitchell River adjoining KANADAYS line. Witnesses: Jesse FRANKLIN and Barnard FRANKLIN. Signed: William AUSTIN.

Page 277. 5 December 1795. North Carolina Grant John MARTIN 400 acres waters Deep Creek adjoining GWIN and Henry SPEER.

Page 277. 5 December 1794. North Carolina Grant Samuel GWIN 200 acres Forbis Creek.

Page 278. 9 July 1794. North Carolina Grant John BURCHAM 50 acres Racoon Branch adjoining Esq. BUMP.

Page 278. 9 July 1794. North Carolina Grant John BURCHAM 50 acres including his improvement on Toms Creek.

Page 279. 9 July 1794. North Carolina Grant David BALLARD 100 acres Branch Bullocks fork including Michael HUFFS old improvement.

Page 279. 9 July 1794. North Carolina Grant David BALLARD 100 acres Bullocks fork Toms Creek including his improvement.

Page 280. 3 November 1794. North Carolina Grant Thomas DUNNAGAN 120 acres Tarrarat River.

Page 281. 18 May 1789. North Carolina Grant Thomas DUNNAGAN 100 acres South side Tarrarat River above his former survey, mouth Flat Shole Creek.

Page 281. 20 December 1791. North Carolina Grant William BERK 100 acres Manners Branch including an improvement made by Peter PRAD adjoining John JINKINS.

Page 282. 18 May 1789. North Carolina Grant Joshua SCRITCHFIELD 100 acres Bullrun.

Page 282. 9 July 1794. North Carolina Grant William HUDSON 100 acres waters Fishers River adjoining Haul HUDSON, Darby RYAN and JARVIS.

Page 283. 20 December 1795. North Carolina Grant Richard
          KERBY 72 acres Grassy Creek adjoining Jacob
SHEPARD.

Page 284. 19 December 1795. Rodham MOORE, Patrick County,
          Virginia, to Joseph JESSOP, 60 pounds, 190½ acres
Archers Creek adjoining Virginia line including plantation
Willis CHEAK now liveth on. Witnesses: Joseph JESSOP, Junr.,
John JESSOP, and Robt. DANNAR. Signed: Rode MOORE.

Page 285. 16 November 1795. Elias TURNER and John TURNER,
          Heirs of Andrew Robert TURNER, deceased, to Henry
SPEER, 100 pounds, 380 acres South side Yadkin River adjoin-
ing William HOGINS; State granted Andrew Robt. TURNER and
John TURNER 9 August 1787 and entered 2 January 1779.
Witnesses: Jo WILLIAMS and Daniel HAUSER. Signed: Elias
TURNER and John TURNER.

Page 286. 10 December 1790. North Carolina Grant Thomas
          CLARK 500 acres Deep Creek adjoining RUTLEDGE
crossing Hoppes Creek and adjoining CLANTON, Edmund REAVIS
and COOK.

Page 286. 30 August 1787. Charles PARKER to Samuel KERBY,
          50 pounds, 100 acres North side Yadkin River and
branch, Bishops Creek adjoining William DOUGLAS, Thomas
SMITH and Leander HUGHES. Witnesses: John LYNCH, Joseph
(X) GENTRY, and John SATER. Signed: Charles PARKER.

Page 287. 7 March 1796. George HUDSPETH, Senr. to Airs
          HUDSPETH, Junr., 150 pounds, 250 acres Yadkin
River to Reed Creek; part GRANVILLE granted to John HOWARD;
from HOWARD to Elijah SKIDMORE; from SKIDMORE to John
HUDSPETH; from John to Ralph HUDSPETH, Senr.; and willed
by Ralph Senr. to his son, David HUDSPETH; from David HUDSPETH
to George HUDSPETH, Senr. Witnesses: A(bner) GREENWOOD and
Drury HOLCOMB. Signed: George HUDSPETH.

Page 288. 16 April 1791. Leonard DAVIS to Edward MOORE,
          100 pounds, 190 acres Fishers River. Acknowledged.
Signed: Leonard DAVIS.

Page 288. 25 November 1791. George LIGET, State of Georgia,
          to John AYERS, 60 pounds North Carolina Currency,
100 acres Yadkin River below WHEELISS. Witnesses: Joseph
WILSON, William (X) FRETWELL, and Samuel WILSON. Signed:
John (X) LIGET.

Page 289. 1 June 1795. Andrew HERRING to James HERRING,
          10 pounds, 200 acres west end 600 acres granted
Henry SPEER 20 November 1791. Witnesses: Joseph SMITH and
Alexander SMITH. Signed: Andrew (X) HERRING.

Page 290. 14 October 1795. John MEREDITH and wife, Frances,
          to William BURCH, Junr., 140 pounds, 50 acres
Yadkin River. Witnesses: William MEREDITH, Philip COOK,
and John BURCH. Signed: John MEREDITH and Frances (X)
MEREDITH.

Page 290.   20 August 1795.   Daniel VESTAL to John MARTIN,
        100 pounds, 100 acres Fesons Branch, waters North
fork Deep Creek.   Witnesses: Levi (X) SHINN and Thomas HINSHAW.
Signed: Daniel VESTAL.

Page 291.   24 November 1795.   Sampson BASS to John BOND, 50
        pounds, 43 acres Branch Deep Creek adjoining 200
acres granted John PETTYJOHN.   Witnesses: William HOUGH and
Jesse VESTAL.   Signed: Sampson (X) BASS.

Page 292.   13 August 1795.   David HUMPHREYS, Elijah HUMPHREYS,
        Solomon HUMPHREYS, and John HUMPHREYS, 100 pounds
Virginia Currency "relinquish all our rights &c in our
Fathers Estate" to Benjamin HUMPHREYS 200 acres; part 400
acres tract originally granted Thomas SMITH "whereon our
Father lived at his decease", both sides Renfroes Creek,
main Hollow road above where David HUMPHREYS now lives.
Witnesses: Samuel LARANCE, Benjamin LAURANCE, and John
LAURANCE.   Signed: David HUMPHREYS, Elijah HUMPHREYS, Solomon
HUMPHREYS, and John (X) HUMPHREYS.

Page 293.   20 May 1795.   Robert JOHNSON, Stokes County, to
        Isaac CARTER, Chatham County, North Carolina, 250
pounds, 283 acres both sides North fork Deep Creek adjoining
Elisha JOHNSON, Simon HADLEY, Hoppes Creek; tract 400 acres
granted Jacob FEREE 3 April 1780; by FEREE and Sheriff to
Henry SPEER; by SPEER to Robert JOHNSON.   Witnesses: H(enry)
SPEER and Airs HUDSPETH.   Signed: Robert (X) JOHNSON.

Page 294.   4 January 1794.   James PARKS to James ROBERTS, 30
        pounds North Carolina Currency, 125 acres near
Beach Creek.   Witnesses: John COX, Hugh ARMSTRONG, and
Stephen K. SMITH.   Signed: James PARKS.

Page 294.   16 June 1794.   Samuel HAGGARD to John HAGGARD, 50
        pounds, 128 acres Boues Creek.   Acknowledged.
Signed: Samuel HAGGARD.

Page 295.   2 January 1796.   Joshua SUMNER to Azariah DENNY,
        50 pounds, 107 acres waters Pilot Creek.
Witnesses: John JACKSON and Joseph (X) WADKINS.   Signed:
Joshua SUMNER.

Page 296.   21 December 1795.   Samuel CROCKET to Stephen LOYD,
        100 pounds, 200 acres waters Deep Creek; granted
said CROCKET 10 October 1783 and adjoining ENAYART.   Witnesses: H(enry) SPEER and Samuel SPEER.   Signed: Samuel CROCKET.

Page 296.   9 February 1795.   Zachariah SPURLIN to Thomas
        HINSHAW, Junr., 30 pounds, 150 acres waters
Greenberry PATTERSONS, Mill Creek, Branch North fork Deep
Creek.   Witnesses: Aaron MOOR and Thomas (X) HINSHAW.
Signed: Zacharish (X) SPURLIN.

Page 297.   31 October 1795.   Sherod BROCK to David TOMASON,
        45 pounds, 100 acres waters Fishers River adjoin-
ing where Peter HAMBLEN now lives on waggon road.   Witnesses:
Peter (X) HAMBLIN, William MEREDITH, and Rezia JARVIS.

Signed: Sherod (X) BROCK and Sary BROCK.

Page 298.   29 October 1795.   George BATES to George RILEY,
        Junr., 55 pounds, 100 acres Harmons Creek adjoin-
ing Jacob HOOAS(?).   Witnesses: Gottfeid (name in German?)
and Thomas COOPER.   Signed: George (X) BATES.

Page 298.   22 November 1790.   Henry SPEER to Abraham SKIDMORE,
        100 pounds, 30 acres Turkey Creek adjoining John
SKIDMORE; part 112 acres granted SPEER 3 April 1780.
Witnesses: Thomas MASON, William SPILMAN, and William
DOWLING.   Signed: H. SPEER.

Page 299.   10 February 1796.   John HORN, Senr. to Reuben
        JACKSON, 300 pounds North Carolina Currency, 100
acres North side Yadkin River, agreed line between HORN and
JACKSON.   Acknowledged.   Signed: John HORN, Senr.

Page 300.   22 April 1795.   Jabez JARVIS, Senr. to James
        MEREDITH, 40 pounds, 400 acres Branch Codys Creek
between Henry SNOW and West MOSELEY.   Witnesses: William
MEREDITH, John CRITCHFIELD, and Jabez JARVIS, Junr.   Signed:
Jabez JARVIS, Senr.

Page 300.   30 June 1795.   Salathiel MARTIN and wife, Mary,
        to William RICHARDS, 11 pounds, 10 shillings,
100 acres South side Yadkin River adjoining SHORE, Peter
SALLEYS old line.   Witnesses: David COOK and William COOK.
Signed: Salathiel MARTIN and Mary (X) MARTIN.

Page 301.   18 June 1795.   Abraham DOWNEY and wife, Mary, to
        William RICHARDS, 45 pounds, 25 acres surveyed for
Gilbert KEEN and now DOWNEYS, waters Yadkin River.   Witnesses:
William COOK and David COOK.   Signed: Abraham (X) DOWNEY and
Mary (X) DOWNEY.

Page 302.   19 June 1795.   William COOK and wife, Kizia, to
        William RICHARDS, 250 pounds, 300 acres South
side Yadkin River, Cobbs Creek, dividing line between Wm.
COOK and his Son, David COOK, adjoining Abraham DOWNEY and
Salathiel MARTIN, Richards Branch.   Witnesses: David COOK,
Elizabeth COOK, and Francis (X) KEATON.   Signed: William
COOK and Kezia (X) COOK.

Page 303.   3 February 1796.   Thomas CLARKE, Spartanburg
        County, South Carolina, to Chas. STEALMAN, 150
pounds, 190 acres; part 500 acres granted CLARK, North side
Deep Creek adjoining RUTLEDGE and REAVIS.   Witnesses: David
DOYLE and Elijzh (X) MARKHAM.   Signed: Thomas CLARKE.

Page 304.   9 May 1796.   William ARMSTRONG and wife, Amelia,
        to Richard LAURANCE, $2,500, 500 acres both sides
middle fork Tarrarat River crossing Bridges Creek.   Witnesses: Thomas A. WORD, Benjamin HUMPHREYS, and Randolph
LAURANCE.   Signed: William ARMSTRONG and Melia ARMSTRONG.

Page 305.   6 February 1796.   Airs HUDSPETH to Meshack GENTRY,
        150 pounds, 150 acres both sides Deep Creek

adjoining MARTIN and HOLCOMBS corner. Witnesses: Allen (X)
GENTRY, Richard PERSONS, and George (X) HUDSPETH, Junr.
Signed: Airs HUDSPETH.

Page 306. 8 April 1796. John MARSHALL to Thomas VESTAL,
100 pounds, 200 acres adjoining said MARSHALLS
corner and ADAMS. Witnesses: David HOBSON and William ADAMS,
Junr. Signed: John MARSHALL and Jemima MARSHALL.

Page 306. 8 April 1796. John MARSHALL to Thomas VESTAL, 60
pounds, 110 acres adjoining said Thomas VESTAL
and ADAMS. Witnesses: David HOBSON and William ADAMS, Junr.
Signed: John MARSHALL and Jemima MARSHALL.

Page 307. 16 March 1796. Thomas HADLEY to Nathan VESTAL,
Chatham County, North Carolina, 300 pounds, 475
acres waters North fork Deep Creek adjoining Iron Work road,
James VESTAL; by Ambrose BRAMLET to Daniel VESTAL; by Daniel
to Thomas HADLEY. Witnesses: Simon HADLEY and Daniel VESTAL.
Signed: Thomas HADLEY.

Page 308. 13 October 1783. North Carolina Grant Salathiel
MARTIN 640 acres North side Yadkin River on Big
Elkin above Spring house, Angels old line, agreed line
MARTIN and John CARTER.

Page 309. 5 April 1796. Joseph DUNNAGAN to Jeremiah WOOTEN,
50 pounds, 100 acres Tarrarat River mouth Flat
Shole Creek; granted DUNNAGAN 20 November 1788. Acknowledged.
Signed: Joseph DUNNAGAN.

Page 310. 1 December 1796. John WILLIAMS to Jane WILLIAMS,
5 shillings, 143 acres waters Deep Creek adjoining
Chas. RUSSELL, RENNOLDS, PETTYJOHN; 100 acres by Peter
MYERS and wife, Mary, to WILLIAMS 5 January 1793 and 43 acres
part 340 acres granted WILLIAMS by State 13 October 1783.
Witnesses: H(enry) SPEER, George C. HOLCOMB, and John GALLYAN.
Signed: John WILLIAMS.

Page 311. 25 April 1796. Jesse REAVIS to Edward REAVIS, 50
pounds, 400 acres waters Harmons Creek. Witnesses:
John (X) MORE and Littleberry BRAY. Signed: Jesse REAVIS.

Page 311. 2 July 1795. Pearra CHIN to John WILLIAMS, 75
pounds, 150 acres waters Forbis Creek adjoining
Halafax ASHBEY, James PILCHERS old place, 320 acres granted
Jacob GALLION now in possession Peary CHIN, part 180 acres
by Abijah ELMORE to CHIN. Witnesses: Michael TURNIDGE and
Ephraim WILLIAMS. Signed: Peara (X) CHIN.

Page 312. 13 September 1795. Hallafax ASHBAY to John
WILLIAMS, 30 pounds, 50 acres waters Deep Creek
on road leads from Shallowford by James PILCHERS old place
in Daniel PILCHERS line adjoining corner 620 acres granted
Jacob GALLION. Witnesses: Ephraim WILLIAMS and Pery CHIN.
Signed: Hallafax ASHBY.

Page 313. 7 May 1796. Thomas WHITLOCK to George MOORE,

Rowan County, 4 pounds, 80 acres Dutchmans Creek adjoining said George MOORE in the Hollow. Witnesses: John REAVIS and William STEELMAN. Signed: Thomas WHITLOCK.

Page 314. 29 February 1796. Thomas COOK, Wilkes County, North Carolina, to George MOORE, Rowan County, 60 pounds, 100 acres Dutchmans Creek, North side in Rowan County line. Witnesses: Jo REAVIS and William STEELMAN. Signed: Thomas (X) COOK.

Page 314. 24 December 1792. North Carolina Grant Joshua BROWN 100 acres adjoining James HOWELL, waters Harmons Creek and John GROCE.

Page 315. 12 November 1794. Patrick COYLE, Bedford County, Virginia, to John BRYSON, Junr., 50 pounds, 50 acres both sides Lovings Creek. Witnesses: Chrisr. ROWLES, Francis BRYSON, and Archibald BRYSON. Signed: Patrick (X) COYLE.

Page 316. 15 September 1789. John CHILDRESS and wife, Nancy, to David DALTON, Rockingham County, North Carolina, 300 pounds, 480 acres both sides Crooked Creek adjoining Wm. MARTIN, Virginia line, Isham COX, and Ambrose HOLT. Witnesses: A. HUGHES, Lea HUGHES, William MARTIN, and Thomas WHITLOCK. Signed: John CHILDRESS and Nancy (X) CHILDRESS.

Page 317. 13 April 1796. William RUTLEDGE to Charles STEELMAN, 60 pounds, 175 acres North side Deep Creek, North Deep Creek adjoining Thomas WILES. Witnesses: Joseph REAVIS and George STEELMAN. Signed: William RUTLEDGE.

Page 318. 9 May 1796. John COOK to John FLETCHER, Patrick County, Virginia, 8 pounds, 12 shillings, 6 pense, 11½ acres North side Yadkin River. Witnesses: William FLETCHER and John BALLINGER. Signed: John (X) COOK.

Page 318. 19 October 1795. Moses BAKER, planter, to Thomas BURKE, Son and Heir of Benjamin BURKE, deceased, 60 pounds, 200 acres waters Forbis Creek adjoining Henry SPEER and Michael BAKER. Witnesses: Jesse VESTAL, Daniel (X) VESTAL, and John Thomas LONGINO. Signed: Moses BAKER.

Page 319. 3 August 1796. Frederick MILLER, Esq., Rowan County, to John MARTIN, 100 pounds, 154 acres waters North fork Deep Creek; part granted Michael HENDERSON and sold said MILLER. Witnesses: Britain Jones HAYMOORE and James MORRISON, Junr. Signed: Frederick MILLER.

Page 320. 8 August 1796. George VANDEVEER to James CARSON, 20 pounds, 16 acres near Forbis Creek; part land from Thomas CARSON to said VANDEVEER. Witnesses: Caleb SAPP and Solomon (X) PHILLIPS. Signed: George (X) VANDEVEER.

Page 320. 3 August 1796. Frederick MILLER, Esq., Rowan County, to James MORRISON, Junr., Rowan County, 80 pounds. 267 acres waters Deep Creek. Witnesses: Britain

Jones HAYMOORE and James MORRISON, Senr. Signed: Frederick MILLER.

Page 321. 26 June 1795. John MOORE, Junr. to George WEBB, 10 pounds cash, 100 acres waters Dutchmans Creek. Witnesses: James REAVIS and John McDANIEL. Signed: John MOORE.

Page 322. 3 August 1796. Fredr. MILLER, Rowan County, to Joseph HINSHAW, 133 pounds, 378 acres waters North fork Deep Creek, top Nobbs adjoining Michael HENDERSON; entry 200 acres granted MILLER and part granted Michael HENDERSON and sold to MILLER. Witnesses: Britain Jones HAYMOORE and James MORRISON, Junr. Signed: Frederick MILLER.

Page 322. 9 August 1796. Thos. A. WORD, Esq., Sheriff, to Humphrey COCKERHAM, Wilkes County, North Carolina, (suit brought by Wm. Terrel LEWIS against Benj. CLEVELAND May Term 1794; nonsuited and said LEWIS liable for cost; also another suit against John JARVIS, nonsuited and no other property of said LEWIS to be found; land lost by said Wm. Terrell LEWIS), (no acreage), Fox Knobs adjoining WOODRUFF; State granted Wm. T. LEWIS 18 May 1789. Acknowledged. Signed: T.A. WORD, Sheriff.

Page 324. 20 July 1795. Jacob SPEER, Senr. to William SPEER, farmer, 5 shillings, 100 acres both sides Elrods Creek, granted said Jacob SPEER, Senr. Witnesses: James SPEER and James (X) STEELMAN. Signed: Jacob SPEER, Senr.

Page 324. 3 November 1794. Henry SPEER to Jacob DOUTHIT, Rowan County, 50 acres waters Deep Creek on Iron Works road adjoining CROCKET and HOWELL. Witnesses: Samuel HOWARD and William HOWARD. Signed: H. SPEER.

Page 325. 9 April 1796. John MARTIN to John BOND, 160 pounds, 200 acres waters North Fork Deep Creek adjoining Jacob BROWN; part 400 acres granted John MARTIN 5 December 1795. Witnesses: Simon HADLEY and Jacob (X) BROWN. Signed: John MARTIN.

Page 326. 24 December 1792. North Carolina Grant George CHAPPEL 100 acres waters North fork Hunting Creek.

Page 326. 17 July 1794. North Carolina Grant Thomas JACKS 50 acres waters Deep Creek.

Page 327. 24 December 1792. North Carolina Grant James ROSS 100 acres Brushy Mountain adjoining William SPARKS including Rich Nob and adjoining REESE.

Page 327. 20 December 1791. North Carolina Grant William CUNNINGHAM 200 acres Wilkes County, Fishers River between Andrew DOUGLAS and James WILLIAMS.

Page 328. 10 August 1796. John MARTIN to Jacob BROWN, 40 pounds Specie, 200 acres waters North Deep Creek adjoining, SPEER, HINSHAW and BOND. Witnesses: Nathan

ARMSFIELD and Thomas LONGINO. Signed: John (X) MARTIN.

Page 329. 22 January 1796. William JOHNSON to Joel BROWN, Orange County, North Carolina, 60 pounds, 129 acres waters Forbis Creek adjoining GWIN and said JOHNSON. Witnesses: William ADAMS, Junr. and Jonathan ADAMS. Signed: William JOHNSON.

Page 330. 20 August 1794. Henry SPEER to Augustine WILLARD, 40 pounds, 120 acres waters Deep Creek adjoining Christian WEATHERMAN, John BARRON and John HUTCHINS; part 200 acres granted WEATHERMAN 10 December 1790. Witnesses: Henry YOUNG, J. CARTER, and Chas. HUNT. Signed: H. SPEER.

Page 330. 7 December 1795. Robin HEAD to James HOLCOMB, 55 pounds, 200 acres Beaver Dam Creek, waters Yadkin River; part 400 acres granted John BRASELL; by BRASSELL to Joseph ALLEN: by ALLEN to Ezekiel REYNOLDS; by REYNOLDS to HEAD. Witnesses: Samuel (X) GENTRY and Isaac (X) CHANDLER. Signed: Robin HEAD.

Page 331. 5 January 1796. John BOURN to William SPILMAN, 27 pounds, 54 acres waters Forbis Creek adjoining John MILLER and old Mill path; granted BOURN 18 May 1789. Witnesses: William DOWLING, John WILES, and William BRUCE. Signed: John (X) BOURN.

Page 332. 6 August 1796. Francis COOMER to John FARMER, 100 pounds, 200 acres waters Yadkin. Witnesses: Nathan FARMER and Jacob GREEN. Signed: Francis (X) COOMER.

Page 333. 20 April 1796. George EARNEST, Rowan County, to Christian EARNEST, Huntsville, 50 pounds, Lot No. 8, High and 2nd Streets. Witnesses: H(enry) YOUNG and M.D. (Marmaduke) KIMBROUGH. Signed: George EARNEST.

Page 333. 16 June 1796. Henry SPEER to Thomas YOUNG, Iredell County, 15 pounds, Lot No. 37, Huntsville, High and 2nd Streets. Witnesses: Calvin WHEATON, Isham YOUNG, and William MacPHERSON. Signed: H. SPEER.

Page 334. 21 July 1796. Airs HUDSPETH, Junr. to Samuel AYERS, 100 pounds, 42 acres North side, North fork Deep Creek adjoining John HUTCHENS, John STANFIELD; part granted John HUTCHENS 1779; also 100 acres adjoining Joshua BROWN and ELMORE; also 40 acres adjoining above, BRUCE, HUTCHENS and STANFIELD. Witnesses: Abner GREENWOOD and George C. HOLCOMB. Signed: Airs HUDSPETH.

Page 335. 7 December 1793. Thomas PATISON to John FORKNER, 50 pounds, 100 acres Southwest side Tarrarat River adjoining GRIFFEYS old line. Witnesses: William FORKNER and Enoch GRIMES. Signed: Thomas (X) PATISON.

Page 335. 20 July 1795. David HUMPHREYS to Lewis FORKNER, 150 pounds Virginia Currency, 100 acres formerly property Thos. SMITH by deed, 3 April 1780, waters Renfroes Creek where public waggon road crosses said creek.

Witnesses: Benjamin HUMPHREYS and Thomas A. WORD. Signed:
David HUMPHREYS.

Page 336. 11 March 1796. Palmer CRITCHFIELD and wife,
            Rebecah, Patrick County, Virginia, to Drury
HOLCOMB, 115 pounds, 200 acres North fork Deep Creek adjoining James JONES near the graveyard and Daniel HUFF. Witnesses: Hugh ARMSTRONG, jurat as to Palmer, Martha ARMSTRONG,
and Thomas HADLEY, jurat as to Rebecca. Signed: Palmer
CRITCHFIELD and Rebecah CRITCHFIELD.

Page 337. 12 May 1796. Drury HOLCOMB to John PATTERSON,
            115 pounds, 200 acres waters North fork Deep
Creek adjoining James JONES near graveyard and Daniel HUFF.
Witnesses: Airs HUDSPETH and William ADAMS, Junr. Signed:
Drury HOLCOMB.

Page 338. 15 May 1796. James DOAK, Guilford County, to
            Thomas CHAMBERLAIN, Senr., 6 pounds, 5 shillings,
15 acres West side Pauls Creek, part granted John McKINNEY
3 April 1780. Witnesses: James BRYSON, A.B. BRYSON, and
Henry HERRING. Signed: James DOAK.

Page 338. 4 February 1795. Joseph HIETT to Abraham HORTON,
            50 pounds, (no acreage), waters Toms Creek adjoin-
ing said HIETT and including plantation where Abr. HORTON
now liveth. Witnesses: Jesse KNIGHTON and Jacob BEALS.
Signed: Joseph HEITT.

Page 339. 16 January 1796. John BURRIS to Joseph JACKSON,
            120 pounds North Carolina Currency, 150 acres
Branch Toms Creek, Yadkin River adjoining Bryans Branch
including John BURRIS improvement. Witnesses: William
TANZEY and John JACKSON. Signed: John BURRIS.

Page 340. 29 January 1796. John MARTIN, Stokes County, to
            John BURRIS, 40 pounds, 300 acres Big Creek of
Dan River adjoining Adam TATE. Witnesses: Jesse KNIGHTON
and Joseph JACKSON. Signed: John MARTIN.

Page 340. 11 March 1795. Joseph JESSOP, Stokes County, to
            Nathan BEALS, 82 pounds, 122 acres both sides
East fork Toms Creek adjoining Curtis JACKSON and said
JESSOP. Witnesses: Curtis JACKSON and Jacob BEALS. Signed:
Joseph (X) JESSOP.

Page 341. 11 March 1795. Joseph JESSOP to Jacob BEALS, 84
            pounds, 100 acres both sides East fork Toms Creek;
part tract entered by Spencer BALL. Witnesses: Curtis JACKSON
and Nathan BEALS. Signed: Joseph (X) JESSOP.

Page 342. 22 November 1794. Benjamin SPEER to William
            HOWARD, 150 pounds, 156 acres Turners Creek
adjoining Jacob SPEER, Arge GARNER, 337 acres GRANVILLE
granted to Roger TURNER, Chas. VANDEVER; part 337 acres
conveyed to Toliver DAVIS. Witnesses: John KELLY and H(enry)
SPEER. Signed: Benjamin SPEER.

Page 342. 16 June 1795. Martin ARMSTRONG, Stokes County, to Gideon EDWARDS, 100 pounds, 640 acres Fishers River called Scull Camp. Witnesses: Jesse FRANKLIN and Peter PERKINS. Signed: Mart ARMSTRONG.

Page 343. 2 March 1796. Airs HUDSPETH to Jacob ELSBERRY, 100 pounds, 200 acres both sides South fork Deep Creek. Witnesses: Thomas WRIGHT and George (X) HUDSPETH. Signed: Airs HUDSPETH.

Page 344. 6 February 1795. Henry HOLSECLAW, Burk County, to James WRIGHT, 15 pounds, 100 acres South side Tarrarat River. Witnesses: James (X) HOLDER, James SOUTHER-LAND, William PINION, Abraham (X) HARRISON, Charity (X) HARRISON, and Jesse PIERCE. Signed: Henry (X) HOLSECLAW.

Page 345. 6 February 1795. Joseph HOLSECLAW, Burke County, to James WRIGHT, 25 pounds, 100 acres Tarrarat River. Witnesses: James (X) HOLDER, James SOUTHERLAND, William PINION, Abrham (X) HARRISON, Charity (X) HARRISON, and Jesse PIERCE. Signed: Joseph (X) HOLSECLAW.

Page 346. September 1795. William COOK, Sheriff, to Thomas Adams WORD (land lost by Garner TUCKER, action brought by Daniel CARLING before James BRYSON and Martin ARMSTRONG, J.P.'S), 101 acres little Fisher River. Witnesses: Joseph WILLIAMS and Henry YOUNG. Signed: William COOK, Sheriff.

Page 347. 12 August 1796. Thomas Adams WORD to John ROBERTS, Junr., 40 pounds, 101 acres Garner TUCKERS corner, East side little Fisher River. Acknowledged. Signed: Thomas A. WORD.

Page 347. 20 March 1795. George REED to William FORKNER, 150 pounds, 200 acres Forkners Creek including Wm. FORKNERS old improvement where George REED now lives adjoining William FORKNERS land. Witnesses: John HUNT, David CHANDLER, and Isaac FORKNER. Signed: George REED.

Page 348. 22 October 1792. Thomas HILL to Benjamin CADLE, 30 pounds, 100 acres Bullrun waters Tarrarat River. Witnesses: Joel MACKEY, James HILL, and Jean MACKEY. Signed: Thomas HILL.

Page 348. 1 October 1795. Edmond WOOD, Green County, Southwest Territory, to John HODGES, 100 pounds, 200 acres Beaverdam Creek. Witnesses: Richard MURPHEY, H(enry) SPEER, and Joe MURPHEY. Signed: Edmond (X) WOOD.

Page 349. 16 November 1795. John STEPHENS to William STEPHENS, 10 shillings Specie, 320 acres Brooks Creek adjoining where Zachariah MARTIN formerly lived. Witnesses: William FORRESTER and Thomas STEPHENS. Signed: John STEPHENS.

Page 350. 17 November 1796. Charles HUNT and wife, Elizabeth, to Peter EATON, Minister of the Gospel, Rowan

County, 400 pounds, Lots Nos. 1 and 2, Huntsville, High Street. Witnesses: Henry YOUNG and John WELCH. Signed: Charles HUNT and Elizabeth HUNT.

Page 350. 11 November 1796. Frederick LONG to Simon GROCE, 75 pounds, 200 acres waters South fork Deep Creek including said GROCE improvement. Witnesses: Thomas WRIGHT and Thomas CLANTON. Signed: Frederick LONG.

Page 351. 10 October 1794. Joseph HUDSPETH to Airs HUDSPETH, Junr., 50 pounds cash, 100 acres North fork Deep Creek adjoining Joshua BROWN and ELMORE. Witnesses: George HUDSPETH, Thos. WILLIAMS, and Benjamin (X) CAIN. Signed: Joseph HUDSPETH.

Page 352. 29 August 1796. Charles VANDEVER and wife, Sarah, to John SMITH, Rowan County, 85 pounds, 4 shillings, 73 acres waters Turners Creek adjoining Andrew and Benjamin SPEER. Witnesses: Thomas BRYAN and Samuel SMITH. Signed: Charles (X) VANDEVER and Sarah (X) VANDEVER.

Page 353. 22 October 1796. William MEECKS to William WALL, 100 pounds, 100 acres both sides Tarrarat River. Witnesses: Sam (X) WOLDRIDGE, Dru (X) WELLS, and Arthe MEEKS. Signed: William MEEKS.

Page 353. 1796. Henry SPEER to Thomas BROWN, 50 pounds, 150 acres adjoining corner Meeting House tract; part 189 acres granted SPEER 4 May 1790. Witnesses: William HOUGH, John BOND, and Jacob (X) BROWN. Signed: H. SPEER.

Page 354. April 1790. John JACKSON, Stokes County, to William JACKSON, 100 pounds, 200 acres Rutledge Creek. Witnesses: Samuel BOND and John JACKSON. Signed: John JACKSON.

Page 355. 17 February 1795. William ADAMS to Jonathan ADAMS, 10 pounds, 60 acres waters South fork Forbis Creek adjoining John MARSHALL and John ADAMS. Witnesses: George ADAMS and Edward BOND. Signed: William ADAMS.

Page 356. 30 January 1796. Henry SPEER to Ephraim WEST, 40 pounds, 160 acres waters Deep Creek near Todds Spring Branch, old Kimbrough Botom adjoining WILLARD, John Miller DEFREES. Witnesses: James (X) PILCHER and Aaron (X) STINSON. Signed: H. SPEER.

Page 356. 16 August 1796. Ephraim WEST to Moses STINSON, 66 pounds, 160 acres waters Deep Creek near Todds Spring Branch, old Kimbrough Bottom, adjoining WILLIARD, John MILLER and DEFREES. Witnesses: H(enry) SPEER, Samuel A. SPEER, and Samuel SPEER. Signed: Ephraim WEST.

Page 347. 10 March 1794. George HOLCOMB, Senr. to John WILLIAMS of Deep Creek, 10 pounds, 10 acres North side said Creek, land said HOLCOMB bought of Peter SPRINKEL on Delilahs ford. Witnesses: Abner GREENWOOD and Jean (X)

WILLIAMS. Signed: George (X) HOLCOMB.

Page 358. 3 September 1796. Mortgage Deed from Michael
            ROMINGER, planter, Stokes County, to Fredr Wm.
MARSHALL, Stokes County (ROMINGER bound $108.75 to be paid 3
September next), 160 acres South fork Deep Creek adjoining
ELLIOTT, Ayres HUDSPETH, land granted 1792 to John WARD; by
WARD to ROMINGER (if paid, above Null and Void). Witnesses:
Gottlieb SHOBER and Jacob REED. Signed: Michael (X) ROMINGER.

Page 359. 20 January 1797. Henry SPEER to Israel HOUGH, 20
            pounds, 63 acres waters Hunting Creek adjoining
RILEY, WINDSOR, James BURNSIDE; part 300 acres State granted
SPEER. Witnesses: Samuel SPEER and William HOUGH. Signed:
H. SPEER.

Page 360. 16 March 1795. Henry SPEER to Daniel HUFF, 10
            pounds, 30 acres waters North fork Deep Creek
adjoining John MARTIN, HINSHAW; part 189 acres granted SPEER
4 May 1795. Witnesses: William HOUGH, John BOND, and Jacob
(X) BROWN. Signed: H. SPEER.

Page 360. 18 March 1796. Isaac EMANUEL to Thomas FITZPATRICK
            of State of Virginia, 20 pounds North Carolina
money, 100 acres waters Double Creek. Witnesses: William
COOK, Thomas COOK, and Daniel DEJARNAT. Signed: Isaac (X)
EMANUEL.

Page 361. 2 March 1796. Jesse VESTAL to Isaac CARTER, 130
            pounds, 100 acres North side North fork Deep
Creek adjoining William HOUGH. Witnesses: John HOUGH and
Joseph (X) CARTER. Signed: John VESTAL.

Page 362. 13 February 1797. Grimes HOLCOMB to George
            Durrum HOLCOMB, 200 pounds, 329 acres North fork
Deep Creek, land sold to Grimes HOLCOMB by George HOLCOMB;
to George by John WILLIAMS (?). Witnesses: Airs HUDSPETH,
Daniel LIVERTON, and James HUTCHENS. Signed: Grimes (X)
HOLCOMB.

Page 362. 31 December 1794. James REAVIS, Senr. to George
            STEELMAN, Rowan County, 200 pounds, 175 acres
Deep Creek adjoining Clanton Spring Branch. Witnesses:
James REAVIS and Chas. STEELMAN. Signed: James REAVIS.

Page 363. 14 November 1795. James REAVIS, Senr. to George
            STEELMAN, 25 pounds, 20 acres both sides Deep
Creek adjoining CLANTON and CLARK. Witnesses: Edward REAVIS
and Charles STEELMAN. Signed: James REAVIS.

Page 364. 15 February 1797. Airs HUDSPETH to Peter MOCK,
            Junr., Rowan County, 200 pounds, 300 acres North
side Yadkin River adjoining COLVARD, Reed Creek; being
GRANVILLE granted to John HOWARD; by HOWARD to Elijah SKIDMORE;
by SKIDMORE to John HUDSPETH; by John to Ralph HUDSPETH and
divolved to David HUDSPETH by Will said Ralph; by David to
George HUDSPETH; by George to said Airs HUDSPETH. Witnesses:
John BURCH and William THORNTON. Signed: Airs HUDSPETH.

Page 365. 11 February 1797. Edwin HICKMAN to William HICKMAN, his Son for love, 40 acres both sides Lovens Creek, middle fork Tarrarat River. Witnesses: Thomas A. WORD, J. MEALAN, and Benajamin BRIGGS. Signed: Edwin HICKMAN.

Page 366. 3 February 1797. Thomas Adams WORD to his Brother, Joshua WORD, Pendleton County, South Carolina, for love and to secure to him that part of his Fathers estate, which the laws of reason says belong to him, 137 acres both sides Lovins Creek, middle fork Tarrarat River. Acknowledged. Signed: Thomas A. WORD.

Page 366. 3 December 1796. George WATKINS to William DENNY, Junr., 50 pounds, 100 acres West side Arrarat River, mouth Bull Run. Witnesses: Lazarus DENNY and Thomas GORDON. Signed: George (X) WATKINS.

Page 367. 15 February 1797. Thompson GLEN to James GROCE, 60 pounds, 151 acres waters Yadkin on small Creek runs through GLENS plantation adjoining LONGINO; part 400 acres granted James GLEN 9 August 1787 and by Heirship left to Thompson GLEN. Acknowledged. Signed: Thompson GLEN.

Page 368. 14 July 1795. James STEELMAN to Zepheniah DOWDEN, 10 pounds, 150 acres waters Deep Creek adjoining former survey of Matthias STEELMAN. Witnesses: H(enry) SPEER, Thomas HARBOUR, and Michael TUNIDGE. Signed: James (X) STEELMAN.

Page 370. 15 September 1796. Stephen JAYNE, Grayson County, Virginia, to Edward LOVELL, 200 pounds, 382 acres both sides Toms Creek adjoining DUNNAGAN and James RITTER. Witnesses: Samuel PARKER and William (X) LOVELL. Signed: Stephen JAYNE.

Page 369. 31 January 1797. Henry SPEER to William ELLIOTT, 20 pounds, 150 acres waters Deep Creek on one of the Brushy Mountains adjoining David HARVEL, Obediah COLLINS, being land granted SPEER 16 July 1795. Witnesses: George (X) HOLCOMB and William ELLIOTT. Signed: H. SPEER.

Page 371. 15 September 1796. Stephen JAYNE, Grayson County, Virginia, to Edward LOVELL, 200 pounds, 50 acres waters Toms Creek on Huckleberry Branch; granted JAYNE 1795. Witnesses: Samuel PERKER and William (X) LOVELL. Signed: Stephen JAYNE.

Page 371. 20 March 1794. Adonijah HARBOUR, Stokes County, to Edward LOVELL, 500 pounds North Carolina Currency, 300 acres North side Yadkin River adjoining John HORN. Witnesses: Alexander KEER, Daniel SCOTT, and Valentine MARTIN. Signed: Adonijah HARBOUR.

Page 372. 5 September 1796. Isaac WELBORN, Senr. to Edward LOVELL, 30 pounds, 2 acres Forbis Creek; part land James CARSON now lives on. Witnesses: William WELBORN and Nicholas BURN. Signed: Isaac (X) WELBORN.

Page 372.   12 May 1796.   William THORNTON, Stephen WOOD, John
          Thomas LONGINO, Jacob SHEPPERD, Joseph WILLIAMS,
William MEREDITH, Thomas BURCH, and Joshua FREEMAN, Commissioners, Town of Rockford, to Edward LOVELL, 17 pounds, 1
shilling, Lot No. 15 in said town on High Street. Witnesses:
Thomas A. WORD and Frederick THOMPSON. Signed: William
THORNTON, Stephen WOOD, John Thomas LONGINO, Thomas C. BURCH,
and Joshua FREEMAN. (No signatures for SHEPPERD, WILLIAMS
or MEREDITH.)

END DEED BOOK F